Landscapes of Memory and Experience

Landscapes of Memory and Experience

Edited by
Jan Birksted

First published 2000 by Spon Press
11 New Fetter Lane, London EC4P 4EE

Simultaneously published in the USA and Canada
by Spon Press
29 West 35th Street, New York, NY 10001

Spon Press is an imprint of the Taylor & Francis Group

© 2000 Selection and editorial matter Jan Birksted, individual chapters,
the contributors

Typeset in Akzidenz Grotesk by Wearset, Boldon, Tyne and Wear
Printed and bound in Great Britain by Biddles Ltd, Guildford and King's Lynn

British Library Cataloguing in Publication Data
A catalogue record for this book is available from the British Library

Library of Congress Cataloging in Publication Data
Landscapes of memory and experience/edited by Jan Birksted.
     p. cm.
    ISBN 0–419–25070–0
    1. Landscape architecture—History. 2. Gardens—History. I. Birksted,
     Jan, 1946– II.
    Title.

    SB470.5 .L36 2000
    712′.09—dc21

                                                        00–063555

ISBN 0-419-25070-0

Contents

Acknowledgements for illustrations

Individuals and organizations

Art Gallery of Western Australia: 1.5
Martine Bouchier: 13.2, 13.8, 13.25, 13.30
British Museum, London: 7.5
Canadian Centre for Architecture/Centre Canadien d'Architecture, Montréal: 10.1
Gérard Chouquer et al.: 13.21
Claremont Teachers' College: 1.6
Collection Musée du Louvre, Paris: 4.2
Courtauld Institute of Art, London: 7.6
Christine Dalnoky: 13.4
Department of Rare Books and Special Collections, McGill University, Montreal: 10.3
Fiske Kimball Fine Arts Library, University of Virginia, Charlottesville: 11.4, 11.7
Getty Research Institute for the History of Art and the Humanities: 7.1
Huntingdon Library, San Marino, California: 7.2–4
Charles Lamb: 13.17
M. A. Lewi: 1.8, 1.9
Marie-Louise Madonna: 13.26
MIT Press, Cambridge, Massachusetts: 9.1
Mitchell Library, State Library of New South Wales: 1.4
Niedersächsische Staats- und Universitätsbibliothek Göttingen: 12.4, 12.5, 12.11
M. Pediconi: 13.19
Sylvia Pressouye: 13.18
Princeton University Libraries, Princeton, New Jersey: 9.2
Réunion des musées nationaux, Paris: 4.2
Royal Institute of British Architects, London: 10.2
Special Collections, University of South Florida Library: 4.1
William Toomath: 2.1–4
Trustees of the Chatsworth Settlement: 7.6
Victoria and Albert Museum, London: 10.4

Publications

Émile Allard, *Les Travaux Publics de la France*, V: *Phares et Balises* (Paris: J. Rothschild, 1883): 6.1, 6.5–9

Émile Allard, *Mémoire sur l'Intensité et la Portée des Phares Comprenant la Description de quelques Appareils Nouveaux* (Paris: Imprimerie Nationale, 1876): 6.10, 6.11

B. di Gaddo, *Le Fontane di Roma* (Genoa: Vitali & Ghianda, 1964): 11.10

Henri Labrouste, *Temple de Neptune à Paestum*, in *Fragments d'architecture antique d'après les rélèves et restaurations des anciens pensionnaires de l'Académie de France à Rome*, ed. H. d'Espouy (Paris: Charles Massin): 4.1

Oeuvres Complètes d'Augustin Fresnel (Paris: Imprimerie Impériale, 1870): 6.3

Henri Révoil, 'Le téléiconographe', in *Gazette des architectes et du bâtiment* (1868): 4.4, 4.5

Léonce Reynaud, *Mémoire sur l'Écairage et le Balisage des Côtes de France* (Paris: Imprimerie Impériale, 1864): 6.2, 6.4

Edmund Sharpe, *Architectural Parallels, or, The Progress of Ecclesiastical Architecture in England Through the Twelfth and Thirteenth Centuries* (London: John van Vorst, 1848): 10.3

Osvald Sirén, *China and Gardens of Europe of the Eighteenth Century* (New York, 1950): 7.7

Felix Summerly [Sir Henry Cole], *Railway Travelling Charts …* (London: Railway Chronicle office, [1845–47]): 10.4

E.-E. Viollet-le-Duc, 'L'aiguille du Midi' (view taken from Pierre-Pontue), from *Le Massif du Mont-Blanc* (Paris, 1876): 4.6–8

Landscape between
memory and experience

In an earlier work, I collected essays by colleagues and friends exploring the ways in which landscape and architecture relate in terms of vision and materiality, and in terms of geometry, form and scale. That collection of essays served the dual process of continuing the documentation of twentieth-century landscape design and of furthering the discussion about the phenomenological experience of landscape.[1] This book is different.

While *Relating Architecture to Landscape* focused on the observation and analysis of *in situ* landscapes and architecture and of their interactions, the present collection of essays — also by friends and colleagues — concentrates on landscape and architecture as *in situ* representations. Their interaction is analysed as a process of meaning, projected and constructed. But precisely this difference makes the work an extension of *Relating Architecture to Landscape*. In a recent review of the growing literature within landscape studies, I discussed the development of theory within landscape studies.[2] The present book is intended as part of the growing analysis of landscape as representation, the problems of which have been discussed elsewhere.[3] And about which I would like to say more.

It has been argued that the history of landscape and gardens has been marginalised from the mainstream of art and architectural history and visual studies because of a lack of engagement with the theories, methods and concepts of these disciplines. J. Elkins, for example, writes that

> [g]arden history, unlike the history of painting, sculpture, and architecture, has no conceptual foundations. . . . Painting, for example, has a recurring set of critical problems, including fictive space, the picture plane, the position and nature of the beholder, and notions of realism and representation. In art history, even the most abstract theoretical accounts of painting dwell on these same topics. The more specialised organs of art history, such as iconology, semiology, formal analysis, and psychoanalytical criticism, all return to these issues as if to a kind of home.[4]

1

This book brings together a collection of essays that discusses landscape from precisely such a standpoint.

But the situation is made more complex because of having to distinguish carefully between the representation of sites (e.g. descriptions and photographs of existing sites and of sites to be realised) and *in situ* sites as representations, and the interaction between these two representations, layered over each other. In the latter, the position and nature of the beholder is not always clear, and representations of sites can, therefore, like ekphrases, be used to provide some semblance of both a stable standing point or at least of a predictable movement.

But in both cases, landscape (in opposition to architecture) is strategically coded. Michael Fried described how Gustav Courbet used landscape (often running water) to represent reality.[5] Georges Didi-Huberman described how painters used the theme of the cloud in opposition to pictorial perspective.[6] Le Corbusier used the woods surrounding the Villa Savoye to represent the 'Virgilien dream'.[7] Landscape, in this respect, represents that other dimension hovering between being other and actually being other, resisting us 'as an encounter not merely as a recognition.'[8]

In this respect, theorising within landscape studies — having made use of analytic procedures poached from neighbouring disciplines — in turn generates new insights and reconnects with the analytical approaches of art and architectural history and of visual studies. Many such landscape studies exist already, but they remain scattered and disconnected from each other because they are spread across various disciplines: social anthropology, art history, cultural studies, visual studies, landscape studies, design history (including photography and film studies), cultural geography, gender studies and architectural history.[9] Theorising landscape studies — in balance between the status of a subject-area and of an analytic tool — would thus be a two-way process in several respects. It would generate new kinds of empirical observations, hence new analytic insights, and so contribute to rethinking processes in visual culture. This would involve reconsidering both aspects of perception (e.g. movement, form, perspective) and of memory. Hence, the structure of this book. These will be briefly outlined.

In perception, vision and touch do not simply overlap but are in active tension with each other: vision and touch interact and operate as a system of spatial and temporal perception.[10] Vision is part of a larger whole such that art and architectural historical discussions of visual culture[11] or of vision as language[12] are necessarily restrictive. If visual perspective is a 'model for thinking',[13] then this model is more complex and less Cartesian. That spatial perception involves both visual and tactile elements has been explored sporadically[14] but never applied in a systematic way, and this needs to be done. Such a concern would clearly expand outwards to other forms of perception, and thus the dominating focus on vision would be questioned.[15]

The development of such insights — what I will call the landscape perspective — would also force rethinking of much art and architecture history and visual studies literature that presupposes the static nature of the object being investigated. Movement through the landscape — and here a connection with film studies seems unavoidable in terms of camera movements as model[16] — puts into question concepts of the 'gaze' and 'glance'. A different kind of seeing is involved when moving.[17] The concepts of perspective, anti-perspective, a-perspective, scenography, anamorphosis, and so on must necessarily be measured against a new and entirely different set of empirical case-studies – which then puts into question basic notions of geometry and of form.[18]

As for notions of memory, the landscape perspective would bring an increased awareness of how memory is 'seen'. Landscape is of course historically linked to the 'arts of memory'.[19] Since vision appears to be natural, it transforms memory into a seemingly natural experience, an experience present in the here-and-now. The interaction between vision and memory in the landscape is thus capable of generating narrative vision that cuts across the very basic distinction between the textual and the visual – a distinction which tends fundamentally to oppose, in art and architectural history, the iconographic approach to the approach of visual culture studies.[20] Hence, also a temporal dimension: transporting the past into the present, blurring past and present, recreating the present as past. Vision of landscape has a temporal dimension and thus brings the temporal dimension into the spatial dimension. The landscape perspective foregrounds time.

These developments would have profound effects on philosophical and methodological issues. A rethinking of the notion of the human subject would develop in so far as the human subject is viewed from the point of view of landscape, that is from the outside. The human subject would not remain as self-centred Cartesian subject – not even as the centrally de-centred subject of deconstructive theory – but would be faced with that 'something that obliges rethinking. This something is the object of a fundamental encounter, not of mere recognition'.[21] It is this situation that Michel Foucault, at the conclusion of *The Order of Things*, mentions as a distant and hypothetical possibility when he writes that:

> humanity is an invention of recent date. And one perhaps nearing its end. If those arrangements were to disappear as they appeared, if some event of which we can at the moment do no more than sense the possibility – without knowing either what its form will be or what it promises – were to cause them to crumble, as the ground of Classical thought did, at the end of the eighteenth century, then one can certainly wager that humanity would be erased, like a face drawn in the sand at the water's edge.[22]

3

Such considerations within landscape studies might also highlight those art and architecture historians – now often marginalised – who concentrated on movement, change and process: August Schmarsow, Aby Warburg, and so forth.[23] Thus, the history and theory of twentieth-century landscape might not only once again share concepts and methods with contemporary art and architectural and design history, but also might in turn influence them.

Indeed, in a shrinking world with increasingly global ecological processes, it is time for landscape studies to become central in the humanities by prioritising the importance of process, change and mobility — on the model of our environment as a mobile and complex process — and thus rethinking our place in it.

It is with these aims in mind that I collected these essays, some specially commissioned, others reworked from several conferences at which I chaired sessions, such as the Exeter conference of the Association of Art Historians (UK), the Houston conference of the Society of Architectural Historians (USA), and the Stockholm DoCoMoMo (Documentation and Conservation of the Modern Movement) conference. I would like to thank Professor George Henderson and Dean Alan Short at De Montfort University for the time which allowed finishing this collection of essays.

The book is organised into several sections that deal with these issues of memory, of vision, of the concepts of 'natural' ('nature' and 'body'), of drawing as representation and, finally, of the aesthetic categories that necessarily underlie all such discussions. I thank the authors for their work in preparing their chapters for publication. I must add that researching this area between architecture and landscape — or rather this interdisciplinary area of both architecture and landscape — has allowed me to make new friends throughout the world, which has been a real pleasure.

When I first started researching landscape studies, I wondered where it would take me. It was Martin Heidegger who explored the dual notion of the *Holzwege*, the paths that meander deep into the forest, leading unsuspecting travellers to nowhere. Seen from the perspective of the forest labourers who make and use them, these paths lead straight to the heart of the forest, allowing new wood to be brought out.[24]

4

Notes

1   Jan Birksted (ed.), *Relating Architecture to Landscape* (London: E. & F. N. Spon, 1999).

2   Jan Birksted, 'Review of *Recovering Landscape*, by James Corner', *Architectural Review Quarterly*, 3/4 (1999), pp. 380–381

3   Jan Birksted, 'Developments in architectural and landscape history', *The Bulletin, AAH* (Autumn 2000).

4   J. Elkins, 'On the conceptual analysis of gardens', *Journal of Garden History*, 13/4 (1993), pp. 189–198 (p. 189).

5   Michael Fried, 'Representing representation: on the central group in Courbet's *Studio*', in *Allegory and Representation*, ed. Stephen J. Greenblatt (Baltimore: Johns Hopkins University Press, 1981), pp. 94–127.

6   For the main argument, see Georges Didi-Huberman, *Devant l'image* (Paris: de Minuit, 1990).

7   Le Corbusier, *Précisions sur un état présent de l'architecture et de l'urbanisme* (Paris, 1930), pp. 136–138.

8   Gilles Deleuze, *Différence et Répétition* (Paris: Presses Universitaires de France, 1986).

9   See, for example, the following six studies, chosen relatively at random, from the fields of cultural studies, art history, social anthropology, landscape studies, architectural studies, cultural geography and film studies: J. Taylor, *A Dream of England: Landscape, Photography and the Tourist's Imagination* (Manchester: Manchester University Press, 1994); W. J. T. Mitchell (ed.), *Landscape and Power* (Chicago: Chicago University Press, 1994); E. Hirsch and M. O'Hanlon (eds), *The Anthropology of Landscape: Perspectives on Place and Space* (Oxford: Clarendon, 1995); Jan Birksted (ed.), *Relating Architecture to Landscape* (London: Routledge, 1999); and A. Berque, *Le sauvage et l'artifice: Les Japonais devant la nature* (Paris: Gallimard, 1986). For a more extended review of the literature, see the Introduction in Birksted, *Relating Architecture to Landscape*. Bringing together the existing, and exponentially growing, literature on landscape and garden history within the critical and visual studies field would provide a real example of a contemporary multidisciplinary field of study, linking together different methodologies and departments.

10 Jan Birksted, 'Thinking through architecture', *Journal of Architecture*, 4 (Spring 1999), pp. 55–64.

11 Svetlaner Alpers, *The Art of Describing: Dutch Art in the Seventeenth Century* (London: Penguin, 1983). Also D. M. Levin, *Modernity and the Hegemony of Vision* (Berkeley: University of California Press, 1993).

12 Hubert Damisch, *L'Origine de la Perspective* (Paris: Flammarion, 1987).

13 *Ibid.*

14 Philosophers such as Merleau-Ponty explored this dimension. Alois Riegl (1858–1905) used notions of the 'tactile' in his art historical analyses. He opposed 'tactile' (or 'haptic') to 'optic' modes of perception. For him, the haptic and the 'optic' were developmentally opposed modes of sensuous experience. The haptic involved a quality of perception comparable with that of touch, i.e. experience of texture and of material solidity, without three-dimensional visual depth. Optic experience, on the contrary, involved visual distance, thus spatial perception of figure against ground.

15 This again is an active field at the moment, highly relevant to landscape studies: D. M. Levin (ed.), *Modernity and the Hegemony of Vision* (Berkeley: University of California Press, 1993). Even if one were to take purely visual space, such visual space would be seen to be more multidimensional since it can involve many different perspectival systems simultaneously. See my study of Cézanne's studio at Les Lauves (Chapter 5 in this volume), which includes simultaneously a distant perspectival and a close-up orthogonal system.

16 For example, Barry Salt, *Film Style and Technology: History and Analysis* (London: Starword, 1992); D. Bordwell and K. Thompson, *Film Art: An Introduction* (New York: McGraw-Hill, 1979).

17 E. Cereghini, 'The Italian origins of Rousham', in *The History of Garden Design: The Western Tradition from the Renaissance to the Present Day*, eds M. Mosser and G. Teyssot (London: Thames & Hudson, 1991), pp. 320–322.

18 E. K. Meyer, 'Landscape architecture as modern other and postmodern ground', in *The Culture of Landscape Architecture*, eds H. Edquist and V. Bird (Melbourne: EDGE Publ. Committee, 1994), pp. 13–34. Also Michel Conan's edited book on movement and landscape (Washington, DC: Dumbarton Oaks, forthcoming, 2001).

19 M. Mosser and P. Nys, *Le Jardin, art et lieu de mémoire* (Vassiviere-en-Limousin: de L'Imprimeur, 1995).

20 Alpers, *Art of Describing*.

21 G. Deleuze, *Différence et répétition* (Paris: Presses Universitaires de France, 1968), p. 182.

22 Michel Foucault, *The Order of Things: An Archaeology of the Human Sciences* (London: Routledge, 1970), p. 387. 'L'homme est une invention dont l'archéologie de notre pensée montre aisément la date récente. Et peut-etre la fin prochaine. Si ces dispositions venaient à disparaitre comme elles sont apparues, si par quelque événement dont nous pouvons tout au plus pressentir la possibilité, mais dont nous ne connaissons pour l'instant encore ni la forme ni la promesse, elles basculaient, comme le fit a tournant du XVIIIe siècle le sol de la pensée classique, æ alors on peut bien parier que l'homme s'effacerait, comme à la limite de la mer un visage de sable'; *idem*, *Les mots et les choses, une archéologie des sciences humaines* (Paris: Gallimard, 1966), p. 398.

23 Michael Podro, *The Critical Historians of Art* (New Haven and London: Yale University Press, 1982); P.-A. Michaud, *Aby Warburg et l'image en mouvement* (Paris: Macula, 1998).

24 'Note de l'éditeur', in Martin Heidegger, *Chemins qui ne menent nulle part* (Paris: Gallimard, 1986).

Section One

The site of memory

Hannah Lewi

1   The commemorative anatomy of a colonial park

Some forty years after the colonial settlement of the Western Australian town of Perth, in the 1870s, a large area of bush encompassing the elevated contour of Mt Eliza was reserved as a future public park. Through the cultivation of Kings Park, as the reserve was later named, the found terrain of Mt Eliza was gradually transformed into an embellished, managed and familiar European-style park. From the turn of the century, the site became a prominent location for the collection and display of monuments, commemorating both imperial histories and collective memories of place. Today, overlooking the city of Perth, Kings Park exists as one of the most enduring and significant urban landscaped places in Australia. Through a dissection of the spaces into adjacent 'zones', the study presented here explores the spatial and visual mechanisms through which this fragment of 'found' Western Australian terrain was assimilated, represented and rendered as commemorative. Furthermore, such colonial processes of place-making are linked to current post-colonial, heritage-driven strategies of remaking place, which attempt to signify and mythologise both colonial and prior indigenous histories of the site.

The creation of the zones of Kings Park exemplifies, in different ways, the process of reconstructing and representing the presumed empty and unfamiliar space of *terra nullius* into an occupied and recognisable place; of transforming an 'exteriorised' space into an 'interiorised' and domesticated place.[1] Intrinsic to this investigation of the cognitive and constructive processes of place-making is a reciprocity between spaces and places.[2] In terms of Australian colonisation, this reciprocity can be inferred as an ongoing and shifting series of cultural negotiations between imperial centres and colonial sites.[3] Michel de Certeau illuminates this transformative relation between spaces to places, generally, as realised through the collective telling of stories and the writing of narratives: 'Stories thus carry out a labour that consistently transforms spaces into places. They also organise the play of changing relationships between places and spaces.'[4] Significant places, suggests de Certeau, are continuously redefined through the 'weight' of cultural signification, spatial occupation and representation. Reflecting on this interpretation of the role of storytelling and narrativisation, this chapter investigates how particular spatial and visual modes of storytelling were transformative in the colonial making and signifying of the place of Kings Park.

The zones of Kings Park are associated with different modes of commemoration and historical narrativisation. These modes include the invention of intentional monuments commemorating particular figures and events of Empire, the preservation of a viewpoint from which colonial settlement was visually constructed, and the mythologising of a found antipodean space that has become testimony to the historical events of settlement and valued as sensually evoking an 'aged' place. In identifying these modes of commemoration and memorialisation, distinctions are made between the investiture of 'intentional' monuments, and the signification of 'unintentional' spatial monuments. These distinctions follow Alois Riegl's conception of a typology of monuments, and his predictions at the beginning of the twentieth century, of their value and role in the formation of modern cultural memory.[5]

The overlaying of distinctive individual and historical associations, memorials and narratives has been, as Edward Harwood discusses, an established feature of picturesque English gardens since the eighteenth century.[6] Similarly, Kings Park can be interpreted as a kind of contemporary metonymic terrain in which monumental markers, or 'simulcra', have been arranged over time within cultivated settings or 'loci'. The historical annotation of the site is currently being further magnified through signs, maps and information boards.[7] Through the ongoing construction of a spatial and visual syntax of commemoration, narratives of shared memories and histories have been rendered palpable and articulate.

What may be termed the technique of picturing, and more particularly the rendering of picturesque landscapes, is also seen as intrinsic to the transformation of found space into recognisable place, within the dominant schema of colonial vision.[8] The technique of picturing is closely linked to the telling of stories of place; for, as John Dixon Hunt has described, the picturesque may be defined as the creation and communication of 'speaking pictures'.[9] The articulation of the picturesque, through images or the design of landscapes, has always operated in close collusion with what Norman Bryson has described as the 'natural attitude'; the seemingly unassisted creation of places, and their seemingly mimetic and realist representation.[10] In this constructive account of the making of a park, such naturalised mechanisms are investigated.

The association of picturing generally with the practice of landscape design is of course long-standing. As Humphry Repton wrote: 'If the knowledge of painting be insufficient without that of gardening, on the other hand, the mere gardener, without some skill in painting, will seldom be able to form a just idea of effects before they are carried into execution. This faculty of fore-knowing effects constitutes the master, in every branch of the polite arts; and can only be the result of a correct eye, a ready conception, and a fertility of invention.'[11] Through the cultivation of a 'correct eye', and the 'fore-knowing' of picturesque effects, the terrain of Kings Park has been assimilated and transformed in two significant ways. First, the elevated eastern edge of Mt Eliza, encompassed by the park, composes a natural frame through which the setting of Perth has consistently been visually apprehended, and thereby represented and constructed. Second, the grounds of the park have been gradually cultivated through the quotation and adaptation of prefigured picturesque scenery and garden design. As this chapter illustrates, such techniques of picturing, and the making of picturesque analogies, were crucial in early episodes of the colonial aestheticising of place.[12] As imperial cognition and vision became more locally accustomed, these modes of picturing were subtly adjusted. Bernard Smith evocatively describes this process: 'Through the broken mirage of English tradition the contours of a new continent were visible, and these contours were to bend and distort the European vision to the ways of a new country.'[13]

To reveal the complex spatial and architectural processes by which the colonial, picturesque landscape of Kings Park has been apprehended, constructed and commemorated, the following historical account dissects the park, through written and drawn descriptions, into four distinct commemorative zones. These spatial and visual zones are delineated as: (1) a viewing edge, (2) cultivated gardens, (3) the siting of monuments and memorials, and (4) the cultural recognition of the native bush, seen previously as a residual or void space awaiting cultivation, and later appropriated and accommodated as a commemorative place (Fig. 1.1). Today these adjacent zones are still experienced as holding distinctive identities and associations.

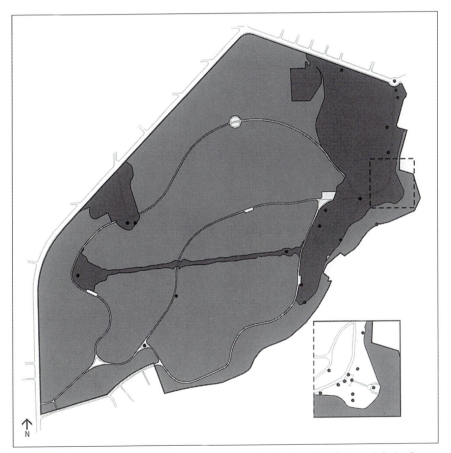

1.1 Zones of significance: plan illustrating the spatial zones as defined in Kings Park. Dark grey indicates the 'garden zone', light grey the 'Bush zone'. (Lewi and Goldswain)

Early encounters

Before entering the interior zones of the park, the colonial scene will be set through a brief description of early encounters with the topography of the scarp. These encounters reveal its emblematic role in the construction of the colonial locale. First, the naming of the scarp as Mt Eliza, on the occasion of the first major English exploratory expedition to the region in 1827, inscribed the first words of European history on the site, and lodged it firmly in the inventory of Empire. As Paul Carter has observed, 'Naming words were forms of spatial punctuation, transforming space into an object of knowledge, something that could be explored and read.'[14] Naming also served to erase and appropriate the site's significance from local, indigenous Aboriginal groups. Second, many of the early explorers record the finding of the wooded scarp as a memorable moment in their journey. After the tentative establishment of the Perth settlement under the shadow of the mount, the following observations were published in a manual of 1835 for 'persons desirous of emigration': 'Passing through a narrow strait at the foot of Mount Eliza, a richly wooded hill on his left … [the traveller] discovers the town of Perth, beautifully situated on one of its declivities and extending along the shore of a somewhat circular bay.'[15] Other early expeditions describe such 'occasional eminences' as the only prominent feature to relieve the monotony of the immense flat western coastal plain.[16]

Therefore, despite its relative topographical insignificance (it is by no means a mountain), Mt Eliza was a strong anchoring element in the developing scene of Perth. Long before the actual consecration of Kings Park, the mount composed a locus of comparative associations with English natural scenes. From this podium, the desiccated coastal plains were viewed as resembling a pastoral landscape, 'turned yellow by the sun'.[17] Other descriptions conjured optimistic images reminiscent of the 'open country' of a vast royal deer park or hunting domain; the quintessential prospects of imperial possession.[18] Such deceptive and purely visual comparisons of the terrain perpetuated imperial allusions.[19] And these allusions were instrumental in reconstructing the perceived empty and unowned landscape of *terra nullius* into a foundation upon which to imagine and cultivate colonial settlement. In the meagre beginnings of this private colonial experiment, these projections of productive and picturesque places were particularly important. As Raymond Williams has described, owing to the impact of industrialisation and colonial trade in the nineteenth century, England began to look to its distant, colonial lands as the new rural parks and prospects of Empire.[20] The traditional relationship between city and country was thus recast on an international scale; and English emigrants sought to recall and recreate in the colonies what was perceived as a threatened rural idyll. However, the reality of the antipodean wilderness found colonial settlers struggling for many decades with the consequences of these early deceptive and idealised images of a ready-made and park-like place.[21]

Zone one – the edge

The scarp of Mt Eliza shaped a significant compositional element in the general scene of the Perth region. The precipitous edge also framed a vast picture window. As evident in the extensive archive of local images — from colonial etchings to photographs and postcards — the elevated and distanced view was exploited for the generation of picturesque urban and natural landscapes. And it is this visual and pictorial vantage that forms the focus of the first commemorative zone of the park (Figs 1.2 and 1.3).

The constructive role of perception in the making of landscapes has been

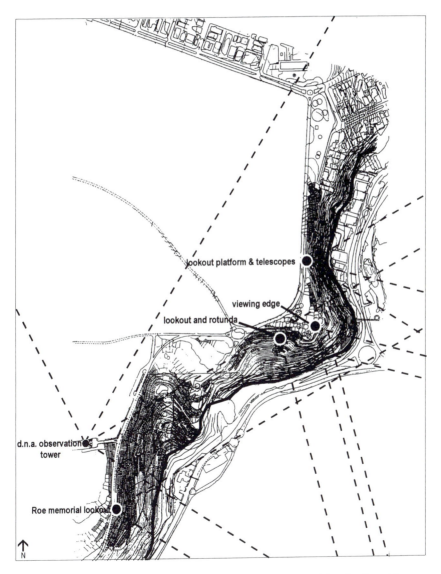

lookout platform & telescopes

viewing edge

lookout and rotunda

d.n.a. observation tower

Roe memorial lookout

N

1.2 Locating the edge condition: the contours of the Mt Eliza scarp dividing the park from the city, and the locations of various viewing devices. (Lewi and Goldswain)

13

elaborated by many recent writings. Karen Burns, for example, writes: 'Perception itself gives rise to the term "landscape", which literally means the portion of land that the eye can compound in a single view.'[22] Williams has suggested that the process of creating picturesque places and imagery is not so much inherent in the particular properties of place, as prefigured in the perceptual modes of viewing and representing: 'The self conscious observer: the man who is not only looking at the land but who is conscious that he is doing so ... and who has prepared social models and analogies from elsewhere to support and justify the experience: this is the figure we need to seek, not a kind of nature, but a kind of man.'[23] Further, Bryson has emphasised the predictive nature of constructive viewing in realist painting: 'Without the instructions that indicate what it is to be observed, observation cannot begin, and it is just this needed set of instructions that the schema supplies.'[24]

Returning to the view from Mt Eliza, colonisers brought with them a history to their vision; a cognitive model of what the place was and should become.[25] In one of many examples recording the painterly sensibilities of colonial vision, an early Perth settler wrote in her diary: 'The scene has been most beautiful; worthy of the pencil of a Claude Lorraine — the moon and the sky dazzling bright, the sea glistening and perfectly smooth, the outline of the shore dark and clear, the lurid flash and curling grey of vermilion and yellow of the fires throwing a bright redness over the scene, investing it with a wildness congenial to the spot and exciting to the imagination.'[26] This analogy to Lorraine is telling. For, as has been suggested by Humphry Wine in an account of landscape gardening and 'associationism', Lorraine's scenographic paintings 'did not so much demand a response from the spectator as leave open space into which the spectator could project his or her own imaginative reactions'.[27] Through the importation of such aestheticised vision, the blank antipodean canvas was modified into pastoral and Arcadian scenes, prior to any physical cultivation. As Dixon Hunt writes, 'potentially unprepossessing scenery' could be 'seen more pleasantly, occupied and visited more safely as if it were thought of as a painting. . . . So it was filtered through sensibilities honed on a study of graphic representations of the world'.[28]

14

As is illustrated by the figures 1.3 and 1.4 included here (which represent only a fraction of the archive of images created), representations made from the natural viewing device of Mt Eliza remain remarkably consistent in their composition; falling somewhere between the panorama, the topographic map and the picturesque, romantic scene. Typically, the flat morphology of the town was documented to a fair degree of detail, and was framed and bounded by a picturesque border of dark exotic flora, a background of still waters, and an exaggerated line of hazy hills behind. In early images, the immediate foreground was often occupied by Aboriginal figures, to be replaced later by local settlers (Fig. 1.3). These colonial images mark a mid-point in what Smith has identified as a transition in nineteenth-century Australian landscape painting from the topographic and scientific record towards the romantic scene. Executed with the European viewer, and buyer, in mind, such paintings satisfied demand for images of both botanically accurate exotica, and productive and safely colonised places. From the distanced and proprietorial vantage of Mt Eliza, viewers were disengaged from the view

1.3 Perth from Mt Eliza, artist unknown, 1842 (courtesy of Mitchell Library, State Library of New South Wales)

1.4 Perth from Mt Eliza, Horace Samson, 1847 (Courtesy of Art Gallery of Western Australia)

before them, rendering the scene as partially abstracted and somewhat 'dispassionately' pleasing (Figs 1.4 and 1.5).[29]

As photography eclipsed painting as the dominant mode of recording places, the duration of the painterly gaze was hastened by the mechanical glance of the camera. Photographs rendered rapid reporting as paramount, casting the viewer as the 'witness' rather than the prolonged visitor.[30] The advent of photography, however, changed the picturesque composition of earlier images very little. The activity of experiencing the

1.5 Perth from Mt Eliza, H. van Raalte, 1912. (The Colonial Eye)

elevated view was, and remains, a popular pastime;[31] people gathering to behold their changing locale, and also to look at themselves as an urban crowd. To enhance the activity of informed 'sight-seeing', various aides such as telescopes, a lookout tower, and orientation maps engraved in panoramic viewing platforms have been gradually assembled along the park's edge.

In figuring the viewing edge of Mt Eliza as the first commemorative zone, it is evident that panoramic and picturesque modes of viewing, and associated techniques of picturing, have been intrinsic to envisioning and structuring the place of the park, and the city below. The schema of the picturesque has continually served to recall and visually to commemorate pre-existing places and imagery. And today the experience of witnessing the picturesque view has become a highly historicised one; the edge condition creating an unbounded and 'unintentional' visual memorial in which visitors locate themselves in a continuous lineage of place-making.[32]

Zone two – the garden

Mt Eliza was gazetted as a public reserve and future urban park in the 1870s. However, in all Australian cities at this time, embryonic parks remained as unmanaged and unmanicured open spaces; described as 'howling wildernesses' holding few attractions for the polite public.[33] The Mt Eliza reserve was, in its early days, largely undifferentiated from the indigenous landscape lying beyond, and pocketed within, the boundaries of the town-site. And while the local landscape may have once resembled a park-like prospect to colonists from a distance, upon more intimate knowledge the deceptions of these pastoral and picturesque visions were revealed. The landscape was far less inviting, romantic or productive than first imagined. Native flora and fauna were seen as anomalies within the known European natural order of things, and the scrubby bush did not conform to any traditional models of beauty. The terrain existed as a somewhat monotonous and unsettling nothingness.

By the 1890s, owing to the rapid expansion of the town and the growing expectations of its gentrified population, a programme had commenced to create a recognisable gardened park across the reserve of Mt Eliza. As Christine Boyer has commented on the cultivation of American urban parks: 'It was believed that parks would spread a desire for beauty and order, spreading a benign tranquillising influence over their surroundings.'[34] The second commemorative zone of Kings Park is here identified as the creation of gardened spaces, which gradually composed a series of small bounded green rooms, carved out of the vast reserve of native bush (Fig. 1). In commemorating the beginnings of this process of cultivation in 1895, the Western Australian Premier John Forrest spoke of the park's present and future significance as: 'one of the signs of the material progress going on from one part of the colony to the other'. He declared his hope that the park would be gradually transformed to: 'a very different place from what it is at present. Even those who remember the ground as it was, will say that some improvements have already been made'.[35] This speech, and other reports of the time, reveal significant themes in the cultivation of the park. First, the entire reserve was seen to be in need of substantial demarcation and delineation. Many reports document concerns about the lack of open, green spaces in the expanding colony. However, such concerns, voiced both at the time and in subsequent historical interpretations, appear to be largely imported from the distant rhetoric of Victorian urban reform. Considered against local realities they appear tenuous. The relatively small town of Perth was still overwhelmed by open green spaces, if of an unfamiliar shade. Diaries document the colony's architecture as still strangely unconnected: buildings floating in undifferentiated open spaces; sandy streets indiscernible from gardens; and surrounding scrub-covered plains still threatening to reclaim the tentatively grounded place. Rather than open space, it was the demarcation and domestication of a bounded place that was of primary concern. Accordingly, one of the first moves in defining the park was the fencing and gating of the entire site.[36] This definition of a manicured and cultivated garden also evoked associations of tamed Arcadia, foregrounding the straggling wilderness beyond. Or, as Simon Schama has described of the composition of the Arcadian character of London's nineteenth-century parks, 'the wild and the tender folded together in the bowl of the same gentle landscape'.[37]

Second, early discussions revealed that the park was seen to be in need of management, so as to create a suitable and comfortable setting for recreation and future collective commemoration. Accordingly, the Parks and Reserves Act 1895 was passed 'for the purpose of controlling and managing local parks and reserves',[38] and a caretaker's lodge and ranger were installed to survey the grounds. In another inevitable gesture of the times, the Native Administration Act 1905 determined that Aboriginals be banned from the Perth metropolitan area, including their sacred site of Mt Eliza, until as late as 1954. Jane Jacobs quotes an aboriginal elder of the area as recalling: 'You wasn't allowed to camp around there at Kings Park by the river on our Homegrounds. … The old people used to talk about Kings Park, all along the river, but you wasn't allowed to stop there.'[39]

Third, the *tabula rasa* of the scarp was regarded as raw ground in need of aesthetic improvement and embellishment. Through the subtle art of landscape gardening, it was envisaged that the character and decorum of both the civic landscape and its visitors would be 'improved'. As illustrated by the writings of Repton, conscious cultivation of the 'character' of landscaped places was also thought to possess the potential to cultivate the character, identity and social decorum of the individual and the collective population.[40] It was initially intended that the entire reserve would be gradually transformed into cleared and gardened scenic arrangements, thus alleviating the discomfort of the dense indigenous scrub. At this time, the Acclimatisation Society in Western Australia zealously assisted in embellishing and improving the found terrain through the importation of all things English, such as deer and foxes, for the reassurance of displaced emigrants.[41] As Schama has aptly commented, the manicuring of landscapes helped to create 'barriers against the beastly'.[42]

However, for a number of decades to follow, only small inroads were made into the vast native reserve. Opportunities for picturesque walks and vistas were first created around 1900 with the laying out of the park's main roads, inscribing an undulating and curvilinear journey across the site. A hierarchy of smaller winding paths and episodic trails, interrupted by shelters, seats and pagodas was gradually implemented in a similar style to many English municipal parks (Fig. 1.6).[43] Where gardens were successfully cultivated in Kings Park, planting generally followed a late Victorian appreciation of

18

1.6 Winding paths and episodic walks in Kings Park today. (Lewi)

eclectic composition and 'gardenesque' style, introducing exotic species to relieve the perceived monotony of the indigenous grey-green prospect. One painter describing the local eucalypts wrote: 'no tree, to my taste, can be beautiful that is not deciduous. What can a painter do with one cold olive-green?'[44]

In composing introduced species, a kind of taxonomical hierarchy was aimed for in which exotic trees and flowers were planted at some distance from the native species to best foreground their special status. Western Australian species were also transplanted and propagated in English parks and gardens for similar eclectic effect.[45] Gradually, further areas of the native reserve were transformed into an arboretum, a series of grassed walks and, later, an extensive botanical garden composed of exotics collected from the countries of the Commonwealth.

Through the importation and adaptation of English park models and plants, and the influence of designers such as John Claudius Loudon and Joseph Paxton, prominent sections of the park were thus recomposed into gardens that held associations, if somewhat remote and perverse, with the memories of more familiar English landscapes. These processes of landscaping reflected an ongoing cultural dialogue between colony and Empire.

Zone three – monuments and memorials

One of the park's founding rationales was the consecration of a suitable public place to house monuments that would 'intentionally' commemorate historical events and allegiances. Kings Park was thereby envisaged to become not only a place of recreation and viewing, but also what Boyer has described as a 'mnemonic device' or 'calendar space' of collective remembering and historical association.[46] Such commemorative associations were often conveyed in English public and private gardens through the sculpting of the existing contours, and through the placement of monuments, follies and historical statuary – sometimes annotated *in situ* with explanatory and poetic texts.[47] The perceived importance of such cultural associations for the cultivation of the colonies was emphasised in writings such as Loudon's article in the *Architectural Review* of 1846: 'The associations which an object so characteristic of British scenery and civilisation is calculated to raise up in the minds of Britons, resident in far distant, and, as yet, scarcely peopled countries, surrounded by primeval forests or wastes, can hardly be conceived by those who have never experienced them.'[48]

So successful was the invention of a public place of intentioned commemoration that today Kings Park is said to hold a greater concentration of named memorials than any other in the Southern Hemisphere.[49] These monuments and memorials, entangled in the formal gardens of the park, compose the third commemorative zone of investigation (Fig. 1.7). Two of the first memorials to be erected were the South African War Memorial of 1901 and an imposing statue of Queen Victoria, prized in its day for its likeness and detail.[50] Draped in her elaborate robe, Victoria was sited imperiously on the edge of the scarp; a Queen surveying her dominions (Fig. 1.8). And in symbolic protection of this Imperial prospect, a preponderance of discarded shells and guns were gradually collected and found their final resting place here.[51] In the founding years of

KEY MONUMENTS:
1. Edith Cowan memorial
2. Queen Elizabeth shell
3. South African war memorial
4. 10th Light Horse memorial
5. Queen Victoria statue
6. Wishing well
7. Leake memorial
8. State war memorial concourse
9. State war memorial

cenotaph
10. HMAS Perth tree
11. Red cross tree
12. Dukes tree
13. Queens tree
14. Karri log
15. Redwood log
16. 2nd/16th battalion memorial
17. Lord Forrest statue
18. Kennedy memorial

19. Old naval guns
20. Minmara guns
21. Pioneer womens memorial
22. Roe memorial
23. Drummond memorial
24. D.N.A. observation tower
25. 2nd/2nd Australian commando squadron
26. 2nd/28th Battalion memorial
27. Vietnam war pavillion

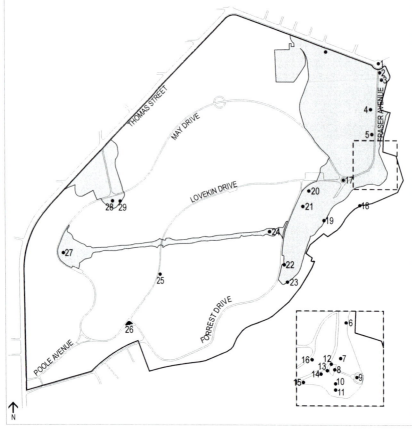

1.7 Monuments and memorials: charting the concentration of monuments in selective areas of Kings Park. (Lewi and Goldswain)

the park, these public monuments predominantly marked distant events and Imperial figures.[52] Commemoration of local histories was noticeably absent; the Australian colonies still seemingly lacked an appropriate language of signification within what Tony Bennett has described as the 'largely Eurocentric lexicons of nationalism and history'.[53] It seems that the overwhelming imperative was the expedient occupation of this perceived historical void with whatever readily came to hand. There was even an Australian literary club whose objectives included the hasty invention of ancient ruins.[54] This consecration of ready-made objects and statues valued for their verisimilitude,

1.8 A Queen surveying her Empire: the statue of Queen Victoria on Mt Eliza scarp. (Lewi)

communicated direct and reassuring connections to the authenticities and heritage of Empire. The formal 'mantelpiece' of the park thus became filled with trophies and souvenirs recalling 'authentic' events and a distant home, 'in that special sense in which "home" is a memory and an ideal'.[55]

After Australia's substantial involvement in the First and Second World Wars, the potentials of war memorials to serve as a catalyst for nationalist sentiment were recognised and many were erected in the park. The most substantial was an impressively sited, if ubiquitous, obelisk commemorating the substantial number of Western Australians who died in both Wars (Fig. 1.9). However, a far more remarkable memorial to fallen soldiers was commenced in 1919 with the planting of a series of tree-lined Avenues of Honour. Exploiting the iconic value of tall trees — often used in American civic memorials — the Avenues of Honour cultivated an enduring scene of undulating Arcadian vistas along the roads of the park. These avenues embodied the close associations held at the time of landscaped places with Australian war memorials; indicating a tendency towards the naturalising of antipodean history, and a lingering sense of unease about commemorating cultural identities in other more permanent ways.[56] In this inter-war period of conservative Australian politics, gardened memorials reflected the strong resurgence of the pastoral vision, as galvanised by the 'back to the land' movement. Good, honest Australian 'men of the bush' were also believed to make good soldiers.[57] Kings Park's avenues were to take these direct associations of nature and nation an important stage further with the trees themselves becoming the very substance of monuments. In large public ceremonies, after both Wars, trees were

21

1.9 War memorial to service in the First and Second World Wars on Mt Eliza scarp. (Lewi)

22

planted with nameplates commemorating individual soldiers who 'laid down a life for King and Country' thus 'keeping green' the memory of individual sacrifice for the future (Fig. 1.10).[58]

The choice of tree species for planting along the Avenues of Honour reflects an interesting shift towards the accommodation of native flora. The first avenues were planted with Royal oak seedlings from the grounds of Windsor Castle. Described by the park's director as being 'migrated for the beautification of Perth',[59] these royal English trees were invested with imperial sentiment, though many died in propagation.[60] Despite the unsuitability of imported species, and a growing interest in Australian iconography generally, eucalypt trees were still not deemed the suitable stuff of monuments. However, after the Second World War, just as writing and painting began to reveal the soul and presence of the Australian Bush, so too were local flora incorporated into the composition of architectural detailing, monuments and gardens, marking a shift in both allegiances and aesthetics. Local eucalypts were eventually chosen for the extensive

1.10 One of the Avenues of Honour planted with local eucalypts. (Photograph by Lewi)

additions to the avenues, which by the end of the 1940s totalled some 1080 trees. Antipodean cultural vision was thus gradually shifting to accommodate local contexts; or, as Smith has aptly described, colonisers 'literally went native, but in ways so subtle and various as often to be imperceptible'.[61]

The establishment of the Avenues of Honour added another important dimension to the commemorative landscape of Kings Park; that of the gardened cemetery. James S. Curl writes: 'the grave and memorial became an essential part of the idealised Arcadian landscape where the living could pay homage, shed decorous tears and reach the dead, for the departed were present, inhabited the landscape, and remained alive in memory'.[62] In Kings Park, these long-standing connections of nostalgia and collective memory within Arcadian landscapes were reinforced both by established Australian associations of melancholy with the native Bush, and the particular sense of loss evoked in the Avenues of Honour.[63] Through commemoration of individual soldiers by trees, the presence of lost soldiers was seen to have been returned from foreign soils. For example, in one report of the time, a visitor to the park is quoted as saying, 'I do not know where my dear boy's body lies, but I do know his soul is here.'[64] Thus, after the Second World War, associations of 'home' began to migrate southwards towards a more peripheral locale.

23

Zone four – the bush

Large-scale garden plans were continually thwarted by a lack of resources and water, and the large native section in the west of the park remained substantially unaltered and 'un-improved' throughout the early twentieth century. However, by the 1940s, the Australian bush was beginning to acquire a more recognisable and comfortable identity. The pastime of bushwalking became popular in Kings Park, as in many other new Australian National Parks. Not only did appreciation grow locally, for the aesthetic of antipodean landscapes gradually filtered back to Britain, fuelling the imagination just as natural resources had fuelled the imperial economy. By the 1960s, the character of the bush had been fully appropriated and accommodated within the evolving vernacular language of the antipodean picturesque. Management of the park turned towards preserving, propagating and informing visitors about native plants. The fourth and final commemorative zone is defined by this now fully recognised and valued bush region of Kings Park (Figs 1.1 and 1.11).

The fact that the flora of this thoroughly managed fragment of bush, adjacent to the city, had been greatly disturbed and recomposed over the years, appeared to matter little. The generalised and 'significant form', to adopt Roland Barthes's term,[65] of the native landscape became a vigorous source of local commemoration. The bush has now come to be exalted for its supposed unaltered 'natural' state. This latest commemorative zone is seen to testify the very history of colonisation; the activity of domesticating and transforming overlooked space into settled and mythologised place. And in a somewhat contradictory fashion, it is thereby seen as commemorating both the sanctioned history of colonial foundation and prior aboriginal inhabitation. Carter writes: 'Just as fence lines could transform the terrifying wilderness into an object of pleasure, so too, the picturesque that foretokened possession could, in retrospect, come to signify wildness and the romance of beginnings.'[66] The investiture of a spatial and 'unintentional' monument to colonial origins reflects what Riegl anticipated as the modern cult of the memorialisation of existing things and places which have acquired the general semblance of the past, the look of 'age', and associations with an irretrievable stage of history.[67] As he suggested, 'every human activity and every human event of which we have knowledge or testimony may claim historical value'.[68]

Unlike most urban parks, this bush zone today does not create a light break in the urban fabric. Rather, it is experienced as a positive 'dark space'; a cool, deep inert void within an overly bright city.[69] And at times this dark and dense bush appears to revert to an unfamiliar or uncanny past state. The darkness touches the senses and imagination of the passer-by, as it drifts across the boundary road of the park. When following the maze of tracks within this region, the presence of others recedes and the visitor can fantasise about being lost in the unsettling 'original' found landscape.

1.11 Native bush zone interrupted by the grassed 'broadwalk'. (Lewi)

Concluding thoughts

By the 1980s, it was concluded in park development studies that there were more than enough specific monuments instituted within the park. The entire park was listed on the Australian National Heritage Register, and management strategies turned towards a programme of conservation and interpretation. Current renovation and enhancement plans include, on the one hand the restoration of existing monuments and architectural structures and, on the other hand, the redevelopment of gardens and botanical sections — in line with a recent bias towards native rather than exotic planting. The intentional memorialisation of military and imperial associations has thus shifted towards more environmental and spatial significations of Australian nationalism.

Within the shifting constructions of this cultivated landscape, the commemoration and representation of place continues. However, rather than being orientated outwards towards the recall and reinvention of other places, techniques are now self-consciously and reflexively focused inwards. Reflecting this shift from colonial improvement to post-colonial historicism, and with the pedagogical and tourist potentials of the park in mind, it has been suggested that resident curators and historians be appointed alongside existing park rangers. The signification of past Aboriginal presence within the site is being fabricated through the reconstruction of grass shelters, located prominently on the exposed face of the scarp. These ethnographic exhibits appear reminiscent of colonial, picturesque images that figured a foreground of controlled 'native' and 'exotic' interest, against the familiar scene beyond. Aboriginality is thus in danger of being appropriated and integrated within a European lexicon of place. Therefore, although no longer concerned with the direct transformation of found space into familiar place, present heritage strategies are still perpetuating adapted picturesque modes of place-making; and creating easily recognisable and comfortable images and stories. Techniques of picturing are also being furthered through the inauguration of 'artist-in-residence' programmes, and the proliferation of souvenirs, which again create easily consumed images of place.

In conclusion, through this chapter's dissection of Kings Park, four spatial and visual zones have been defined which, although spatially adjacent and at times intertwined, are seen to represent mutually exclusive commemorative stories and places. Such differences and contradictions are potently discerned in the experience of the park today. The intentional monuments scattered across the front of the park still actively hold their collective historical values and memories, and are continually renewed through local ceremonies. The picturesque gardens and views, from the edge of Mt Eliza, are still appreciated as recalling other familiar cultivated places. And the bush zone is fervently preserved as mythologising the making of the particular place of Perth itself. However, it may be concluded that such commemorative distinctions are being eroded. Current heritage strategies of historical interpretation, including the display of maps, texts and signs, are endeavouring to annotate and narrativise the readings of these distinct zones into a single place, evidential of a coherent historical story.

1   *Terra nullius* here refers to the (fictitious) imperial legal assumption of the Australian land as having no prior ownership or by inference history.

2   Some Australian writers have discussed this notion of the translation of antipodean spaces in terms of colonial exploration, specifically, for example, Paul Carter, *The Road to Botany Bay* (London: Faber & Faber, 1988).

3   Peter Beilharz, *Imagining the Antipodes: Culture, Theory and Visual in the Work of Bernard Smith* (Cambridge: Cambridge University Press, 1997), p. 110; and Carter, *Road to Botany Bay*.

4   Michel de Certeau, *The Practice of Everyday Life* (Berkeley: University of California Press, 1988), p. 118.

5   Alois Riegl, 'The modern cult of monuments: its character and its origins' [1902], repr. *Oppositions Journal*, no. 25 (Fall, 1982), pp. 21–51.

6   Edward Harwood, 'Humphry Repton and the idea of Association', *Journal of Garden History*, 16/3 (1996), p. 197.

7   For an explication of the classical 'art of mnemonics', see Francis Yates, *The Art of Memory* (London: Routledge & Kegan Paul, 1966), pp. 2–6.

8   'Technique' is used here in reference to Ian Hunter's discussion of the construction of culture through various social techniques or apparatus: I. Hunter, *Culture and Government: The Emergence of Literary Education* (London: Macmillan, 1988), p. ix.

9   John Dixon Hunt, *Gardens and the Picturesque: Studies in the History of Landscape Architecture* (Cambridge, MA: MIT Press, 1992), p. 13.

10 Norman Bryson writes of the 'natural attitude': 'Essential to the work of naturalisation and the "habitus" is the mobility of the place at which the "join" between cultural and natural worlds lies hidden, as a kind of blind spot or blank stain within social consciousness: travelling through time and across the shifting cultural spaces, its invisible accompaniment and participation is vital to the process of cultural reproduction'; N. Bryson, *Vision and Painting: The Logic of the Gaze* (London: Macmillan, 1983), p. 14.

11 John Claudius Loudon (ed.), *The Landscape Gardening and Landscape Architecture of the Late* Humphry Repton, *Esq.* (London: Longman & Paternoster Row, 1836 [first reprinted edn]), p. 30.

12 For example, Isaac Scott Nind, describing the south-west of Australia in 1828, wrote: 'The general appearance of the country, although of a very barren nature, is very picturesque.' A visual atlas of Australia was produced in the 1880s called 'The Picturesque Atlas'; B. Chapman (ed.), *The Colonial Eye*, exh. cat. (Perth: Art Gallery of Western Australia, 1979), pp. 36, 64.

13 Bernard Smith, *Place, Taste and Tradition: A Study of Australian Art Since 1788* (London: Oxford University Press, 1979), p. 53.

14 Carter, *Road to Botany Bay*, p. 67.

15 Extract from Captain Irwin's manual for emigration to Western Australia of 1835; quotation in George Seddon, *A City and its Setting* (Freemantle: Freemantle Arts Centre Press, 1986), p. 108.

16 Captain Stirling's description of the view from the Darling Scarp, in 'Captain James Stirling's first report on his survey of the Swan River district together with his "Narrative of Operations" and "Observations on the Territory"', New South Wales, April 1827; repr. Malcolm Uren, *Land Looking West* (Melbourne: Oxford University Press, 1948), pp. 267–291.

17 *Ibid.*, p. 273.

18 Tom Williamson, *Polite Landscapes: Gardens and Society in Eighteenth-Century England* (London: John Hopkins Press, 1995), p. 93.

19 For discussion of such pastoral and park-like illusions, see Carter, *Road to Botany Bay*, p. 230; and Simon Ryan, *The Cartographic Eye: How Explorers Saw Australia* (Cambridge: Cambridge University Press, 1996), p. 75.

20 Raymond Williams, *The Country and the City* (London: Hogarth, 1986), p. 281.

21 G. C. Bolton, *Spoils and Spoilers: Australians Make their Environment* (Sydney: Allen & Unwin, 1981), p. 15.

22 Karen Burns, 'On site: architectural preoccupations', in A. Kahn (ed.), *Drawing/Building/Text* (New York: Princeton Architectural Press, 1991), p. 160.

23 Williams, *Country and the City*, p. 121.

24 Bryson, *Vision and Painting*, p. 32.

25 A sense of prior 'history' in Australian vision is discussed with regard to Australian painting, see Beilharz, *Imagining the Antipodes*, p. 29.

26 Diaries of Louisa Clifton, extract from an entry in 1841, as cited in Chapman, *Colonial Eye*, p. 6.

27 For discussion of Claude Lorrain by Wine, see Harwood, 'Humphry Repton and the idea of Association', p. 197.

28 Hunt, *Gardens and the Picturesque*, p. 5.

29 For the distant abstraction of Cartesian perspective painting as imposing 'mathematically regular, spatio-temporal order filled with the natural objects that could only be observed from without by the dispassionate eye of the neutral researcher', see Martin Jay, *Force Fields: Between Intellectual History and Cultural Critique* (New York: Routledge, 1993), pp. 116–118.

30 For the act of witnessing and reporting a scene through the frame of the camera, see Paul Virillio, *The Vision Machine* (Bloomington, Ind.: Indiana University Press and London: British Film Institute, 1994), p. 1.

31 The Western Australian novelist Elizabeth Jolly remembers: 'My father liked what he called a splendid view. He would dismount from his high bicycle and, parting the hedge, he would exclaim on the loveliness of what he could see'; E. Jolly, 'A sort of gift: image of Perth', in D. Modjeska (ed.), *Inner Cities* (Melbourne: Penguin, 1989), p. 201.

32 As Jacobs comments in reference to a similar lookout site of Mount Coot-tha in Brisbane, which is relevant to the present site under discussion: 'here colonisation could be repeatedly re-visioned'; J. M. Jacobs, *Edge of Empire: Postcolonialism and the City* (London: Routledge, 1996), p. 139.

33 Tim Bonyhady, 'A useable past: the public trust in Australia', *Environment and Planning Law Journal* (October 1995), p. 131.

34 For a discussion of the American context where the 'back to nature' movement spread across the country in the late nineteenth century, see Christine Boyer, *Dreaming the Rational City* (Cambridge, MA: MIT Press, 1984), pp. 34–39.

35 Transcript of Premier John Forrest's Foundation Speech of 1895, courtesy of the Kings Park Board archives.

36 The fences and gates were subsequently removed in the 1950s.

37 Simon Schama, *Landscapes and Memory* (London: HarperCollins, 1995), p. 576.

38 For the Act, see M. McCoombe, 'Kings Park', unpublished thesis, University of Western Australia, Nedlands, 1955.

39 Jacobs, *Edge of Empire*, p. 108.

40 For a discussion of Repton's notion of 'character', see Harwood, 'Humphry Repton and the idea of association', p. 201.

41 The Society was formed in the 1860s in most Australian colonies. For a description of its aims as 'stocking our waste waters, woods and plains with choice animals making that which was dull and lifeless become animated by creatures in the full enjoyment of existence, and lands before useless become fertile with rare and valuable trees and plants', see Geoffrey C. Bolton, *Spoils and Spoilers: Australians Make Their Environment* (Nedlands: University of Western Australia Press, 1981), p. 97.

42 Schama, *Landscape and Memory*, p. 7.

43 Hazel Conway, *People's Parks: The Design and Development of Victorian Parks in Britain* (Cambridge: Cambridge University Press, 1991), p. 165.

44 Comments from the painter and explorer Barron Field's 'Geographical Memoirs' (1825), cited in Bernard Smith, *European Vision and the South Pacific* (London: Oxford University Press, 1960), p. 182.

45 Conway, *People's Parks*, p. 164.

46 For a discussion of the role of monuments as defining calendar spaces, see Christine Boyer, *The City of Collective Memory* (Cambridge, MA: MIT Press, 1994), p. 343.

47 For example, Harwood describes an eighteenth-century garden whose statue pedestals contained additional pictures and texts about the commemorative subject of the statues; Harwood, 'Humphry Repton and the idea of Association', p. 193.

48 George Hersey, 'J. C. Louden and architectural Associationism', *Architectural Review*, CXLIV/858 (August 1968), p. 89.

49 *Kings Park and Botanic Garden Centennial Enhancement Project*. Draft Framework Plan (Perth: Kings Park Gardens, 1995).

50 McCoombe, 'Kings Park', p. 12.

51 Some quick-firing missiles from the *Queen Elizabeth* were also donated to the park's first director by the British Admiralty; Hon. A. Lovekin, *The Kings Park* (Perth: Wigg & Sonn Printer, 1925), p. 13.

52 Representations of the far-flung dominions of Empire were also evoked in some British, Victorian parks. For example, in Glasgow Green Park, a statue of Victoria incorporated into an ornate terracotta fountain was ornamented with representations of the colonies of South Africa, India, Canada and Australia. Australia is represented by a gold-digger resting on his spade and by a female figure carrying a sheaf of wheat, resting her hand on a sheep, with a vine growing beside her. Thus, the Australian landscape was seen purely in terms of productive, natural resources and economic significance; Conway, *People's Parks*, p. 162.

53 Tony Bennett, *The Birth of the Museum: History, Theory, Politics* (London: Routledge, 1995), p. 139.

54 The Dawn and Dusk Club; Tom Griffiths, *Hunters and Collectors: The Antiquarian Imagination in Australia* (Cambridge: Cambridge University Press, 1996), p. 153.

55 Williams, *Country and the City*, p. 281.

56 John Fiske, Bob Hodge and Graeme Turner, *Myths of Oz* (Sydney: Allen & Unwin, 1987), p. 139.

57 John F. Williams, *The Quarantined Culture: Australian Reactions to Modernism 1913–1939* (Cambridge: Cambridge University Press, 1995), p. 129.

58 Lovekin, *Kings Park*, p. 63.

59 'Editorial', *Western Australian Daily News* (4 August 1919).

60 Other early efforts also to Europeanise the park flora and fauna, perhaps thankfully, failed, including a gift from Victoria of deer intended to run in the park, which were instead kept in the new Perth Zoo.

61 Antipodean cultural vision was thus gradually shifting to accommodate local contexts; or, as Beilharz describes, in reference to Bernard Smith's writing, colonizers 'literally went native, but in ways so subtle and various as often to be imperceptible'; Beilharz, *Imagining the Antipodes*, p. 44.

62 James S. Curl, 'Young's *Night Thoughts* and the origins of the garden cemetery', *Journal of Garden History*, 15/1 (1995), p. 97.

63 Bishop suggests that the Western aesthetic of nostalgia and longing is ultimately pastoral in inspiration: 'To encounter nostalgia is always to enter a particular landscape, a particular aesthetic, in a specific mood: the pastoral'. See Peter Bishop, *An Archetypal Constable: National Identity and the Geography of Nostalgia* (London: Athlone, 1995), p. 57.

64 Quotation in Lovekin, *Kings Park*, p. 28.

65 'Significant form' refers to Barthes's analysis of the construction of cultural myths and the relationship of mythical concepts to the 'significant forms' appropriated to signify these myths; Roland Barthes, *Mythologies* (New York: Noonday, 1988), pp. 109–158.

66 Carter, *Road to Botany Bay*, p. 250.

67 Riegl, 'Modern Cult of Monuments', pp. 21–51.

68 *Ibid.*, p. 21.

69 Anthony Vidler writes of dark spaces: 'space is assumed to hide, in its darkest recesses and forgotten margins, all the objects of fear and phobia that have returned with such insistency to haunt the imagination's of those who have tried to stake out spaces to protect their health and happiness'; A. Vidler, *The Architectural Uncanny* (Cambridge, MA: MIT Press, 1992), pp. 167–175.

Paul Walker

2   A new monument in a new land

In 'The end of modernity, the end of the project?', Gianni Vattimo discusses briefly what he calls 'a new monumentality': 'It is as if to say that the need for monumentality makes itself felt when architecture and planning, in their reciprocal relation, no longer respond clearly to immediate needs – shelter, clothing ... but are left in that indefinite state that derives from the principle of reality having been worn away.'[1]

The phrase 'a new monumentality' is not itself new to architectural discourse. It was first coined in the 1940s by Sigfried Giedion who raised the issue of the monumental in a series of texts whose purpose was to argue that functionalism was not enough: 'People desire buildings that represent their social, ceremonial, and community life. They want these buildings to be more than a functional fulfilment. They seek the expression of their aspirations in monumentality. . . . Monumentality springs from the eternal need of people to create symbols. . . .'[2] This 'need' became the subject of ongoing debate between Giedion, Lewis Mumford and other architects, artists and theorists.

Now the concern with monumentality that appeared around the period of the Second World War is not exactly the same as Vattimo's. But there is a relation: the discussion Giedion initiated is symptomatic of an early recoiling from instrumentality which followed on from the uses to which 'rational' technologies were put in the war years. This left a problem: if not by rationality, how should design work be legitimated? In relation, perhaps, to a much more problematic realm of values, where legitimation is necessarily weak because it is difficult to make design intention and subsequent interpretation commensurate. This issue arises simultaneously in the theoretical discourses typical of but not exclusive to the intellectual centres of Europe and America, and in design practice as it came to be conducted everywhere in the post-war years.

I want to extend these comments by focussing on a series of apprehensions and misapprehensions surrounding the design of a particular project for a monument – a war memorial garden – in a location apparently remote from metropolitan locations: Wellington, New Zealand. This is not so much a matter of tracing the dissemination of ideas from a putative origin to the periphery, but rather of employing the language thrown up by debates conducted in one sphere to articulate what was happening in a more specific situation, and using the latter to reflect on the former. Utility and monumentality could not so easily be distinguished. Equally problematic, the monumental—functional binary pair came to be overlaid with another, that of the local versus the international. How did all this bear on design practices, and the practices of reading designs?

Utility/monument

Planning for a memorial to commemorate the Second World War started in Wellington in 1948, proceeding exactly at the same time as monumentality was being debated on the other side of the world. But just at the moment Giedion attempted to move modern design past the narrowly defined tenets of functionalism, there was an apparently general acceptance of just such utilitarianism. As post-war plans for memorials proceeded in New Zealand, the propriety of the 'purely' monumental was weighed in the newspapers, articles and letters-to-the-editor, against the advantages of more functional memorials such as halls, gymnasiums, swimming pools, and so forth.[3]

Early public submissions on what the Wellington memorial should be demonstrate a range of positions from the purely utilitarian to the purely monumental. Some cited conventionally monumental precedents: the Canberra war memorial; the Statue of Liberty; a 'purely symbolic memorial on the lines of that at Edinburgh'. The Wellington Returned Services' Association submission was one that called for the new memorial 'to take a utilitarian form' to serve the needs of former service men and their families. Other suggestions were more inventive: a proposal to cover Mt Victoria (a prominent feature in the city's landscape) with rosemary for remembrance, and indigenous pohutukawa trees whose red summer flowers have come to symbolise Christmas in New Zealand; another to silence all radio stations for one day a month for ever more; even a proposal for more beautiful homes for everyone, to be made possible in part through endowments for architectural scholarships.[4]

The proposal selected was one made by the newly established Wellington Architectural Centre. The Centre's idea was for 'a "Memorial Park" set apart from the stream of city life; modest and informal and not a monumental show place. A simple stone or plaque within the Park to commemorate World War II'. Following the Centre's decision not itself to provide a design for the garden, the City Council organised an architectural competition, for a site near the top of the city's botanic garden.

Few entries were received for the competition to design the Wellington Garden of Remembrance. Six registrations were sent in, and then only three designs arrived. The winning scheme was by William Toomath, a young local architect, in collaboration with landscape architect Odo Strewe. Strewe had come to New Zealand from Central Europe just before the Second World War, like other designers who were to have notable careers in Wellington and Auckland. He arrived from Berlin in 1938, bringing direct experience of mid-European modernity with him.

The very limited interest in the competition is notable. Although the Centre did not want 'a monumental show place', perhaps their proposal for a memorial garden did not escape this condition in the minds of most architects. Indeed, the reception given to the Centre's proposal seems to reflect misgivings around Giedion's call for a new monumentality which were most clearly articulated by Mumford. Did this coolness in Wellington derive from direct knowledge of the international discourse on the monument? The most likely source of any such knowledge was the *Architectural Review*, an extremely influential journal in New Zealand. It has been described as having been 'the gospel' to architects of the post-war generation: in 1947, the programme of the Architectural Centre was, on its foundation, articulated in terms of the *Architectural Review*'s agenda of visual re-education. The Centre would later publish *Design Review*, its own journal, that borrowed its vigorous graphics — and even its name — from its English model.[5]

But with regard to the debate on the monumental, the influence of the *Architectural Review* on the situation in Wellington in 1948 must be a moot point. Mumford's most sustained critique of Giedion's position appeared in the *Review* in April 1949; the Wellington design competition was announced in September 1948. Dis-ease about the monumental was almost certainly generated locally.[6]

Local/international

Giedion's position on the monument served to promote a conception of architectural modernity as a kind of formal abstraction. This was a view of architectural design advanced most strongly by the Museum of Modern Art, notably through its International Style exhibition of 1932. In arguing the legitimacy of a new monumentality, Giedion cited the work of artists such as Pablo Picasso (his *Guernica*), Fernand Léger, Hans Arp, Georges Braque and Joan Miró, whose work had become closely associated with MoMA.[7] Stanford Anderson has pointed out that Giedion's argument for a new monumentality was, because of its association with an institution powerfully promoting a new international visual culture, inevitably entwined with arguments about precisely that internationalism and the resistance that began to emerge to it in the years following the Second World War.[8]

This emerging interest in the local is most clearly exemplified in the series of books *Brazil Builds*, *Switzerland Builds*, *Sweden Builds* and *Italy Builds* that appeared between 1943 and 1955.

But these localisms were not necessarily purely local in their provenance. Thinking the local necessarily entails a self-conscious awareness of the international. Some of the earliest words on the idea of a regionally specific modern architecture to be published in New Zealand were written by the *English* critic J. M. Richards in 1946, the text of a BBC talk broadcast by a Wellington radio station: 'An interesting modern tendency is for modern buildings to look as if they could belong nowhere but where they do, for buildings in England to look more English, just as Swedish buildings will look more Swedish, which is interesting seeing that modern architecture began by taking a special pride in its international characteristics.'[9]

The clearest contemporaneous call for an architecture specific to New Zealand came in the manifesto *On the Necessity for Architecture*, issued by the Architectural

Group in Auckland, also in 1946: 'overseas solutions will not do. New Zealand must have its own architecture, its own sense of what is beautiful and appropriate to our climate and conditions'. But to seek endorsement for this call for the local, the Group sent its manifesto to that place whose solutions would not do. They sent it overseas, to California. In the first issue of their magazine *Planning* (it was also the last), the Group published a letter in support of its manifesto from Richard Neutra in Los Angeles.[10] *Planning* also featured an epigram from Mumford and an article by a local Austrian émigré, Ernst Plischke, though the Group architects found the polish of his work — flat white surfaces that in New Zealand had to be made of painted wood — problematic. He in turn was uncomfortable with their self-conscious desire for the local: it smelt to him, he was later to say, of blood and soil.[11]

Whether it was viewed as good or bad, was this desire for the local really local? Eschewing polish for what they considered straightforwardness and economy, inevitably the Group was still looking overseas: the thirty or so houses they designed in the late 1940s and 1950s clearly owe a great deal to contemporary Californian architecture, particularly to that of the Bay area.[12]

Both Strewe and Toomath had connections to the Auckland Group: Toomath was one of its foundation members;[13] Strewe was later to commission a house from them, and design the garden for one of their most important domestic projects.[14] As the Group apparently looked to California, so did Strewe. His design work was clearly influenced by that of Garrett Eckbo, first known in New Zealand probably through its publication in *Architectural Review*.[15] Strewe's description of the completed design for the Group's Catley House as 'the integration of the uncovered space [land] with the covered space [house]' suggests just this influence: Marc Treib and Dorothée Imbert's recent book on Eckbo has emphasised that *his* conception of the residential lot was precisely this spatial one.[16] Eckbo's philosophy that the whole of the lot should be designed as 'a co-ordinated series of rationally connected and related indoor and outdoor rooms' was cited by Strewe in articles he later wrote for promotional literature published by the Auckland plant nursery Palmers.[17]

Bearing in mind the influence of experiences belonging to other locations on attempts to derive a peculiarly New Zealand design mode, the definition of the local with regard to formalism and the international can not be thought of in purely oppositional terms. (Giedion himself was increasingly to acknowledge the 'regional' in successively revised editions of his *Space, Time and Architecture*,[18] and in 1950 he even provided the introduction to *Switzerland Builds*.) The local and the international, the monumental and the utilitarian: these ideas become mutually embedded in the formations of post-war architectural discourse. If some designs worked one line exclusively, perhaps others which resisted doing this were more interesting even if problematic. I want to claim just this of the Strewe and Toomath design for the Wellington memorial garden.

Mechanical and personal

In his elaboration of the consequences of Vattimo's weak ontology for architecture, Ignasi Solà-Morales focuses on issues of reception by referring to Walter Benjamin's

'The work of art in the age of mechanical reproduction'. In particular, he cites Benjamin's description of the distracted mode of attention, a mode facilitated when the auratic, totalising aspect of the work has disappeared (as, Benjamin argued, typically it has in cinema — and architecture), and when it has instead become multiplicitous in its readings and its consequences.[19]

Solà-Morales particularly associates the manifoldness and tangential quality of the work of art in the contemporary situation with its decorative qualities. Vattimo himself deploys the idea of new monumentality to get at this condition. There are no longer any singular ways of legitimating the work:

> the task posed is to find legitimations for the project that no longer appeal to 'strong', natural, or even historical structures. For example, one can no longer say that there is a golden number, an ideal measure that can be used in the construction of buildings or the planning of cities, nor even that there are natural needs, since it is increasingly absurd to try to distinguish them from new needs induced by the market and therefore superfluous, not natural.[20]

It is precisely this that differentiates Vattimo's formulation of monumentality from Giedion's. Both acknowledge the displacement of utility as the principal means by which design is to be validated. But for Vattimo this is not replaced by another fundamental while for Giedion it is: 'the eternal need of the people to create symbols'.

Mumford's critique of Giedion relates to this point. In his *The Culture of Cities* (1938), Mumford had already set out an argument against the monument, claiming that the modern city was to have a dynamism that came from being based in the architecture of the 'dwelling house, or the House of the Living', as opposed to the 'older order of architecture, … the House of the Dead'.[21] Following on from this, he suggested in his *Architectural Review* article of 1949 that the modern period had deflated symbolism itself, and therefore monumentality. The only powerful symbol this had left was the machine. But, he argued, new cultural exigencies were arising 'in which the mechanical will give place to the biological, the biological to the social, the social to the personal'.[22] (Mumford found the personal epitomised in the work of Frank Lloyd Wright and in the Bay Region style of California, coincidentally admired by the Group and other New Zealand architects.[23]) Design's motivations are multiple, both in the labour of bringing the work into being, and in its subsequent interpretation.

Strewe and Toomath's joint design for the Wellington memorial garden was simple and even severe in its formal arrangement. It was, however, not simplistic, featuring a relatively complex interplay of diagonal plan elements within an axially arranged overall composition (Fig. 2.1). Toomath has identified an interest in Wright in this arrangement, not the specific influence of some particular scheme but a sense that Wright's work represented of modern possibilities other than those of the International Style.[24]

A series of terraced garden beds was proposed along a path stepping down a hillside, terminating in a pool backed by a pierced screen. It was to be at one of the

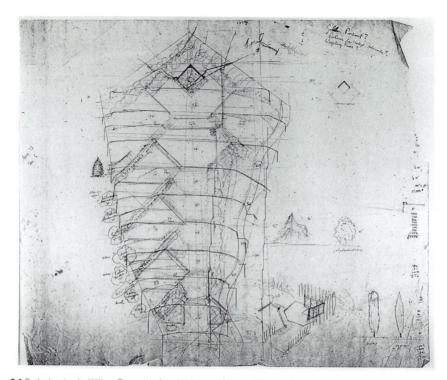

2.1 Early drawing by William Toomath of the Wellington Garden of Remembrance

highest points in the botanic garden's vertiginous topography. Views to the north-east across Wellington Harbour would be had from the termination of the path, and to its eastern side.[25] Each terrace was designated to stand for a geographical area in which New Zealanders had been involved in fighting: Britain, the Middle East, Greece and Crete, Europe, the Pacific (Fig. 2.2). Strewe contrived a detailed planting scheme for each of these specific gardens. As well, the whole was supposed to have 'an overall symbolism'.

And yet the adequacy of the representational gestures implied in Strewe and Toomath's design was, like Giedion's calls for a new monumentality, problematic – both in the disposition of forms and in the choices of plant materials. For example, the plants chosen for the Pacific were mostly lush-leafed, but included a row of standard azaleas presumably to stand for Japan. Weeping cherry trees elsewhere in the garden, supposed to represent the ongoing sorrow of the war, could as easily have read as Japanese. Meanings are multiple. Meanings slip and slide: they will not be fixed in place.

In further considering Strewe and Toomath's Wellington garden design I want to employ the two poles of the range of terms Mumford raised in his response to Giedion's new monumentality: the mechanical and the personal. I will consider these specifically in relation to the garden's planned siting.

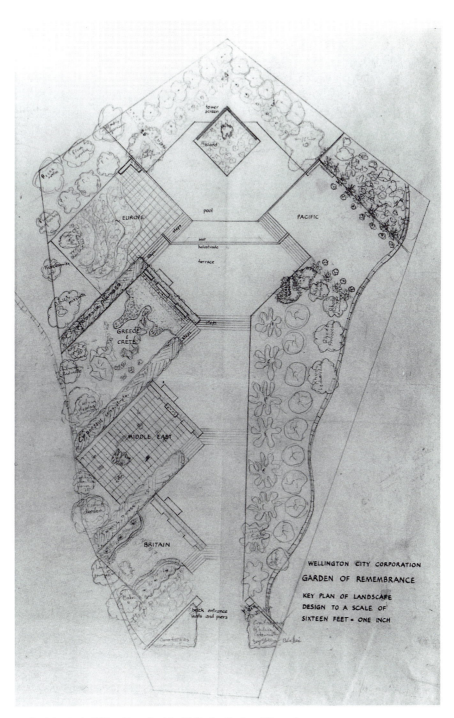

Within the plan, labels appear including: tower screen, island, pool, PACIFIC, EUROPE, step, seat, balustrade, terrace, GREECE & CRETE, steps, MIDDLE EAST, BRITAIN, brick entrance walls and piers.

WELLINGTON CITY CORPORATION
GARDEN OF REMEMBRANCE
KEY PLAN OF LANDSCAPE
DESIGN TO A SCALE OF
SIXTEEN FEET = ONE INCH

2.2 Final drawing by William Toomath of the Wellington Garden of Remembrance

The problematic of the mechanical — of the machine — is raised in particular by the proposed location of the Strewe/Toomath design at the top of the botanic garden. This area of the garden was (and remains) occupied by various utilitarian and scientific enterprises: the terminus of a tramway, an observatory, a seismology office, meteorological devices. Together, these are remnants of the instrumental ideology on which the Wellington botanic garden had been founded as a department of the Colonial Museum in 1869.[26] Though they seem alien to the picturesque pleasure grounds that the garden has subsequently become, it was precisely to the making of the New Zealand landscape amenable and homely — identifiable as the colonial subject's own — that the acclimatisation and economic researches of the scientific botanic garden of the nineteenth century had been devoted. The adjacency of Strewe and Toomath's memorial garden to these things suggests it too was an instrument: it prescribed a particular mode of use. Toomath and Strewe's description of the putative visitor's approach and movement along the memorial makes this overt:

> A broad symbolism runs throughout the Garden of Remembrance. Movement past the sunken gardens represents progress through the war towards the goal seen ahead. The other side of the avenue is bordered by a row of weeping Japanese cherry trees — the accompanying sorrow. Just as the thorny shrubs at the entrance endeavour to symbolise the thorny path at the beginning of every war.
>
> The path to most war memorials leads up, but in this case the steps lead the visitor down. The climax of the garden consists of the pierced screen enclosing a group of weeping birch trees. At its base stands an apparent island in a dark pool. As the visitor draws nearer to the climax of the gardens the 'V' symbol is seen to form in the profile of the top of the screen, silhouetted against the sky. The sense of separation and loss is heightened by the intervening water, making the island and the screen unobtainable by the living. The high screen, with pierced panels seen normally against the light, conveys something of the division between the living and the dead. In this way the Air Force is represented by the loftiness of the screen, the Army by the land of the island, and the Navy by the water.[27]

Start at the top of the path; move to the bottom. Water: navy, land: army, sky: airforce, V: victory. It is prescriptive and mechanical. As much as the telescopes in the observatory nearby Strewe and Toomath's Garden of Remembrance was to be a device for framing out and looking beyond its context.

But in considering a particular aspect of its context a very different and much more personal, intimate and provisional reading of this garden is possible. This relates to Strewe's own wartime experiences. When he arrived in New Zealand before the Second World War, he did not have the status of an official refugee. He was therefore interned for the duration of the war as an enemy alien despite his known anti-Nazi activities. The site of this internment was Somes Island in Wellington Harbour. There, the New

Zealand government had impounded any nationals of enemy powers who were in the country without appropriate documentation. Among the internees from Germany and Austria were not only Nazi sympathisers, but also many fervent anti-Nazis who had escaped to the end of the earth, but without the correct papers. On their island prison, they fought out the battles of the war in miniature. Strewe was a vigorous participant in these activities.[28]

Views of Somes Island could have been had from the lofty location of the memorial garden and its vicinity. Strewe and Toomath noted in the report they submitted with their design competition entry that the harbour view was to be a dramatic element in the scheme, 'to be revealed suddenly as the visitor reaches the climax of the Garden. If desired, the acacia trees beside the end of the avenue could be omitted to provide a broader view of the harbour. . . . The view from the "Pacific" garden is, fittingly, completely freed'. Completely freed, the view from the Pacific garden — the only one of the geographical areas placed east of the main plan axis of the Garden of Remembrance — would have included Somes in the middle of its open panorama. This garden had been located that way precisely to get the open view. I do not want to claim that Strewe purposely inlaid his own life story somehow in the garden he designed. But the conjunction of the garden design and aspects of his life story leads one to think of him with that harbour view before him, Strewe all at once Somes dreaming, Pacific dreaming, California dreaming. . . .

Tangents

Its designers felt the problematic quality of the memorial garden design. Toomath had doubts, withdrawing from the project because he had been persuaded by his friends' criticisms of the whole proposition of a war memorial. He wavered, however, later trying to reassert his interest in the project.[29]

Apparently Strewe had fewer qualms: he published the project in one of a series of articles he contributed to the popular, monthly magazine *Home and Building* where he intimated that he had initiated the collaboration with Toomath. What underwrote his confidence in the project? In the only published analysis of Strewe's design work he is described by the New Zealand design historian Douglas Lloyd-Jenkins as a formal modernist, his aesthetic characterised as abstract and likened to that of Henry Moore, Barbara Hepworth, and Arp. Lloyd-Jenkins also maintains that the plants Strewe was interested in were only ones that could be seen in dramatically sculptural terms — his favourites reputedly including the rubber tree and the monstera — and that he disliked changing seasonal effects.[30]

But the planting lists Strewe published with his designs in magazines and the Palmers catalogues do not bear out the formalism ascribed to him. (Perhaps this insistence by contemporary historians on the abstract in twentieth-century landscape designs is a way of asserting the intellectual credibility of these designs. Treib's characterisation of Eckbo's work entirely in terms of its connections to modern formalist art and complete dismissal of any consideration of its regionalist content is another case in point.)

Strewe's planting plans are notable for their variety and for their eclecticism: a single scheme might contain things as different as a cluster of birches, with their connotations of the cool 'north', and philodendrons with theirs of lush tropicality.[31] Gardens for Strewe were artifices, even if some times artifice had the purpose of making things sign 'nature' to acculturated eyes.

The plant lists for the geographically representational terraces in the Wellington Garden of Remembrance are consistent with this: they are complicated, whimsical, with various fleeting seasonal qualities. The garden representing Greece and Crete was to feature cypresses, which might seem suitably Hellenic and monumental, and crocuses and tulip species, which might also have certain Greek connotations. But why such oddities as the New Zealand tree *Libocedrus bidwillii*, or the Australian *Agonis flexuosa*, or Japanese *kurume* azaleas? (Fig. 2.3). Bulbs feature in the Middle Eastern garden, but mostly they are South African. And so on. These gardens are almost weedy in their lack of overall coherence. They have a quality tangential to slipping past the formalism attributed to their designer.

Strewe recognised that interpretations vary, slip. In an essay published in 1958, he discussed the problem of what constituted a beautiful garden. The difficulty of achieving consensus on this he attributed to differences in the interpretations of words, and in particular in this case of the word 'beautiful'.[32] He cited C. K. Ogden and I. A. Richards' *The Meaning of Meaning*, which lists sixteen definitions of 'beauty', for example.

The Meaning of Meaning was later to form an important reference in attempts to formulate a semiotics of architecture, in the volume *Meaning in Architecture*, edited by Charles Jencks and George Baird (1969).[33] Indeed, Giedion's diagnosis of a human desire for symbols is an important precursor of the semiotic theories of architecture that would be formulated in the 1960s and 1970s. A comparison between language and architecture is always implicit in these. In the *New Yorker* article in which he promotes the Bay Area style, Mumford raises just this metaphor: 'it was time that some of our architects remembered the non-mechanical and non-formal elements in architecture, that they remembered what a building says as well as what it does'.[34]

40

But what can things say? Words are like the elements that architects and landscape designers work with not least in the *evasiveness* of their meanings. Among Strewe's manuscript papers is a very interesting document, a kind of key of plants and poetry. It takes the form of a chart with a list of plant names and poems in which those names are important references. Mostly they are English poets and the plants of English gardens, but titles of a few pieces by New Zealander A. R. D. Fairburn are entered by the names of plants typical of the New Zealand countryside. Just what occasioned this list to be made is unknown, but it may have been a design commission: alongside some of the plant names are entered not only poems, but also what seem to be references to plan locations.[35] Whatever Strewe's purpose was in compiling this key, it suggests a certain complexity in the way plant materials might be construed in a landscape design, just as there is complexity in the way words might be construed in a poem.

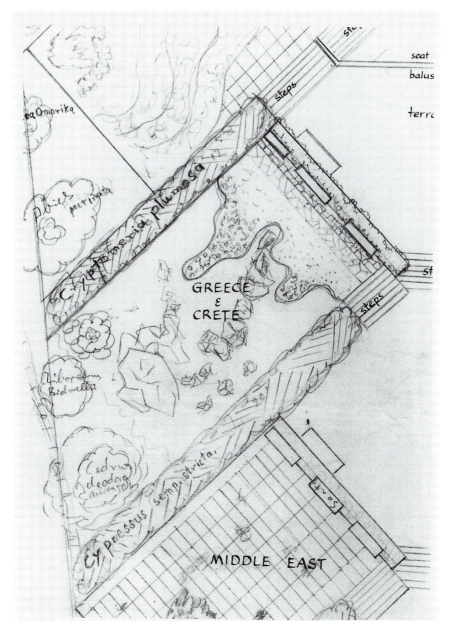

Labels visible in drawing: seat, balus, terr, steps, GREECE & CRETE, MIDDLE EAST, Cryptomeria Plumosa, Cypressus Semp. stricta, Cedrus deodara aurea 50?, Libocedrus Bidwillii, Picea perinata, Picea Omorika, steps, st

2.3 Detail of Fig. 2.2

Plants, of course, have a relationship to the more architectural aspects of landscape design that could be thought of precisely in terms of the tangential, the decorative. But an evasive, tangential quality can be found as well in the architectural elements of the Garden of Remembrance: those diagonal plan elements, derived according to Toomath from Wright, suggest other modes of movement than the

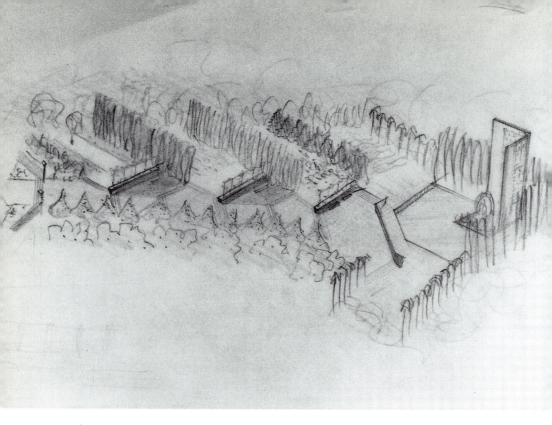

2.4 Sketch by William Toomath of the Wellington Garden of Remembrance

straightforward one in the project descriptions, imply sideways looks as well as the 'proper' one along the plan axis and down (Fig. 2.4). They entail, that is, some resistance to the formal, monumental, qualities of the project, inviting different experiences, different interpretations.

42

Conclusion

Such distinctions as those between the local and international, the monumental and the utilitarian are stronger in the saying than in the doing. Designs like Toomath and Strewe's Wellington memorial garden evade such artificially categorical differences. This is especially apparent insofar as it is a project whose status and proposed location are obscure enough that it has not been subject to the kind of critical exegesis that would decide on a canonical interpretation, determine on which side of any such critical division it belonged.

The garden did not come to be built. A new government elected in New Zealand in 1949 imposed a deadline of 30 June 1953 after which it would not allow any subsidies to local authorities to build memorials. But the public of Wellington could not be persuaded: a street appeal in September 1951 collected only £1000; a concert arranged by the Air Force Association of New Zealand in the Wellington Town Hall raised a paltry £49.[36] Did they not feel Giedion's eternal need for symbols? Perhaps the problem was obversely that the garden was useful: it was a proposal that had been accepted by the authorities as suitable for a subsidy, which meant it satisfied their requirement that it be utilitarian. Or was it simply all too slight?

As a design strategy, evasiveness is risky: construction rhetorically demands its own kind of certainties. But the tangential and the slight may have strength of their own. As Solà-Morales puts it: 'for the work of art — sculptural or architectonic — an acceptance of a certain weakness, and thus of relegation to a secondary position, may possibly be the condition of its greatest elegance and, ultimately, its greatest significance and import'.[37] How can significance — the meaning of meaning, the meaning of identity — be figured in a project such as the Wellington Garden of Remembrance? Perhaps it could be thought of as a mediation, or experience of mediation, movement *between* different registers: formal, symbolic; mechanical, personal; architectural, horticultural; woody, herbaceous; international, local; built, drawn; monumental, ephemeral; structural, ornamental. The relationship of these registers and their terms could be characterised as one of ongoing mutual deferral, the shifts between them occurring distractedly.

1   Gianni Vattimo, 'The end of modernity, the end of the project?', in Neil Leach (ed.), *Rethinking Architecture: A Reader in Cultural Theory* (London: Routledge, 1997), p. 153.

2   Sigfried Giedion, 'The need for a new monumentality' [1944], in S. Giedon, *Architecture, You and Me* (Cambridge, MA: Harvard University Press, 1958), pp. 27–28.

3   For example, 'Editorial: War Memorials', *The Dominion* [Wellington] (23 August 1947).

4   The documentation relating to these proposals is held in the Wellington City Archive, WCC TC 60/4232.

5   For a discussion of the influence of *Architectural Review*, see Justine Clark, '"The Book": representing a New Zealand modernism', unpublished paper presented at the '(In)visible Languages' conference, National Library, Wellington, August 1997. For key articles on monumentality that appeared in the journal in the 1940s, see 'In search of a new monumentality', *Architectural Review*, 104/626 (1948), pp. 117–128; and Lewis Mumford, 'Monumentalism, symbolism and style', *Architectural Review*, 105/628 (1949), pp. 173–180.

6   Toomath does not recall being aware of the debate on monumentality being conducted between Mumford and Giedion at this time, despite his general familiarity with the international scene.

7   Giedion, The 'need for a new monumentality', pp. 32–35.

8   Stanford Anderson, 'The "New Empiricism–Bay Region Axis": Kay Fisker and postwar debates on functionalism, regionalism, and monumentality', *Journal of Architectural Education*, 50/3 (1997), pp. 197–207.

9   J. M. Richards, 'Architecture in evolution', *New Zealand Listener* (13 September 1946), p. 20; repr. of a BBC radio talk broadcast in Wellington.

10 Richard Neutra, 'Letter', *Planning*, no. 1 (1946), p. 33.

11 Linda Tyler cites a letter Plischke wrote to Nikolaus Pevsner in 1960 that uses the phrase 'Blood and Soil'; Plischke archive, Vienna. L. Tyler, 'Off the record: Plischke visits Hawke's Bay', unpublished paper, Conference of the Society of Architectural Historians, Australia & New Zealand, Auckland, October 1996.

12 The influence of California was confirmed by Emeritus Professor Allan Wild, who was an active member of Group Architects, in a discussion of their work that occurred at The Modern World Conference, Unitec School of Design, Auckland, 18 November 1995. However, Pevsner compared New Zealand unfavourably with California, noting with regard to New Zealand architecture's crude detailing:' … California is not all that old and yet is quite capable of taking its details seriously'; N. Pevsner, 'New Zealand,' *Architectural Review* Commonwealth Special 1, 126/752 (1959), cited in Clark, '"The Book"'.

13 The Group was founded on 3 April 1946. Toomath's signature is one of six that endorse the Group constitution formulated on that occasion.

14 He wrote of the approach along the road to this house: 'Long before we could see the section, the house itself was visible. There was no doubt by the visible forms of construction of this dwelling it could have only been designed by Group Architects … who, to the delight of any landscape architect, place the house in such a way that it is not forced on to the section, but is integrated with it'; Odo Strewe, 'Garden for a sloping section', *New Zealand Modern Homes and Gardens* (Summer 1959–60), pp. 135–137.

15 Garrett Eckbo, 'Landscape design in the USA as applied to the private garden in California', *Architectural Review*, 105/625 (1949), pp. 24–32.

16 Marc Treib and D. Imbert, *Garrett Eckbo: Modern Landscapes for Living* (Berkeley: University of California Press, 1997), pp. 20–21. Just as Strewe was influenced by US design, so was

Toomath. In fact, Toomath has published an important study on the influence of American precedents on New Zealand house design in the nineteenth and early twentieth centuries: *Built in New Zealand* (Auckland: HarperCollins, 1996).

17 Odo Strewe, 'Landscaping – an introduction', in *Palmers Winter Planting Guide* (Auckland: Palmers, 1962(?)), p. 1; *idem*, 'Your garden', *Palmers Catalogue* (Auckland: Palmers, 1967), p. 1. Toomath's domestic designs feature a similar commitment to the complete and integrated design of house and garden as a series of connected spaces. The design for his parents' home, undertaken in 1948–49, is clearly organised on these principles. 'A house at Lower Hutt', *Design Review*, 4/1 (1951), pp. 9–11.

18 Alan Colquhoun points this out in 'The concept of regionalism', in G. B. Nalbantoglu and C. T. Wong, *Postcolonial Space(s)* (New York: Princeton Architectural Press, 1997), p. 14. Colquhoun also comments on the construction of national cultures in various European countries in the nineteenth century, noting that in Finland 'an eclectic architecture representing "Finnishness" was put together from various stylistic sources, some indigenous, some external (for example, one of its main sources was the English Arts and Crafts movement)' (p. 16).

19 Ignasi Solà-Morales, 'Weak architecture', in I. Solà-Morales, *Differences: Topographies of Contemporary Architecture* (Cambridge, MA: MIT Press, 1997), p. 70; Walter Benjamin, 'The work of art in the age of mechanical reproduction', in *Illuminations* (London: Jonathan Cape, 1970), pp. 41–42.

20 Vattimo, 'End of modernity, the end of the project?', p. 151.

21 Lewis Mumford, *The Culture of Cities*, offset edn (London: Secker & Warburg, 1940), p. 433.

22 Mumford, 'Monumentalism, symbolism and style', pp. 177–178.

23 For Mumford's comments on the Bay Region style, see L. Mumford, 'The sky line: status quo', *New Yorker* (11 October 1947), pp. 94–99, cited by Anderson, '"New Empiricism–Bay Region Axis', p. 198. Also 'Bay Area domestic', *Architectural Review*, 104/622 (1948), pp. 164–170.

24 William Toomath, comment to the author, 9 September 1994.

25 For a description of the selected site, see a letter from the Secretary of the Architectural Centre to the Secretary of the Wellington Citizens' War Memorial Committee, dated 29 November 1948; Wellington City Archive, WCC TC 60/4232.

26 Winsome Shepherd and Walter Cook, *The Botanic Garden Wellington: A New Zealand History 1840–1987* (Wellington: Millwood, 1988).

27 This description is from Odo Strewe, 'Proposed garden of remembrance', *Home and Building* [Auckland], 14/9 (1952), pp. 30–31, 59. A similar description is in the article on the garden that appeared in the *Evening Post* (15 December 1949), where the words are attributed to Toomath. Both were drawing from the report submitted with their competition entry, held at the Wellington City Archive, WCC TC 60/4232. Also 'Proposed war memorial for Wellington – a garden of remembrance', *Design Review*, 2/6 (1950), p. 116.

28 For a novel about the Somes Island internees, in part based on archival records of Strewe's experiences there, see Maurice Gee, *Live Bodies* (Auckland: Penguin, 1998).

29 These matters are dealt with in letters from Toomath to the Secretary of the Wellington Citizens' War Memorial Executive Committee, dated 15 November 1950 and 23 May 1951; Wellington City Archive WCC TC 60/4232.

30 Douglas Lloyd-Jenkins, 'Odo Strewe: modern homes, modern gardens', in Matthew Bradbury (ed.), *A History of the Garden in New Zealand* (Auckland: Viking, 1995).

31 Silver birches were much admired by Strewe when planted in groups, though because the winters are too warm for the trees they do poorly in Auckland where most of Strewe's projects were realised.

32 Odo Strewe, 'Understanding design in landscaping', *New Zealand Modern Homes and Gardens* (Summer, 1958), pp. 137–139.

33 C. K. Ogden and I. A. Richards, *The Meaning of Meaning*, 7th edn (London: Kegan Paul, Trench, Trubner & Co., 1945 [1st edn 1923]); Charles Jencks, 'Semiology and architecture', in Jencks and Baird (eds), *Meaning in Architecture* (London: Barrie & Rockliff, the Cresset Press 1969). For a critique of Jencks's use of Ogden & Richards, see Diana Agrest and Mario Gandelsonas, 'Critical remarks on semiology and architecture', *Semiotica*, 9/3 (1973), pp. 252–271.

34 Mumford, 'Sky line: status quo', p. 96.

35 Odo Strewe, 'A key to poetry and landscape', ATL MS Papers 5921–065, Alexander Turnbull Library, Wellington.

36 Wellington City Archive WCC TC 60/4232. At least £5000 was needed before the project could receive its government subsidy and proceed.

37 Solà-Morales, 'Weak architecture', p. 70.

Anne-Catrin Schultz

3 Carlo Scarpa: built memories

Primarily located in the Veneto region in Northern Italy, the work of Carlo Scarpa (1906–78) tells stories about his background, perceptions and memories. Scarpa's buildings are architectural inventions, set into the historic context of and around Venice which carefully reinterpret features characteristic of the city. This sensibility underlies Scarpa's key role in the architecture of the twentieth century: he is recognised for his unique ability to integrate formal influences into his language. Several architectural movements crystallise in Scarpa's work: he is inspired by Frank Lloyd Wright (and, correspondingly, Japanese aesthetic culture), the Viennese Secession and the Dutch De Stijl, and he merges these influences into his own expression (Fig. 3.1). Just as Scarpa's projects reinterpret architectural precedents and local traditions, architects today quote, transform and draw inspiration from Scarpa's work.

Especially critical to Scarpa's language is the context of his buildings, the ageing and deteriorating structures of Venice. Scarpa's architecture itself must be understood as part of the historic process, decaying and changing. He often employed delicate construction techniques, fine details and sensitive materials that easily deteriorate or fall into disrepair, and as a result some of his projects are in poor condition. This problem is aggravated by an absence of restoration efforts, despite Scarpa's important position in contemporary architecture.

The ageing of the city: buildings in time

The expression of built objects at every scale, from cities to buildings to details, changes with time and use. Understanding the ageing process and the corresponding developments of structures, as opposed to merely analysing formal design ideas, allows a more profound interpretation of the building in context of the past and the future. Human memory draws references to places and pulls images from the past, facilitating predictions about the future. Images of the past can relate to buildings or events that were part of the life span of a generation and are therefore part of recent past included in direct personal memory. Buildings or events outside of direct memory are considered a part of history and can be perceived through oral or literal documentation as well as

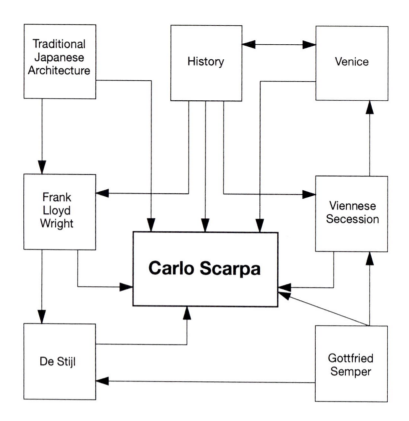

3.1 Influences on Carlo Scarpa

48

built references. They may be existing, or they might be demolished, possibly rebuilt, or merely preserved in images and other documentation (Fig. 3.2). Although not directly expressed, content in the form of memory or association can be incorporated into built objects. There are two kinds of memory: direct, referring to the building's original shape or style; and indirect, a narrative component evoking historic places or elements. The conscious handling of indirect and direct memory incorporates narratives into buildings. These components add profound meaning to architecture that exceeds merely fulfilling practical functions. Symbols and details give coherence to a building and connect it with its historic and local context.

> One has the impression that memories most carefully built up with memory architecture, with architectural places reflected within. The art of memory is an invisible art, it reflects real places but is about, not the places themselves, but the reflection of these within the imagination.[1] (Francis Yates)

Cities undergo a continuous process of change and modification that includes the conscious decision, based on social conditions, to delete or preserve existing structures

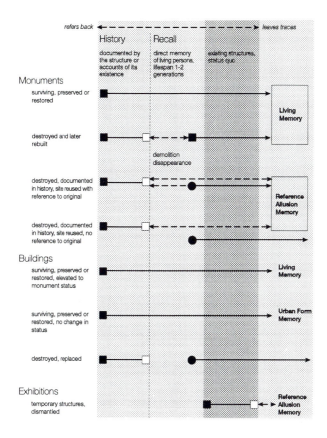

or landscapes. In many historic cities, the process of continuous change has ceased and has been replaced by ongoing preservation without any possibility for modification or innovation. The popularity of these cities derives from their beauty and the presence of historic traces. In being vestiges of different periods of time, political systems and lifestyles, historical buildings convey information about the life of people as well as their tastes and aesthetic attitudes. Buildings therefore can act as materialised memories, memories that relate to the observers' knowledge and experience.

The maturing of a building follows a complex sequence. It may begin with an innovation in form, function or style as it did for the Centre Pompidou in Paris by Renzo Piano and Richard Rogers (1971–77). Through time and use, this non-contextual structure has become an accepted part of the urban system. As the building enters its second generation, it begins to take on the qualities of renovation and repair as well as of functional upgrades for contemporary exhibition and security requirements. The physical makeup of urban systems is comprised of buildings, streets and places. Through these elements, the city conveys information about its history, culture, function and users as coexistent strata that overlay, interact and communicate. As the city travels through time, modifications leave traces of former configurations and connect them into a layered time–space narrative. As John Ruskin notes, buildings are the repositories of memories: 'It is as the centralisation and protectress of this sacred influence, that architecture is to be regarded by us with the most serious thought. We may live without her, and worship without her, but we cannot remember without her.'[2]

Memory in the city is the recollection of past situations and places or buildings through the quotation of materials, forms or even details. Woven together, elements in the city fall into layers created in different times, simultaneously referring to historic incidents and cultures as well as their adaptation to later actions and lifestyles. The urban environment includes direct memory through historic buildings or reused fragments integrated into more recent structures, while indirect memory is formed through the quotation of historic buildings, fragments or single forms. Such quotation transforms building elements into a symbol or representation of the original object. The architects Venturi and Rauch have championed the practice of indirect memory, evoking historic precedents by exaggerating obvious motifs or referring to their contour lines. In his Wexner Center (Ohio State University, 1983–85), Peter Eisenman invents an artificial historic process, adding an archaeological layer to his architecture, where newly built objects evoke their removed precedents. Memories in the city come to life through the existence of historic structures and the reinterpretation of form in new buildings. However, mere reconstruction avoids the complexity of time by replicating a destroyed object and thus pretending a continuous existence (Fig. 3.2).

The life of the perception of a building is characterised by three phases. It begins as being visually challenging and searching for a future style, is followed by acceptance and integration into, daily life, and finally it could become a memorial, monument or landmark. Existing buildings are references for scale, size and orientation: historic architecture has an important impact on architectural theory and subsequent directions in style.

Referring to architecture typology, Aldo Rossi developed the 'analogous design process'.[3] For him, history provides types that in analogies formulate a continuous line connecting yesterday and today, integrating fragments and personal history in new buildings, forming the 'analogous city'.[4] Rossi describes the layering of perception and time: 'The overlapping of the individual and the collective memory, together with the invention that takes place within the time of the city has led me to the concept of analogy. Analogy expresses itself through a process of architectural design whose elements are pre-existing and formally defined, but whose true meaning is unforeseen at the beginning and unfolds only at the end of the process.'[5]

Built analogies — the original object as well as the representation or symbolic recreation — evoke associations: they indicate a broader context than the building itself, allowing the building to be understood as part of a legible system. These analogies can refer to details originating from different places and times. Often, elements change or lose their function over time but are retained in new works as purely formal features. Specific forms or details occur frequently and help describe the character of the place. Application of these elements in contemporary architecture expresses the acceptance of their cultural and artistic value, their engagement in a system of perception that evolves through time. The stories told through architecture's appearance and details that harbour indirect or direct memory are continually narrated by signs of past use and traces of modifications. Parallel to a building's physical ageing, the surrounding social understanding and criticism changes over time. Interpretations of references gain clarity with the benefit of hindsight regarding an architect's *oeuvre* and the times itself.

Venice: layers of memory

> The experience and memory of humankind are laid down in layers in the physical environment, concretely and graphically. Every new part exploits ancient forms, materials and ways of making. Building is, at base, a sign of hope, a sign of society's belief in future, a gesture forward in time.[6] (Aldo Rossi)

An illustrative example of the complex process of ageing, Venice is a city rich with multiple readings of memory. Layers created and sedimented over time represent the built history of the city. Its complex mercantile history meets a geographically extreme marine place, with each force evident in the architecture. The city's location in a lagoon historically made the transportation of new materials cost prohibitive, a fact that favours reuse and recycling of existing structures and materials. This recycling intensifies the layering of which there are three kinds: Spatial Layering, Material Layering and Associative Layering. Spatial and material layers are essentially physical–material witnesses of the passage of time, spatial layering in urban contexts involves the overlapping of spaces and spatial sequences. Material layering, best exemplified in representative façades facing the Grand Canal, has a long tradition in Venetian design (Fig. 3.3). Associative layers refer to a broader content of buildings, associations that awaken memories of something else, allowing the concurrent presence of completely different sites and times. In the case of Venice, memory has the function to connect the different periods of time in history as well as the change of the city's functions and their architectural appearance into one system of buildings, the city fabric.

For Scarpa, Venice serves as a reference system, a reservoir for his ideas and applications, and a model for his layered compositions (Figs 3.3 and 3.4). He quotes such forms as the typical Venetian chimney, applies local materials like the Istrian sandstone as decorative and stabilising elements (Figs 3.5 and 3.6), works with water both as a material and as a foil to bridges and details; and is a master of Venetian light. He builds narrow canals as miniature reminders of the city (Fig. 3.5) and incorporates such historic forms as the Byzantine window.

In contrast to Rossi, Scarpa does not refer to abstract architectural archetypes. He instead recreates direct and idiosyncratic experiences, existing form, material and atmosphere as a base for his personal design process. Scarpa weaves individual memories and experiences into his design approach and reinterprets the associations he draws into new architecture. This, in a similar fashion as layering, is a fundamental aspect of Scarpa's architecture.

The play of memory is most provocative in instances where original objects undergo transformation. In working with existing buildings, Scarpa's interest was

3.3 Venice: layered façades along the Grand Canal

3.4 Castelvecchio, Verona by Carlo Scarpa, layered walls (1958–1964)

3.5 Fondazione Querini-Stampalia, Venice by Carlo Scarpa, Canal in the Inner Courtyard (1961–1963)

3.6 Brick wall on the Island of Torcello (detail)

didactically to point out the changes those buildings experienced during their existence. He brings the movement of time to the fore in the finished project. The addition of memory as an immaterial component to buildings is Scarpa's way of touching what might be called the 'soul' of the building, the part that is capable of telling stories about itself and its location.

Carlo Scarpa: built memories

> Remembering is like constructing and then travelling again through a space. We are already talking about architecture. . . . Memories are built as a city is built. It could be said that architecture, from its beginnings, has been one of the ways of fixing memories.[7] (Umberto Eco)

Architecture communicates memory; the intensity of memory activation however, is closely related to the cultural involvement of the observer. When there are no associations to recognize, aesthetic values move to the foreground in the absence of the ability to decode the associative layers, and perceived beauty can mark the profoundness of the design. By rearticulating what he has seen before, Scarpa transforms objects into new form as indirect memory combines the source of inspiration with contemporary means of expression and his personal handwriting.

Scarpa's *oeuvre* is going through the same changes as all Venetian buildings over time: interventions, modifications and renovations, even partial or complete demolition. The first changes happen through the weathering and ageing of the material and the applied details. Memories are the connection to immaterial expression in architecture, the narrative aspect that contains what the building wants to communicate. Parallel to its function in the city, memory can refer to the direct context of a building (like its history) as well as to a broader complex of interest.

> The profound affinity between architecture and place results in an intensified mimesis between building and environment, between redefinition and genius loci. The remodel of the Fondazione Querini is a project which shows Scarpa's handwriting more than many other projects; at the same time it embodies the unmistakable artistic metaphor of the city of Venice.[8] (Vittorio Amagnago Lampugnani)

53

One of Scarpa's well-known buildings, the Fondazione Querini, can be seen as a scaled-down metaphor of Venice. The first floor serves as exhibition space, while the upper floors house a library, office and storage space. Located on a canal, the building had to endure the periodic Venetian floods. Instead of undertaking measures to keep the water out, Scarpa lets it in, constructing drainage canals along the walls of the interior spaces themselves and elevating the floor levels. By inviting the water into the building, Scarpa recreates the play of light and shadow found throughout the city. Unfortunately, floods have reached higher levels than he anticipated, damaging the raised wall panels and

3.8 Fondazione Querini-Stampalia, Venice by Carlo Scarpa, layered stair leading to the library (1961–1963)

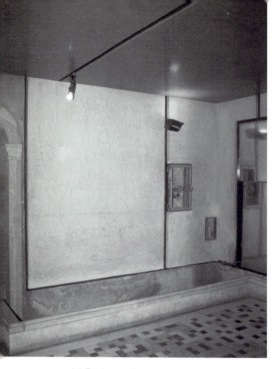

3.7 Fondazione Querini-Stampalia, Venice by Carlo Scarpa, entrance area with stucco panels (1961–1963)

leaving traces of water on the coloured stucco. The affected panels simultaneously demonstrate the ageing of the building, as well as reiterating the original design intention. By documenting an actual flood in the building's history, the panels evoke direct memory of Venice and its nature (Fig. 3.7). In other details, Scarpa makes use of indirect memory, referring to the surrounding city and its unique features. The entrance bridge to the Fondazione Querini is constructed from wood and metal, similar to bridges on the island of Murano. The handrail pieces are put together with a 'connector', an element derived from the stone bridges. In the stair to the library, Scarpa exposes the layers of old and new, adding treads to the existing stair and allowing both to simultaneously exist (Fig. 3.8). In the backyard, a small canal continues the microcosmic analogy of the city (Fig. 3.5). Scarpa arranges concrete blocks into different levels, treating their corners in a manner similar to the brick walls on the island of Torcello, stabilising their edges with white stone (Figs 3.5 and 3.6). Through careful geometrical articulation, Scarpa exaggerates these Istrian sandstone forms, calling attention to their function and beauty at the same time. Also in the backyard, a small canal distinguishes the planted area from the paved lower area. Together, these single pieces integrate the building into the aesthetic and functional systems that formed Venice itself. Despite Scarpa's transformations, motifs remain familiar, and the building comes to life as part of an existing family rather than as solitary intrusion into an historic urban fabric.

Beyond this narrative of historic context, Scarpa's architecture carries a strong didactic component, a quality most apparent in his design of numerous exhibitions, as well as several museums. Temporary in nature, exhibitions are immune to the physical ageing process. Once taken down, their memory is bound to written and photographic documentation that allows the influence of the exhibition to live on. Scarpa often crafted his exhibitions as an added layer to the containing building, altering its spatial organisation to fit the sequence and character of the exposed objects. This approach further enhanced the visitor's understanding of the exhibition by illustrating the objects and developing a specific formal language for them. Scarpa's involvement in the organisation and design of the Venice Biennale spanned from 1948 to 1972. In the Giardini, the site of the Biennale, a few small interventions permanently remain from this period as does the Venezuela Pavilion. Each of these projects engage in indirect memory, alluding to Venice through marine details and the use of water and light as formable materials. A small garden in the Italian Pavilion recalls the 1952 Biennale; however, sculptures on display have long been removed, leaving behind a deteriorating roof and a water basin (Fig. 3.9). Working on museums with permanent exhibitions, Scarpa interprets the exhibition through his architecture instead of creating a neutral box. The visitor's attention is lead by a carefully planned sequence of details pointing to the exposed objects. Scarpa designed his intervention in the Castelvecchio in Verona (1958–64) not only to surround the museum's displayed artefacts, but also to expose the building's history and associated layers. Separating and connecting mechanisms comprise a complex system of walkways that embrace the whole complex at the River

3.9 Sculpture Garden in the Italian Pavilion, Venice Giardine della Biennale, by Carlo Scarpa (1952)

Adige. The *percorso* through the museum acts like a network of connections that overlay the existing building's organisation. Scarpa uses this overlay to allow the building to reflect upon its own history, emphasising transformations that took place over time. With these transformations, the castle is almost a patchwork of original pieces combined with later interpretations and replicas. This effect is apparent even at the large scale, as different buildings were connected and disconnected depending on the political and military context. Scarpa points out the joints between different layers (Figs 3.10 and 3.12) and exposes historic walls, such as the Roman sections underneath the museum floor. He reconnects the two parts of the castle divided by the street leading to the Adige bridge; he also alludes to the internal historic moat by quoting it in the landscaping of the internal courtyard. Scarpa reveals the main façade as a separate construction, one that had been installed during a remodel (1923–26) using Gothic pieces from a demolished palace unrelated to Castelvecchio. By separating its edges from other façades, he distinguishes this façade as a separate piece. He alters the rigid symmetry of the façade by shifting the entrance and adding a small exhibition space, the *sacello*. In Castelvecchio, Scarpa creates an obviously

56

3.10 Castelvecchio, Verona by Carlo Scarpa, separation of different volumes through layering (1958–1964)

didactic restoration primarily through making direct memory an association to the building itself and its evolution.

He writes: 'I thought of the water surrounding the wall of the castle. That gave me the idea of making a negative seam. The floor of each room was individualized, as if they were a series of platforms. I changed the material of the edge, from slate to a clearer stone in order to better define the square. In this way, the movement was modulated.'[9]

The building does not only physically lead the visitor to its historically important places, it also acts as a guide through the exhibition, paying attention to special pieces. Some references reach further using indirect memory of somewhere or something else: many interior walls are covered by stucco panels that allude to Venetian *stucco lustro*, while the glass layers Scarpa added to the window openings recall Piet Mondrian's paintings (Fig. 3.11). The second floor ceiling treatment follows the space modulation of

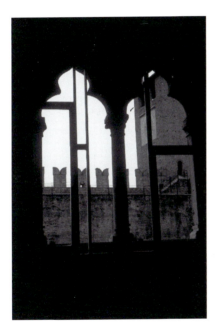

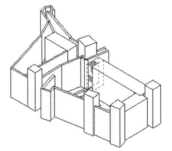

3.11 Castelvecchio, Verona by Carlo Scarpa, window design (1958–1964)

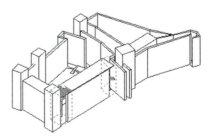

3.12 Castelvecchio, Verona by Carlo Scarpa, separation of different building elements through layering (1958–1964)

57

Japanese *tatami* mats. Also the separate double stepstone coming back down at the end of the *percorso* seems to be inspired by Japanese tradition. The composition of associations and the choice of familiar forms and materials integrates the museum into both a regional and a wider cultural context that engage many visitors.

The future of masterpieces

Through analysis of the interaction Scarpa's buildings have with their immediate and urban contexts, it is evident that each subsequent modification brings profound changes of meaning. This begs the question of how to add to the architect's work, how to transform it without destroying his system of memories and meaningful layers. Scarpa's *oeuvre* exists in many stages of transformation, with some projects, such as the Casa Zentner in Zurich and the Casa Scatturin in Venice being well maintained, while others continue to age and still others are indiscriminately modified. Public buildings that enjoy wide visitor attention (Castelvecchio, Fondazione Querini, Negozio Olivetti) remain largely intact, with minor changes. Castelvecchio, for example, undergoes restorations to prevent the decay of the ageing materials. It is difficult to adhere to the quality of the original, as these renovations use less expensive and less time-consuming detailing. The Venezuela Pavilion has been modified several times. The effort to protect the building from structural failures through the installation of a new roof has caused a counter intervention: removing the concrete slab from the glass openings reaching horizontally over the roof. Modifications in private homes serve to increase comfort or update to contemporary lifestyles.

The continuing narrative of Scarpa's influence demands skilled designers who can work in an historic environment. Interventions have had mixed success: the Fondazione Querini added flight stairs in addition to the existing stair. An example turning out less well is the former Negozio Olivetti, a small but formally dense showroom Scarpa built in Piazza San Marco. Trying to mimic Scarpa's detailing, the shop has become a caricature of itself in the interest of marketing souvenir art and Scarpa memorabilia. One might argue that this is the same fate as most of Venice, and that the only way to maintain Scarpa's work here is to embrace his drawing power to architects and other international visitors. However, an unfortunate but predictable side-effect of this architectural tourism is the loss of fragments of buildings to individuals desiring mementoes, their own personal direct memory, as is happening in the Cemetery Brion.

While Scarpa freely adapted the historic and cultural context in which he operated, the tendency is toward strict conservation of all built work declared historic. Once a building receives official monument designation, it becomes untouchable, and no further formal language can be integrated into it. Scarpa interpreted historic buildings such as the Castelvecchio, where he exposes the museum's objects as well as narrating a story of the building.

Twenty-one years after Scarpa's death in Sendai, the role of his architecture in twentieth-century architectural history remains unclear. Their relative youth removes Scarpa's buildings from the scrutiny of conservation and renovation, and many of them are still undergoing changes. They remain part of the narrative process of ageing, transforming, and even dying. While recognition of the significance of Scarpa's *oeuvre* pre-empts the loss of important works, a rigid protection would interrupt their life process and freeze them in time, a notion counter to his spirit.

One can view memory in Scarpa's work from multiple perspectives. There are the associations of an indirect memory, allusions to Scarpa's own personal perception history. And there are direct memories, references to the place and precedents of the building. In the course of time, the building itself becomes an object of history, reminding us of its original shape and splendour. Through this process the building also becomes a repository of indirect associations, as architects all over the world quote details and refer to Scarpa's work.

Scarpa's *oeuvre* today is in an ambiguous position. He did not follow a certain style, yet he produced recognisable projects. The factor of memory as a conscious part of the design process involves issues that are beyond fashion or building conventions resulting in a design that is independent from formal language and therefore applicable today. Instead of limiting Scarpa's influence to formal reference, it would be more appropriate to learn from his process of form finding and contextualisation.

The continuous appeal of Carlo Scarpa's work is based not only on his ability to integrate his design process into the flux of tradition and history, but also on his capacity to allow different elements to coexist. His non-hierarchical layering of planes is capable of accommodating fragments of building or elements of exhibitions. Because so much emphasis is given to layered façades or building skins, Scarpa's strategies remain continually relevant, especially when urban diversity calls for mechanisms of coexistence and variety, of maintaining as well as overcoming history and memory.

Notes

1   Francis Yates, 'Architecture and the art of memory', *Architectural Association Quarterly*, 12/4 (1980), p. 5.

2   John Ruskin, *The Seven Lamps of Architecture* (London: J. M. Dent & Sons, 1913), p. 181.

3   Peter Eisenman, 'Editor's introduction', in Aldo Rossi, *The Architecture of the City* (Cambridge, MA: MIT Press, 1982), p. 10.

4   Rossi, *Architecture of the City*, p.18.

5   *Ibid.*

6   Marja-Riitta Norri, 'Six journeys into architectural reality', *Architectural Review*, CXCIX/1190 (1996), p. 71.

7   Umberto Eco, 'Architecture and memory', *Architecture and Literature VIA* [Journal of the Graduate School of Fine Arts University of Pennsylvania], 8 (1986), p. 89.

8   Vittorio Amagnago Lampugnani, 'Einleitung', in *Carlo Scarpa Architektur* (Stuttgart: Gerd Hatje, 1986), p. 15 (present author's translation).

9   Carlo Scarpa, 'Furniture', address delivered at the Academy of Fine Arts, Vienna, 16 November 1976; in Francesco dal Co and Giuseppe Mazzariol, *Carlo Scarpa: The Complete Works* (Milan: Electa, 1985).

Section Two

Vision and optical instruments

Paula Young Lee

4 'The rational point of view': Eugène-Emmanuel Viollet-le-Duc and the *camera lucida*

In 1827, French architect Antoine-Laurent-Thomas Vaudoyer (1756–1846) suggested in a letter to his son, Léon (1803–72), then travelling in Italy as a winner of the prestigious Prix de Rome, that a popular sketching aid known as the *camera lucida* could aid his study of Roman ruins. Irritated, Léon retorted: 'Is it with a *camera lucida* that one draws the entablatures and capitals which are sent to you each year?' (Fig. 4.1). Certainly not, he huffed:

> 'I measured that of Jupiter Stator and I can judge how much effort it represents to measure, to restore, to trace, and to render. Is it with a *camera lucida* that [Louis] Duc and [Henri] Labrouste made their trip to Pompeii, from which they returned, not with sketches and picturesque views, but with plans and sections measured and redrawn? … Our manner of working today is not a fashion; it is scientific and incontestably superior to that of our predecessors'[1]

A serious student of architecture, Léon spurned the fickle whims of 'fashion' for the superior rigors of 'method'. In his opinion, a *camera lucida* was only suitable for an amateur's amusement because it encouraged the observation of superficial effects.[2] Yet, less than four decades later, architect and rationalist theorist Eugène-Emmanuel Viollet-le-Duc (1814–79) advocated the use of this device precisely because it lent scientific credibility to architectural drawings made on site (Fig. 4.2). For Viollet-le-Duc, the instrument facilitated an accuracy of measure that the younger Vaudoyer had concluded was suppressed or denied by its use.

What had changed? The answer was not the technology. Even today, the *camera lucida* remains essentially the same instrument patented in 1806 by British chemist and physician William Hyde Wollaston (1766–1828). The simple, portable device consisted of a small prism mounted on an adjustable stem (Fig. 4.3). The prism's refractive properties made it possible for the user to see a landscape or any object in front of him as if it were projected onto the page. Crucially, however, the sight was an optical illusion. The *camera lucida* differed from the *camera obscura* – a device with which it is often

4.1 Henri Labrouste, *Temple du Neptune à Paestum*, in *Fragments d'architecture antique d'après les relevés et restaurations des anciens pensionnaires de l'Académie de France à Rome*, ed. Hector d'Espouy (Paris: Charles Massin, 1905), I, pl. 24. (Photograph Special Collections, University of South Florida Library)

confused — precisely in that it cast no image forward. As historian Larry Schaaf has stated, 'A person standing beside the artist [using a *camera lucida*] will see nothing.'[3] If the prism did not project light onto a planar surface, how did the *camera lucida* help its user produce a drawing? Wollaston explained: when the eye was placed 'so that only a part of its pupil may be intercepted by the edge of the prism', half of the eye would see the landscape in front of it, while the other half would see the paper and pencil

4.2 E.-E. Viollet-le-Duc, *Paestum. Interior of the Temple of Hera, called the Temple of Neptune*, brown wash and graphite, 24 July 1836. (Collection Musée du Louvre, Paris. Photograph Réunion des musées nationaux, Paris)

positioned directly beneath it.[4] The resulting overlay was akin to seeing your reflection in a windowpane while looking through the glass to the outside world at the same time. The effect made it possible for the user to directly trace what he was seeing in his mind's eye.

Arguably, it was that evocative possibility that made the device so attractive for Viollet-le-Duc, whose use of the *camera lucida* provided a tangible and highly expressive link between his architectural thought and his geological studies of Mt Blanc. Why would an architect devote his time to geology (more precisely, to tectonics)? What compelled him to study this mountain? His importance as a rationalist theorist is well known, thanks in part to Sir John Summerson's key article of 1949, 'Viollet-le-Duc and the rational point of view'.[5] The ensuing five decades of architectural scholarship have paid increasing attention to Viollet-le-Duc's interest in geology, comparative anatomy and scientific methods in general.[6] His use of the *camera lucida* has only been of tangential concern in these later studies, largely because the supposed scientific status of the instrument simply reinforced the foundations of Viollet-le-Duc's rationalism. However, historians of science have questioned the presumed neutrality of viewing aids such as the *camera lucida* along with other, more familiar instruments such as barometers and air pumps, arguing that their contributions to scientific inquiry were neither passive nor self-justifying. Most recently, Thomas Hankins and Robert Silverman have suggested that instruments do not 'merely follow theory' but are capable of

Paula Young Lee
'The rational point of view': Eugène-Emmanuel
Viollet-le-Duc and the *camera lucida*

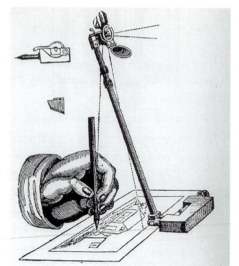

4.3 *Camera Lucida* by William Hyde Wollaston, London, 1826

determining it.[7] Moreover, a complicity between the user and any instrument, be it paintbrush, pump or prism, expects and even imposes agreement between perception and performance. Instruments that have survived the test of time owe their legitimacy to cultural circumstances as much as to careful planning. (Ever heard of an 'ocular harpsichord' or a 'sunflower clock'? Such devices were as pedigreed as the microscope in their origins, yet their essential character now seems eccentric rather than utilitarian.[8]) As the correspondence between Vaudoyer *père* and *fils* indicates, the *camera lucida* had begun to make a tentative segue from frivolous amusement to serious tool by the 1820s. Despite a certain measure of success in this regard, it was quickly forgotten as a quaint fad a few decades later, and had fallen entirely out of use in all but one telling area of study, geology, when Viollet-le-Duc began working with a version of the instrument. All told, its shifting status over the course of the nineteenth century clearly makes the point that there was nothing intrinsically 'scientific' about it.

What, then, did it represent to Viollet-le-Duc? Considering his drafting skills, what use could he have had for the instrument? Arguably, it made it possible for him to externalise and establish visual controls that reflected a rational process of thought. 'It is neither with the pen nor with the pencil that one draws, but with the intelligence', he stressed repeatedly.[9] Consistent with this belief, he asserted that one could not 'draw well' with a *camera lucida* unless one could already draw well without it.[10] Viollet-le-Duc had no quibbles with the use of instruments *per se*, given that for him 'the eye is nothing but an instrument that communicates an impression to the brain', just as 'the mechanism of the hand is only an accessory [to intelligence]'.[11] His comments reflected a dualistic position inherited from René Descartes, who characterised the human body itself as a machine, directed by the reasoning mind. Thus, Viollet-le-Duc understood that the drawing hand was nothing more than a 'docile servant' which obeyed the reigning power of intelligence.[12] His position was clear: 'Every artist who does not draw with his brain will be no more than a pantograph'[13] — that is to say, a mere copying device (an open eye, a labouring hand), regardless of whether a man-made instrument was actually employed.

Such explicit comments regarding the separate but interdependent roles of mind and body in the drawing process begin to suggest why the *camera lucida* appealed to him. Among other things, its particular configuration of prism and drawing board, which suspended the observing eye directly over the drawing hand and insisted that the higher organ constantly survey the lower appendage, formally codified the conceptual distance separating intellectual activity from manual work. Viollet-le-Duc's contempt for the pantograph is thus highly revealing. Much like the pantograph, the *camera lucida* reduced the drawing process into a matter of making a trace. Both instruments promised to save the user time and effort on that basis, and Viollet-le-Duc himself turned to the *camera lucida* as a 'sure' and 'expedient' means to obtain 'exact reproductions'.[14] What each of the two instruments allowed its user to 'reproduce', however, was not of the same nature. Whereas the pantograph made it possible to make multiple, essentially identical copies of a pre-existing image set on paper, the *camera lucida* enabled its user to trace the physical contours of the natural landscape as he saw them in his mind's eye. The user traced an interior vision instead of a visible line. Consequently, as simple as the act of direct tracing sounds, the *camera lucida* was, unlike the pantograph, quite difficult to use. The earlier description of the 'split-pupil' technique alone suggests why many novices threw the 'good for nothing' instrument away in frustration.[15] Lack of patience and coordination aside, the user still had to compensate for parallax distortion and the loss of focus around the edges of the visual field once the balancing act was mastered.[16]

Viollet-le-Duc was quite aware that the *camera lucida* posed numerous 'difficulties'. But, he accepted them calmly. A solution was at hand. As these problems inevitably confronted the 'view of each [user]', he noted, it was necessary to find the '*point*, that is to say, the distance where the eye must be held from the prism' (emphasis in original). Once that point was determined, then the drawing could proceed.

* * *

Manuals and brochures describing the advantages of the *camera lucida* sometimes noted that it allowed the user to draw 'in true Perspective'.[17] However, the claim was somewhat deceptive. The instrument neither imposed a boundary frame around visible space nor supposed a 'box of space' that could be entered. In contradistinction to the mathematical predictability of perspectival space, the depiction of a landscape through the prism of a *camera lucida* was the aggregate product of incidental, surface marks. Any illusion of spatial depth emerged as corollary effect, generated by the tendency of the user's eye to register a variety of surfaces inside a layered field of vision. Because a

Paula Young Lee
'The rational point of view': Eugène-Emmanuel
Viollet-le-Duc and the *camera lucida*

camera lucida did not assign the user a particular place relative to the observed landscape, any movement of the head ruptured the integrity of what was essentially a contour drawing. Yet, it was impossible to maintain absolute stillness over any stretch of time. To remedy the problem, the user marked his spot by placing a small dot on the drawing surface that 'fixed' the exact position of the suspended pupil. The dot could appear anywhere on the page, but, once placed, it served as an absolute point of reference. Without it, the drawing dissolved into an incoherent jumble. This 'viewing point' sat turgidly on the surface of the paper, and functioned in many respects as the inverse of the symbolically laden 'vanishing point', the crux of perspectival space.

This shift is suggestive. First, the invention of linear perspective is traditionally credited to an architect, Filippo Brunelleschi. Others before him had noted the illusion of orthogonal convergence, but Brunelleschi was the first to attach the observation to a representational method that has since become synonymous with the Renaissance as a whole. As Hubert Damisch has argued, the method was less significant as a means of pictorial representation than as a model of thought linked to the Renaissance construction of a 'desiring subject' – a subject that was, via Brunelleschi's hand, lodged firmly inside an architectural matrix.[18] Following Damisch's lead, it might be suggested that the very configuration of the *camera lucida* split the desiring subject of the Renaissance into two parts: intellect (observing eye) and sensuality (drawing hand). Nominating the perceptual division of mind and body theorised by Descartes, it brought the dual position of the 'rational subject' forward, and substituted a viewing point for a vanishing point in the process.

Given the peculiar emphasis Viollet-le-Duc placed on that '*point*' (the word is etymologically unremarkable and its translation unproblematic), its representational function in the drawing process merits further elaboration.[19] Throughout his life, Viollet-le-Duc was deeply and actively engaged with the principles of drawing because of its central role in a well-rounded artistic education. In the 1860s, Viollet-le-Duc engaged in a series of polemical debates with Ludovic Vitet on the subject of drawing at the Ecole des Beaux-Arts. Citing the dangers of following 'tradition' at 'the expense of thought', Viollet-le-Duc argued that it was not sufficient for a student to rely upon plaster casts, Old Master drawings and nude models in the studio. In order for a pedagogical program to 'enlarge, to raise the intelligence of the pupil', it must recognise that 'the ideal [model] is none other than nature'.[20] Once the student's attention was turned towards the correct subject, the 'true draftsman [*dessinateur*]' did not merely copy the model in front of him, but adopted the critical position of an 'observer' who studied this unmediated model to discern what lay beyond external appearances. To such an observer, nature would yield the 'secrets' of its 'logical order'.[21]

It was during this period that Viollet-le-Duc began his mountaineering expeditions up Mt Blanc in the Western Alps, commencing his studies of the structural origins of mountains. It was also when he began using a variation of the *camera lucida* introduced by architect Henri Révoil, an associate of the Commission des monuments historiques, who had attached a *lucida*-type prism to a surveyor's scope (Fig. 4.4).[22] This small modification made it possible to '*reproduce at a grand scale [those] images from which one is separated by a very large distance*'.[23] As Viollet-le-Duc noted in an article of 1868, otherwise inaccessible sculptural details of the Château de Pierrefonds could be drawn more accurately with its help, as demonstrated by the tiny 'before' versions (A', B', C', D') drawn with a *camera lucida*, and the large 'after' versions (A, B, C, D) drawn with the 'téléiconographe' (Fig. 4.5). Viollet-le-Duc continued to use the *téléiconographe* in his geological treatise *Le Massif du Mont-Blanc, étude sur sa construction géodésique et géologique, sur ses transformations et sur l'état ancien et moderne de ses glaciers* (Paris, 1876) (The Peak of Mont-Blanc, A Study of its Geodesic and Geological Construction, its Transformations and the Former and Present State of its Glaciers). 'With the help of this instrument', he explained, 'I could, from the summits of Brévant, Grands-Mulets and the Grand Plateau, securely recognise the mode of structure and dislocation by retreat of the large crystals that make up the summit of the Aiguille du Midi, and draw the curves that complete this summit' (Figs 4.6 and 4.7).[24] The instrument made it possible for him to see distant mountains at a large scale, and to 'grasp the silhouette' of pinnacles disguised by the reflective whiteness of snow.[25]

On the surface, his reasons for using the téléiconographe seem straightforward. However, more was at stake in the choice to use the instrument than the desire to draw distant details. (The younger Vaudoyer's comments made it plain that the *camera lucida* held no allure for an architect who preferred to put his faith in the objective numerics of a plotted space rather than the divided perceptions of a single pupil.) Use of the téléiconographe not only allowed Viollet-le-Duc to state his location (this is Maudit mountain, as seen from the top of Plan-Prez, using a téléiconographe enlarged at a setting of four[26]), but also his interpretive position (this is a reconstruction drawn by a critical observer). It also permitted him to do something more: namely, it allowed him to retrace building processes that had taken place in the distant past, and to subsequently

4.4 Henri Révoil, 'Le téléiconographe', in *Gazette des architectes et du bâtiment* (1868), fig. 118

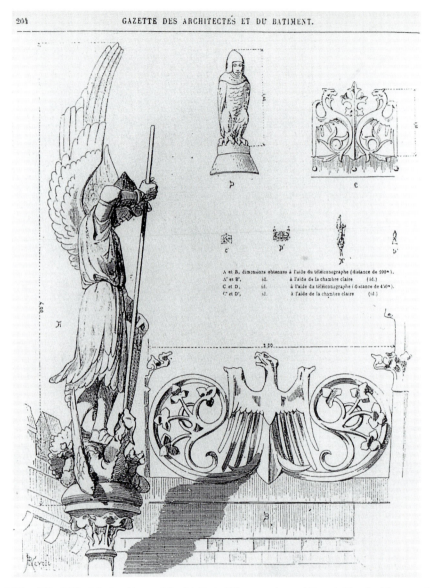

4.5 Henri Révoil, 'Résultats d'expériences faites à l'aide du téléiconographe au château du Pierrefonds', engraved by Tomaszkiewicz, in *Gazette des architectes et du bâtiment*, fig. 119 (Paris, P. Morel 1868)

indicate the lost geometry of the 'ruined parts' through the convention of a punctuated line (Fig. 4.8). The eloquence of the dotted line comes from its brave uncertainty: it describes what could not be seen directly but could be deduced, based on the observation of extremely large historical patterns and sustained by the belief that nature has its own logic. To discern the patterns of mountain formation was, for Viollet-le-Duc, to give oneself up 'to a methodical work of analysis' that was analogous to the labours

Paula Young Lee
'The rational point of view': Eugène-Emmanuel
Viollet-le-Duc and the *camera lucida*

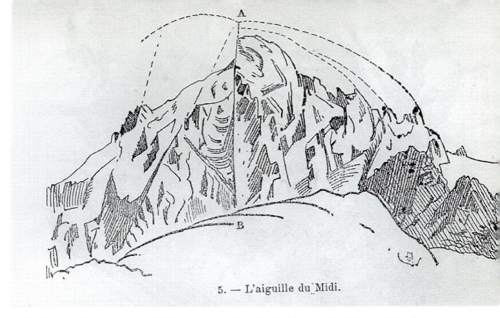

5. — L'aiguille du Midi.

4.6 E.-E. Viollet-le-Duc, 'L'aiguille du Midi' (view taken from Pierre-Pontue), from *Le Massif du Mont-Blanc* (Paris, 1876), p. 8, fig. 5. Drawn with a *camera lucida* (*téléiconographe*), p. 7, n.2

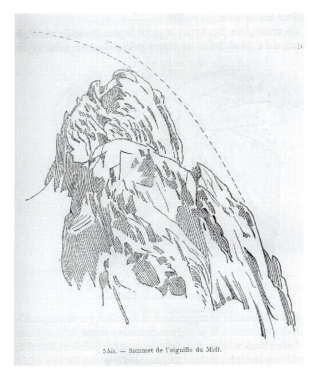

5 *bis*. — Sommet de l'aiguille du Midi.

4.7 E.-E. Viollet-le-Duc, 'Sommet de l'aiguille du Midi' (taken from Pierre-Pontue), from *Le Massif du Mont-Blanc* (Paris, 1876), p. 9, fig. 5 *bis*. Drawn with a *camera lucida* (*téléiconographe*), p. 7, n.2

71

Paula Young Lee
'The rational point of view': Eugène-Emmanuel
Viollet-le-Duc and the *camera lucida*

CHAPITRE IV.

B

A

C

(l. — Le mont Maudit. (P. 81.)

4.8 E.-E. Viollet-le-Duc, 'Le mont Maudit', from *Le Massif du Mont-Blanc* (Paris, 1876), p. 81, fig. 41

of an architect or archaeologist who 'deduces the form of monuments', but 'on a much greater scale'.[27]

72   Following his own imperative to seek out nature's secrets, Viollet-le-Duc climbed, studied and exhaustively analysed Mt Blanc, but he also understood that the analogy was reciprocal. 'Our globe is but a great edifice of which all parts have a reason for being', he observed. Elevated, enlarged and separated by great distances from the human presence on earth and in history, the massive mountain – itself a synecdoche for the inexorable forces that shaped the terrestrial globe as a whole – presented the kind of challenges the *camera lucida* was configured to meet. The mediating presence of the instrument kept the viewer outside and apart from the overwhelming subject, acknowledging the temporal limits of his tiny presence while claiming the timelessness of reason. The resultant drawings reconstituted a geological process rather than the topography of a mountain, thereby expressing an interpretive position that adopted a 'scientific' rather than 'historical' point of view.

     As a viewing device and drawing tool, the *camera lucida* broached the conceptual gap between what could be perceived and what was actually present. Posing a glistening barrier between viewer and viewed, the prism transposed a visual impression into a complex metaphor of perceptual and intellectual possession: with hand extended, yet with touch denied, it traced a vision that was only available in, and to, the reasoning mind. Viollet-le-Duc was fully aware that 'the *camera lucida* does not reproduce images as the eye sees them',[28] but this was precisely its advantage. For any user to draw with a *camera lucida* exposed his spatial and geographical orientation in the real world, even as it made an internal process of observation visible to others through the careful tracing of lines. In Viollet-le-Duc's hands, the *camera lucida* not only occupied a critical, symbolic juncture between architecture and landscape, but also the mental and physical demands the instrument placed on the user also allowed him to express, through the very act of drawing, a rational point of view.

Paula Young Lee
'The rational point of view': Eugène-Emmanuel
Viollet-le-Duc and the *camera lucida*

Notes

1   J'ai mésuré celui de Jupiter Stator et j'ai été à même juger toute la peine que cela donne, à
    mésurer, à restaurer, à rapporter, et mettre au net. Est-ce que à la chambre-claire que Duc
    et Labrouste ont fait leur voyage de Pompéia dont ils ont rapporté non pas des croquis et
    des vues pittoresques, mais des plans et des coupes levées et rapportées; on ne fait plus de
    minutes comme autrefois que l'on ne rapportais jamais et qui restent au portefeuille sans
    être jamais consultées. On arrive à Paris aujourd'hui avec un voyage complet, tant sur
    l'antique que sur le moderne et dont on peut jouir immédiatement; notre manière de
    travailler, aujourd'hui, n'est pas un mode; elle est positive et incontestablement supérieur à
    celle de nos prédecesseurs. Léon Vaudoyer, letter of 4 April 1827, to his father A. L. T.
    Vaudoyer, quoted and translated in David Van Zanten, *Designing Paris* (Cambridge, MA:
    MIT Press, 1987), p. 6. The French original is on p. 253, n.19.

2   As described by Barry Bergdoll: 'Vaudoyer *père* produced "picturesque sketches", whereas
    the drawings of Vaudoyer *fils* were "more coldly analytical" '; B. Bergdoll, *Les Vaudoyer*
    (Paris: Réunion des musées nationaux, 1990), pp. 38–39.

3   Larry Schaaf, *Tracings of Light: Sir John Herschel and the Camera Lucida* (San Francisco:
    Friends of Photography, 1990), p. 12; Brian Warner and John Rourke, *Flora Herscheliana:
    Sir John and Lady Herschel at the Cape, 1834 to 1838* (Houghton: Brenthurst, 1998), pp.
    75–85. On the history of the *camera lucida*, see John Hammond and Jill Austin, *The Camera
    Lucida in Art and Science* (Bristol: Adam Hilger, 1987). Modernists are chiefly familiar with
    the term '*camera lucida*' via Roland Barthes, *Camera Lucida: Reflections on Photography*
    (New York: Hill & Wang, 1981). However, Barthes refers to the *camera lucida* to exploit the
    term's poetic possibilities (*lucida*, lucidity). The technology of the *camera lucida* bears no
    relation to photography.

4   William Hyde Wollaston, 'Description of the *camera lucida*', *Philosophical Magazine*, 27
    (1807), pp. 343–347.

5   Sir John Summerson, 'Viollet-le-Duc and the rational point of view' [1949], in *idem, Heavenly
    Mansions* (London: Cresset Press, 1949); repr. *Eugène-Emmanuel Viollet-le-Duc,
    1814–1879* (London: Academy Editions, 1980), pp. 7–13.

6   Recent contributions include Laurent Baridon, *L'imaginaire scientifique de Viollet-le-Duc* (Paris:
    l'Harmattan, 1996); Jean-Michel Leniaud, *Viollet-le-Duc ou les délires du système* (Paris:
    Mengès, 1994); and Martin Bressani, 'Opposition et équilibre: le rationalisme organique de
    Viollet-le-Duc', *Revue de l'art*, no. 112 (1996), pp. 28–37. For earlier forays into the subject,
    see Bernard Thaon, 'Viollet-le-Duc, pensée scientifique et pensée architecturale', in *Actes du
    colloque international Viollet-le-Duc Paris, 1980* (Paris: Nouvelles Editions latines, 1982), pp.
    131–143; and Philippe Junod, 'La terminologie esthétique de Viollet-le-Duc', in *Viollet-le-Duc,
    centenaire de la mort à Lausanne* (Lausanne: Musée historique de l'Ancien Evêché, 1979).

7   Thomas Hankins and Robert Silverman, *Instruments and the Imagination* (Princeton:
    Princeton University Press, 1996), p. v. On optical devices in the nineteenth century, see
    Jonathan Crary, *Techniques of the Observer* (Cambridge, MA: MIT Press, 1990); and Gerard
    L'E. Turner, *Nineteenth-Century Scientific Instruments* (London: Sotheby's Publ., 1983).

8   Various chapters in Hankins and Silverman, *Instruments and the Imagination*, discuss the
    ocular harpsichord, cat piano and other fascinating 'failures'.

9   E.-E. Viollet-le-Duc, *Réponse à M. Vitet à propos de l'enseignement des arts du dessin*
    (Paris: A. Morel, 1864), p. 36.

10 E.-E. Viollet-le-Duc, 'Le téléiconographe', *Gazette des architectes et du bâtiment*, no. 20
    (1868), p. 203: 'Pour bien dessiner à l'aide de la chambre claire, il faut savoir bien dessiner
    sans son secours; c'est là un point qui n'est pas discutable.' Many other users made the
    same observation. For example, as William Henry Fox Talbot described in 1833: 'I was
    amusing myself on the lovely shores of the Lake of Como in Italy, taking sketches with
    Wollaston's *camera lucida*, or rather, attempting to take them: but with the smallest amount
    of success. After various fruitless attempts I laid aside the instrument and came to the

conclusion that its use required a previous knowledge of drawing which unfortunately I did not possess.' W. H. Fox Talbot, *The Pencil of Nature* (London, 1844–46), quotation in Beaumont Newhall, *The History of Photography* (New York: Museum of Modern Art, 1988), p. 19.

11 Viollet-le-Duc, *Réponse à M. Vitet*, p. 36.

12 Viollet-le-Duc, in *Débats et polémiques à propos de l'enseignement des arts du dessin, Louis Vitet, Eugène Viollet-le-Duc* (Paris: Ecole nationale supérieure des beaux-arts, 1984), p. 100. Viollet-le-Duc directly refers to René Descartes's *Discours de la méthode* in *Entretiens sur l'architecture* (Paris: A. Morel & cie, 1863–72). Other works, such as *Histoire de l'habitation humaine* (Paris: J. Hetzel, 1875), can be seen to respond to Cartesian thought. Although it treats the British case, the historical discussion offered by Steven Shapin and Barry Barnes of the social hierarchy embedded in the division of mental and manual work provides a theoretical basis to explore the related case in France; S. Shapin and B. Barnes, 'Head and hand: rhetorical resources in British pedagogical writing, 1770–1850', *Oxford Review of Education*, 2/3 (1976), pp. 231–254.

13 Viollet-le-Duc, *Réponse à M. Vitet*, p. 40.

14 Viollet-le-Duc, 'Le téléiconographe', p. 203: 'La chambre claire n'est (pour les personnes qui savent manier le crayon) qu'un moyen sûr et expéditif d'obtenir des reproductions exactes. Il n'en faut pas moins, même pour les dessinateurs, une certaine pratique, si l'on prétend utiliser la chambre claire; mais cette pratique n'est pas longue à aquérir.' Viollet-le-Duc's remarks were originally published in the *Journal officiel*, but I am unable to locate the full citation.

15 *Ibid.*, p. 203.

16 *Ibid.*: 'Les difficultés qui se présentent au dessinateur sont de trois natures: 1o difficulté de voir la pointe du crayon en même temps que l'objet reporté par le prisme sur le papier; 2o déformation des objets aux extrémités du champ de vision; 3o difficulté de dessiner les objets, par suite de la parallaxe ou de la variation apparente de l'image.'

17 From an instruction sheet accompanying a *camera lucida* held in the Science Museum, South Kensington, London. Quoted in Hammond and Austin, *Camera Lucida in Art and Science*, p. 19.

18 Hubert Damisch, *The Origin of Perspective*, trans. John Goodman (Cambridge, MA: MIT Press, 1994), pp. 58–74.

19 Viollet-le-Duc owned several treatises on perspective and the mechanics of vision, such as Jean Pélérin ('Le Viateur'), *De Artificiali Perspectiva* (Paris: Librarie Tross, 1860/61), as well as an original edition of Sébastien Leclerc, *Discours touchant le point de vue, dans lequel il est prouvé que les choses qu'on voit distinctement ne sont que d'un oeil* (Paris: Thomas Jolly, 1679). Other related texts owned by Viollet-le-Duc include R. Gautier de Maignannes, *Invention nouvelle et briève, pour reduire en perspective ... toutes sortes de plans et corps*, 1648; and F. Lasseré and Père Cherubin d'Orléons, *La dioptrique oculaire ou la théorique, la positive et la mechanique de l'oculaire dioptrique en toutes ses espèces* (Paris: Thomas Jolly & Simon Bernard, 1671).

20 Viollet-le-Duc, *Réponse à M. Vitet*, pp. 42, 43.

21 Viollet-le-Duc, in *Débats et polémiques*, p. 100: 'Veuillez croire, messieurs les amateurs qui vous donnez tant de peine pour nous apprendre les secrets d'un art que vous ne pratiquez pas, que pour l'art du dessin comme pour l'art d'écrire, la première chose à faire, c'est de s'adresser à l'intelligence, qui est la vraie et la seule souverain, que quand l'intelligence s'est longtemps exercée à comprendre la forme, à la choisir, la main n'est plus qu'un serviteur docile. La véritable dessinateur n'est pas un photographe reproduisant un modèle posant devant lui, mais un observateur étudiant ce modèle, de façon à en connaître si bien la forme, la raison d'être, de se mouvoir, les diverses apparences suivant les circonstances extérieurs.'

22 Viollet-le-Duc, 'Le téléiconographe', Révoil's invention did not receive much attention, largely because Cornelius Varley had done much the same several decades earlier by attaching the

Paula Young Lee
'The rational point of view': Eugène-Emmanuel
Viollet-le-Duc and the *camera lucida*

prism to a telescope. C. Varley, *A Treatise on Optical Drawing Instruments* (London: Horne, Thornthwaite & Wood, 1845).

23 Viollet-le-Duc, 'Le téléiconographe', p. 203 (emphasis in original).

24 E.-E. Viollet-le-Duc, *Le Massif du Mont-Blanc, étude sur sa construction géodésique et géologique, sur ses transformations et sur l'état ancien et moderne de ses glaciers* (Paris: J. Baudry, 1876), pp. xi–xii: 'A l'aide de cet instrument, j'ai pu, du sommet du Brévent, des Grands-Mulets et du Grand-Plateau, reconnaître sûrement le mode de structure et de dislocation par retrait des grands cristaux qui compose le sommet de l'Aiguille du Midi, et dessiner les courbures qui terminent ce sommet.' On Viollet-le-Duc and Mont-Blanc, see Robin Middleton, 'Viollet-le-Duc et les Alpes: la dispute du Mont-Blanc', in *Viollet-le-Duc, Centenaire de la Mort à Lausanne* (Lausanne: Musée historique de l'Ancien-Evêché, 1979), pp. 101–10; Pierre Frey, *Viollet-le-Duc et la montagne* (Grenoble: Glénat, 1993); and *idem* (ed.), *E. Viollet-le-Duc et le Massif de Mont-Blanc, 1868–1879* (Lausanne: Payot, 1988). Mott Greene's excellent survey, *Geology in the Nineteenth Century: Changing Views of a Changing World* (Ithaca: Cornell University Press, 1982), includes a brief discussion of Viollet-le-Duc's study.

25 *Ibid.*, p. 212.

26 *Ibid.*, p. 81.

27 *Ibid.*, p. xv–xvi: 'Je devais en quelques mots, à ceux qui voudront me lire, expliquer comment et pourquoi un architecte a laissé de temps à autre l'architecture pour entrer dans un domaine qui semble n'être pas le sien./ De fait, notre globe n'est qu'un grand édifice dont toutes les parties ont une raison d'être; sa surface affecte des formes commandées par des lois impérieuses et suivies d'après un ordre logique./ Analyser curieusement un groupe de montagnes, leur mode de formation et les causes de leur ruine; reconnaître l'ordre qui a présidé à leur soulèvement, les conditions de leur résistance et de leur durée au milieu des agents atmosphériques, noter la chronologie de leur histoire, c'est, sur une plus grande échelle, se livrer à un travail méthodique d'analyse analogue à celui auquel s'astreint l'architecte praticien [sic] et archéologue qui établit ses déductions d'après l'étude qui établit ses déductions d'après l'étude des monuments.'

28 'Le téléiconographe', p. 203: 'Mais, jusqu'à ce jour, la chambre claire ne reproduisait les images que comme l'oeil les voit; elle ne les rapprochait les images que le fait la longue-vue; il s'agissait donc de trouver un appareil facilement transportable et réunissant les avantagesf de la longue-vue et du prisme.'

Jan Birksted

5　Cézanne's property

Given the canonical Modernist status of Paul Cézanne's landscapes, can his work illuminate the modernist architectural concept of landscape as quasi-wilderness? Cézanne in fact not only painted paintings of Arcadian scenes 'of an imaginary realm of perfect bliss'[1] with 'the late forest landscapes of timeless peace and breathless quiet'[2] in his attempt to 'Redo Poussin after nature', but also he inhabited and worked in it, and he created in its midst a quasi-wild garden: 'J'ai fait construire un atelier sur un petit terrain que j'ai acquis à cette intention. Je poursuis donc mes recherches.'[3] This plot of land that Cézanne purchased, with its studio and garden which he himself designed, is, of course, Les Lauves, and is indissolubly associated with Cézanne's late work. There Cézanne was protected from the mistral, warmed by the winter sun, and benefited from those extensive prospects towards Mt Sainte-Victoire to the east and Aix-en-Provence to the south, which are now the very fabric of art history. Cézanne's Arcadian plot of land, Les Lauves, was initially an uncultivated and overgrown scrubland, described in the Land Register as 'un terrain à usage de chasse'.[4] And Cézanne, while he was working on his 'harmonies parallel to nature', was deliberately to retain it as a tangled mass of overgrown vegetation, tended and nurtured in this state by his gardener Vallier. The original wilderness of Cézanne's garden, now intentionally restored to that condition, is such that the curator of Les Lauves questions not only the significance of the garden, but also even the applicability of the concept of 'garden':

> Le jardin de Cézanne ne ressemble à aucun autre, et s'il est un jardin historique dans le sens que, lié à l'Historie, et de plus à l'Historie de l'Art, c'est bien par le biais le plus inattendu qu'il s'impose à nous … puisque c'est celle … d'un éternel retour de la nature. Le jardin de Cézanne a échappé à toutes les intentions hormis celles de la nature … ce n'est plus l'Homme, mais son oubli, qui est à son écoute.[5]

Indeed, such absence of human intervention problematises the word 'garden'. Cézanne's tangled mass of unkempt vegetation stands in absolute contrast to those of other

5.1 Paul Cézanne's studio and garden at Les Lauves. (All photographs by the author)

contemporary artists' lovingly tended provençal gardens: to Pierre Bonnard's garden at Le Bosquet above Cannes, with its terrace shaded from the midday heat by fig, palm and pine, with its south-facing flowerbeds arranged in small terraces linked by paths and stairs, and with its almonds, olives and mimosas through which the distant Mediterranean shimmers in the heat; to Auguste Renoir's garden above Cagnes, also overlooking the Mediterranean, with its rose beds and bamboos and lawns and goldfish pond, its gardeners and their shears and watering cans. But then Cézanne himself, as the self-proclaimed 'first primitive of a new race',[6] stands in absolute contrast to Bonnard and Renoir. In opposition to their luxuriant and sumptuous garden paintings, Cézanne's paintings of Les Lauves often leave large, unpainted areas of canvas. Cézanne's paintings of his garden thus mirror the garden itself, eschewing conventional representation. And so there is a paradox: Cézanne designs — if the term is appropriate at all — a garden that is a precursor of the modernist garden in the 'Corbu style', a garden which anticipates Le Corbusier's ideal description: 'Les habitants, venus ici parce que cette campagne agreste était belle avec sa vie de campagne, ils la contempleront, maintenue intacte. . . . Leur vie domestique sera inserée dans un reve virgilien.'[7] Thus, Cézanne, who in his art 'took the ideology of the visual to its limits and breaking point',[8] also took his garden at Les Lauves to its limits and breaking point. The question inevitably resurfaces: can an understanding of Cézanne's garden help one to clarify the modernist tradition of quasi-wilderness? What, then — if not simply an insignificant tangle — are we looking at?

Looking in more detail at Cézanne's property at Les Lauves, access is through a solid timber door set into the stone wall, which hides the garden from the road. A short gravel path becomes a narrow terrace in front of the house. From this terrace, demarcated by a stone parapet, a small staircase leads down into the tangled thicket of trees pressing up against it. Paths meander through this dense undergrowth. Here and there are clearings. Unexpectedly, a path leads back to the terrace. On entering the house, a staircase leads up to a first-floor landing that opens into Cézanne's studio. The studio, now the Museum Atelier Cézanne, still contains those items that appear in Cézanne's paintings: bowls, plates, bottles, skulls, the Puget plaster cast, and so on. On

5.2 Cézanne's studio, views towards Aix

5.3 Cézanne's studio, views towards the woods

79

5.4 Cézanne's studio, furniture

the north side is a very large conservatory-type window against which presses a dense thicket. Two casement windows, facing south, overlook the garden beneath and, beyond, the surrounding countryside with Aix-en-Provence in the distance. Looking out over this garden, it is not that it contains little of interest, but rather that any singularity is denied to every specimen by their entanglement with others such that 'un foisonnement d'arbustes en a pris d'assaut la place …'.[9] This tangle of unkempt vegetation is reminiscent of statements about Cézanne's paintings according to which they stand as 'powerful forms of refusal or negation … against the grain of established culture'[10] in that 'the very absence of Academic competencies … [is] a kind of competence in itself'.[11] Just as Cézanne's paintings are 'peculiarly resistant to being translated into a form of words',[12] so the garden remains resistant to a sequential and narrative description.

It is in this respect that Cézanne's garden corresponds to the quasi-wild modernist landscape, which also inhibits analysis.[13] Le Corbusier too wanted to convey the impression that the landscape was untouched and naturally wild, and he specifically represented the landscape as if without human design. Thus, apparent lack of order is a purposeful design strategy. Le Corbusier's landscape strategies resemble strongly Cézanne's 'technique of originality'[14] in which he 'avoided hierarchical organisation. Many of his decisions were negative ones: he did one thing as if to escape doing another; he strove to deny all established academic principles'.[15]

What was Les Lauves like during Cézanne's lifetime? Judging from photographs and written descriptions, little has changed since Cézanne worked there. Les Lauves originally consisted of a ruin surrounded by an overgrown piece of land. Cézanne commissioned an architect in Aix-en-Provence — a Monsieur Mourgues whom Cézanne's father had used regularly[16] — to design a new house. The ruins were therefore cleared and the construction of the new house started. Cézanne then discovered to his fury that the new house was designed *dans le style Suisse* — as a Swiss chalet — with large roofs overhanging at different levels and much ornamentation. Cézanne had the beginnings of the new house torn down, paid the architect the fee already incurred and then himself drew up the plans for the existing house which his builder constructed. The garden was left wild, apart from a few fruit trees towards the west of the property, a line of yuccas beneath the low wall separating the terrace from the garden, and the flowerpots on the wall. Jules Borély described Cézanne's garden in 1902 as 'Au delà d'un fouillis d'oliviers et d'arbres desséchés….'[17] Nor has Les Lauves changed much since John Rewald's 1977 description:

> The plain, two-story structure he built there — it was ready in September 1902 — contains small rooms on the ground floor while the second floor is taken up almost entirely by a large studio, more than twenty-three by twenty-five feet and a little over thirteen feet high, its north wall made up of a huge window next to which there is a long, narrow slit through which big canvases can be moved. On the opposite wall are two tall windows (the third lights the stairwell) that afford a magnificent view of Aix and, in the far distance, the misty blue mountain range,

the Chaine de l'Etoile, with its protruding, square Pilon du Roi.

There is a twenty-foot-wide terrace in front of the studio, bordered by a low wall, separating it from a small garden that descends towards a narrow canal. An old gardener, Vallier, took care of the grounds. Behind the studio a wooded plot, belonging to a neighbour provided a green curtain for the large window. . . .

He furnished it [the studio] sparsely but brought along many of the objects (quite a few are still there) that he liked to use for still life compositions. Among them were four or five skulls, a blue ginger pot, old bottles, green olive jars, various containers and crockery, as well as a rather ugly rug or table cover made of some kind of heavy felt. … He also took to the studio a small wooden table with scalloped apron that he had already used over a decade and on which he liked to assemble still lifes. It is still there. Preserved also are the white plaster putto, *L'Amour*, attributed to Puget…'.[18]

When visiting Les Lauves, the terrace in front, which separates the studio from the overgrown property, takes on a central importance. The paths through the overgrown property start from there and, as in a labyrinth, erratically lead back to it. This terrace is both entrance yard and patio space, both private and public space: it fulfils several opposing functions, simultaneously as 'circulation space' and 'room'. This compression and overlaying of different functions creates a sense of tension. A similar quality is also found inside the studio. Between the two windows overlooking the garden and facing Aix-en-Provence to the south, and the large northern conservatory-window with the vegetation pressing up against it, Cézanne's studio is itself like a transition space, a space between the panoramic vision to the south and macroscopic vision to the north. The south and north windows offer different perspectival experiences. Spatial compression is generated from the direct juxtapositions of these different visualities. In addition, the portrait-format southern windows accentuate the amplitude of the landscape format panorama towards Aix-en-Provence, in opposition to the north-facing metal-grid window that highlights the tactile qualities of the vegetation pressing up against the glass. The studio is thus in tension between opposing visual and tactile qualities.

81

5.5 Cézanne's garden

5.6 Cézanne's garden

Cézanne's studio becomes an intermediary space between prospect and aspect. But in this process of cancellation of a transitional garden between interior studio and indivisible nature, that transitional garden space migrates into the interior studio, which

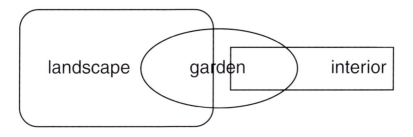

itself becomes a richly cluttered landscape of still-life objects disposed on a surrounding shelf extending the full length of the wall, extending the horizon of Aix-en-Provence, as well as on the often painted scalloped table and on the floor, against and on the walls.

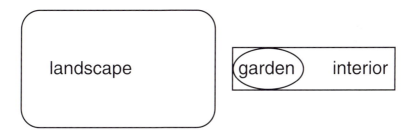

The studio itself becomes like a garden. Thus, it would seem that in the triad the garden must appear somewhere. If it cannot appear as a transitional space outside in the landscape, it will reappear, as a kind of 'return of the repressed', inside the interior: And here are found exactly the three basic features of Le Corbusier's modernist gardens and landscapes. First, the semi-wild uniformity of the thickets and the meadow surrounding the Villa Savoye. It is precisely this quality of the landscape as foil to the architecture that is so noticeable and that one finds so perfectly expressed in several studies: 'Architecture was placed in what I consider a paysage-type, a generic landscape framed by calculated openings; its shape was less important than its evocation of nature. Seldom were the scenery and vegetation more than an unaltered backdrop.'[19] Second, the exterior becomes a landscape indivisible and wild, with the result that the transitional space of the garden becomes integrated into the interior of the building as *jardin suspendu*. According to this modernist notion, the cultivated garden is banished: wilderness becomes 'an imaginary realm of perfect bliss'.[20] Nature thus becomes a separate and autonomous system, scenographic instead of perspectival. Third — as scenographic — landscape becomes a separate standard and takes on an epistemological and moral character. In this respect, landscape can no longer be mimetically referred to. Instead of image, landscape becomes a process. Le Corbusier stated precisely this view when describing how 'L'achitecture est la première manifestation de l'homme créant l'image de la nature, souscrivant aux lois de la nature.... Les lois physiques primordiales sont simples et peu nombreuses. Les lois morales sont simples et peu nombreuses.'[21] Thus, landscape and nature become transcendentals of truth and morality, unattainable transcendental ideals to be strived towards. This wilderness, by its brut appearance, resists conceptual analysis. Apparently untouched by human design, resistant to the mind through its primitiveness and vegetal Otherness, this Modernist landscape is a landscape of resistance. Seminal Modernist landscapes are, so to say, invisible since they present themselves as quasi-wildernesses specifically made to look undesigned and untouched, therefore without very much to be said about them at all. Indeed, the Modernist Arcadian quasi-wild landscape register is in the register of the unreferable through avoidance of historical allusions, evacuation of narrative reference and through a particularly significant form: formlessness....

According to the Modernist notion from which the cultivated garden is banished, Arcadia becomes a transcendental ideal: Cézanne's 'promised land' and Le Corbusier's 'primordial laws'. In his analysis of the notion of Arcadia, Erwin Panofsky unearths behind Nicolas Poussin's elegiac 'I, too, lived in Arcady', the altogether different original meaning of 'Death is even in Arcadia'.[22] Perhaps if one therefore revisited the quasi-wilderness of Cézanne's 'late forest landscapes of timeless peace and breathless quiet'[23] while considering this Modernist gift of idealised transcendental nature with its exclusion of the garden, the reverse meaning of the word 'gift' becomes transparent.

Notes

1   Erwin Panofsky, *Meaning in the Visual Arts* (London: Penguin, 1955), p. 343.

2   Fritz Novotny, 'The late landscape paintings', in William Rubin (ed.), *Cézanne: The Late Work* (London: Thames & Hudson, 1977), pp. 107–111 (p. 111).

3   'I have had a studio built on a plot of land which I purchased specially. And so I am continuing my investigations'; quotation in R. M. Bourges, *Le Jardin de Cézanne* (Aix-en-Provence: Ville, 1984), p. 16.

4   A 'hunting reserve'; *ibid.*, p. 18.

5   'Cézanne's garden resembles no other, and if it is a historic garden in the sense of being linked to art history, it commands our attention by a most unexpected twist, namely that of a return to the state of nature. Cézanne's garden has managed to avoid all intentions except those of nature itself. It is not so much human presence that makes itself felt here, but the very freedom from human involvement'; *ibid.*, p. 5.

6   Cézanne, quotation in John Rewald, *Paul Cézanne Letters* (New York: Hacker Art Books, 1984).

7   'The inhabitants, having come here in pursuit of the rural countryside with its pastoral life, will contemplate it in its untouched purity.... Their domestic life will be framed by a virgilien dream'; *Le Corbusier, Précisions sur un état présent de l'architecture et de l'urbanisme* (Paris, 1930), pp. 136–138.

8   T. J. Clark, *The Painting of Modern Life: Paris in the Art of Monet and his Followers* (London: Thames & Hudson, 1984), p. 17.

9   '[A] tangle of underbrush has taken over …'; Bourges, *Jardin de Cézanne*, p. 12.

10 Charles Harrison, 'Impressionism, modernism and originality', in F. Frascina, N. Blake, B Fer, T. Garb and C. Harrison, *Modernity and Modernism* (New Haven and London: Yale University Press and the Open University, 1993), p. 207.

11 Harrison, 'Impressionism, modernism and originality', p. 206.

12 *Ibid.*, p. 213.

13 It could be argued that, rather than quasi-wilderness, Cézanne's garden simply falls into the same category as the gardens of the Impressionists, informal *jardins à l'anglaise* specifically rejecting the *jardin à la française*? If so, this would explain Cézanne's apparently undesigned garden, the very embodiment of his notion of a 'chaos irisé'; (Cézanne, quoted in Bourges, *Jardin de Cézanne*, p. 28). But in this respect Cézanne's garden would then belong to the same category as Bonnard's garden with its informal profusion of colour and texture, not to mention Claude Monet's Giverny. Indeed, these Impressionist gardens have been described as acts of resistance, 'deliberate, if less obvious or aggressive, representations and accommodations of the modern world'; John D. Hunt, 'French Impressionist gardens and the ecological picturesque', in J. D. Hunt, *Gardens and the Picturesque: Studies in the History of Landscape Architecture* (Cambridge, MA: MIT Press, 1992), p. 256. But, of course, Cézanne's garden is precisely not like these Impressionist gardens with their carefully cultivated picturesque qualities and their social activities, which provide 'disclosure of social unease or even fracture'; *ibid.*, p. 270. Cézanne's garden is not a carefully cultivated picturesque setting, and no social activities took place in it. Cézanne's garden, as seen, is uncultivated. Cézanne poses his models against the garden in front of the boundary wall separating house from garden. The garden is not where life takes place, but the backdrop to the figures involved.

14 Richard Schiff, *Cézanne and the End of Impressionism: A Study of the Theory, Technique, and Critical Evaluation of Modern Art* (Chicago: Chicago University Press, 1984).

15 *Ibid.*, p. 199.

16 Personal communication from the Curator at Les Lauves.

17 A 'tangle of olive trees and other desiccated trees'.

18 John Rewald, 'The last motifs at Aix', in Rubin, *Cézanne: The Late Work*, pp. 95–102.

19 Dorothée Imbert, *The Modernist Garden in France* (New Haven and London: Yale University Press, 1993), p. 148.

20 Panofsky, *Meaning in the Visual Arts*, p. 343.

21 Le Corbusier, quotation in Marc Perelman, *Urbs ex Machina* (Paris: Passion, 1986), p. 35: 'Architecture is the first human manifestation which creates the image of nature and underwrites nature's laws.... The primordial laws of physics are simple and few. Moral laws too are simple and few.'

22 Panofsky, *Meaning in the Visual Arts*, p. 343. And, curiously, Cézanne was struck down by illness after being caught in a thunder- and rainstorm, and Le Corbusier died while swimming in the Mediterranean.

23 Novotny, 'The late landscape paintings', p. 111.

Edward Eigen

6   Subject to circumstance: the landscape of the French lighthouse system

> Pour le marin qui se dirige d'après les constellations, ce fut comme un ciel de plus qu'elle fit descendre. Elle créa à la fois planètes, étoiles fixes et satellites, mit dans ces astres inventés les nuances et les caractères différents de ceux de là-haut.[1]

During his 1669 visit to Bordeaux, Claude Perrault, the architect of the Paris observatory and naturalist, first viewed the famed Cordouan lighthouse from an advanced point on the coast through a telescope (an instrument to which he once likened the human eye).[2] The weather being fine, his party resolved to embark the following day for a closer look at the 'marvelous edifice', built on an isolated shoal in the mouth the Gironde River (Fig. 6.1). More than once had a visitor lamented that such a superb monument was situated in 'the most barren place in the world'; evidently, lighthouses were not meant to be seen like other works of architecture or features of the man-made landscape.[3] That evening, Perrault engaged a ship ready to take his party in the morning, but overnight the weather changed. The very sound of the agitated sea woke him, and with this synesthetic alert to the senses, the plan was abandoned; the opportunity to approach the tower was indefinitely delayed.

What came to pass between the evening and the morning was an unforeseen change in the weather, an example of the circumstances that 'distribute' themselves, in Michel Serres's notion, around any instance of seeing.[4] The focus here will be the study of these circumstances carried out by the French Lighthouse Commission, which was established in 1811 to determine the 'best distribution and arrangement' of lighthouses along the entirety of the littoral.[5] For the Commission, distribution referred to the topographic placement of towers, but this chapter is also concerned with the distribution of light itself, which was to hinge on a variable of transparency, a measure of the visual character of the atmosphere itself. The era of modern illumination began at Cordouan in 1826 with the installation of Augustin Fresnel's recently invented lenticular system (consisting of concentric bands of prismatic glass), replacing the tower's traditional reflectors. Despite their polished precision, however, there could be no optical correction

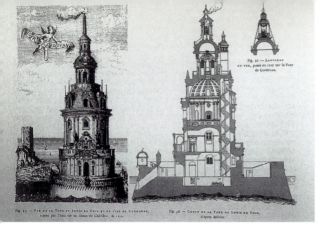

6.1 Claude Chastillon, 'View of the Tower of Cordouan' (1612) from Emile Allard, *Les Travaux Publics de la France – V Phares et Balises* (Paris: J. Rothschild, 1883), fig. 35, p. 30

for the uncertain circumstances into which its light was cast. The circumstances Perrault encountered over 150 years earlier persisted, even if they manifested themselves just as unpredictably.

In determining the distribution and arrangement of lighthouses, the Commission had to instruct itself in the fatality of place. The unknown relationship between lights and the irregularities of the terrain was unwittingly revealed by the boast of the great astronomer François Arago, who equated the brilliance of a single Fresnel lantern to one-third of that produced by all the street lamps of Paris, its department stores and its theatres.[6] Where these lights made the city imageable, marking its major venues and centres of attraction, the lighthouse was poised above a trackless sea, marking but not illuminating features cloaked by darkness or permanently submerged.

Arago, along with Fresnel, the engineer Léonce Reynaud, and officers of the navy, was an original member of the Commission, which scrupulously consulted sources to establish which places posed the greatest threat to navigation. The sources included hydrographic charts, memoirs written by seasoned sea captains and coastal pilots, shipwreck statistics and oral histories of coastal residents. From this analysis a plan emerged, consisting of channels of communication and routes of safe passage knowable by the luminous signals which occupied a stratum of air. Following the long tradition of the Corps des Ponts et Chaussées, faults in the countryside – chasms, occluded watercourses, etc. – were corrected with the civic armature of roads, bridges, canals and finally lighthouses.[7] Yet it is in Arago's discussion of getting one's bearings, more so than questions of topography, that one can begin to see how the question of distribution of a signal system, with all its constituent variables, was laden with significance. To begin with, it will be necessary to replace the notion of a geographic fatalism by recovering a particular form of possibilism, evident in the very movements of the air.[8] Some of the first stirrings of a modern understanding of a mediated landscape can be registered in this context, and with it the increasing difficulty of establishing one's bearings.

Arago describes the terror felt by those unfamiliar with the art of navigation when their ship loses sight of the shore and has only the stars and the ocean currents to orient them. The view of the most inhospitable stretch of the coast dissipates, as if by a spell, the indefinable fears which being out to sea inspire.[9] The seasoned navigator, however, knows that it is near the shore that the greatest dangers lie – dangers that could include, incidentally, light sources themselves.[10] The 'prudent' navigator never approaches a coast without first receiving a signal, especially if 'unfavorable skies' deprived him of the means of establishing his position. How were the lights along the coast to be read? First of all they had to be distinguished from 'such planet or such star that is largest as its rises or sets, or fires unpredictably lit [*feux accidentels*] along the coast by fishermen, woodcutters, charcoal-burners'; Arago referred to the failure to do so as a 'fatal misprision which is often the cause of deplorable wrecks'.[11] More common, however, was the problem of mistaking one lighthouse for another. Distribution, then, also involved creating a coherent syntax of distinctive 'characters' – first, second and third order of intensity; fixed, turning or flashing – by which the identity (and location) of a light could be understood. The navigator's fate does not depend on gaining sight of a 'hospitable signal', as Arago wrote, adopting a familiar literary image, but making sense of the system of signs. Though lights were placed where it was calculated they were most needed to guide the navigator, the sky played an uncertain role in their very legibility.

The signal takes place between its point of origin in the optics of the lighthouse and its terminus on the retina, somewhere in the night sky. To examine its place in the order of visual knowledge one must understand the laws that in effect 'suspend time'. (*Suspendre le temps*; it is indispensable to note that in French *temps* means both time and weather or season of year.[12]) The example Serres uses to discuss distribution as such, even when abstracted from his vertiginous project of understanding different orders of order, is revealing in this regard. In classical discourse, distribution, which was cognate with 'economy', referred to the proper use of materials no less than the ordered composition of parts; yet in the nineteenth century, for Serres, distribution was another name for disorder: water, steam, fuel constitute fluctuating groups.[13] One can begin *in media res* with what he described as a particular 'instance' of looking to the sky. The regular periodic order of the celestial system allowed an astronomer to calculate the exact moment of an eclipse.[14] But he did not know, nor could he predict, whether he would be able to view it. For at the very instant of its passage, a cloud, for instance, might interpose itself between the phenomenon and the observer. Although his station is precise in time and place, his view is blocked. Unforeseen clouds threaten to conceal the order of the world. Serres limns the simple construction of circumstance, from *circum*, or that which surrounds, and *stans*, that which stands. For our purposes, the architectural mass of the tower, the axial fulcrum for its light, makes it easily identified as that which stands. One might locate the lighthouse, then, as occupying an uncertain place between two 'fields of disorder': the first is the 'chaotic distribution' of the stars and galaxies beyond the orderly Solar System; the other more proximate one is 'meteorological chaos'.

The passing from a classical to a meteorological understanding of forms and

Edward Eigen
Subject to circumstance: the landscape
of the French lighthouse system

phenomena is evident in various efforts to observe and even to explain the appearance of the sky and its atmosphere. At the beginning of the nineteenth century, the British chemist Luke Howard suggested the first 'methodical nomenclature' of clouds based on the Linnaean binomial system.[15] To emphasize the fact that he was basing his classification of clouds on their 'visible character, as in natural history', he consciously assigned names — cirrus, cumulus, stratus — from the Latin, to distinguish them from the use of Greek in chemistry to identify invisible entities.[16] Nomenclature was essential to making communicable the 'experience' of atmosphere, which is gained by those whose labours depend on its state, the husbandman and mariner in particular. For unlike the natural philosopher who, in attending his instruments, takes the 'pulse' of the atmosphere, their respective habit of frequently observing the countenance of the sky better allows them to make predictions, connecting present and future conditions. They become practised in prevision. Howard's system for understanding the appearance of clouds was much appreciated by Johann Wolfgang von Goethe, who wrote that it touched on the possibility of seeing 'the formless formed'.[17] Goethe made numerous sketches of clouds so as 'to fix an ever-mobile subject on paper in accord with the concept'.[18] Applying Howard's principles to every season and different barometric conditions, his illustrations sought to show the 'characteristic forms' of visual experience of the sky.

The formless was to reassert itself as a theme, if not a natural fact, for seemingly the nature of clouds was undergoing a sea change at century's end. John Ruskin's *The Storm-Cloud of the Nineteenth Century* (1884), which began as two lectures delivered at the London Institute on 4 and 11 February 1884, spoke of phenomena of which there could be no historical 'experience', having been seen only by 'now living, or *lately living* eyes'.[19] None of the verses of Homer or Virgil — or so Ruskin maintained — offered a sense of them. Evidently the skies had darkened since the writing of his *Modern Painters* twenty years earlier, in which the outlines of clouds could be seen to follow perspectival projection lines. Lately, however, there was to be seen an increase in storms, of turbulent winds, intermittent rain, what in the parlance of Victorian solar physics would be understood as an increase in entropy. The latter term would nowhere enter as such into Ruskin's discussion; instead, he wrote vividly, 'It is a wind of darkness … a malignant quality of wind, unconnected with any one quarter of the compass.'[20] Its coming prefigures the passing of the classification sought optimistically by Howard into a state of randomness: the storm cloud marked the end of the distinction between states of things. 'In the old days, when the weather was fine, it was luxuriously fine; when it was bad — it was often abominably bad, but it had its fits of temper and was done with — it didn't sulk for three months without letting you see the sun.'[21] The gravest peril imagined by Ruskin was the final dying of the light.

The immediate threat that such an inconsistent and inconstant cloud as Ruskin dreaded posed to communication was captured by the painter Claude Monet in his *The Signal* (1877), from his series of railroad pictures. The drama of the scene is in the visual signal being lost amid the steam driving the locomotive it was meant to direct. In maintaining a system of signals, the Commission was obliged to come to terms with the

90

predictably unpredictable, circumstances which in reality consisted of dust, fog, rain, thunder and optical effects. Reynaud's claim that one can represent graphically the relation between the intensity of a light and its scope in an atmosphere of a given transparency, is all the clue one needs for how the literal mi-lieu (between places) of the cloud figured into their system.[22] Indeed, the experiments Fresnel carried out on his lenticular system brought into the view the circumstances that could defeat its potential to produce a clear and distinct signal.

The results of these tests, carried out before the system's installation at Cordouan — the changed appearance of which mariners were alerted to in the pages of the *Annales Maritime* — amount to a running caption of the onset of the circumstances that would degrade the luminous signal to the point of indifference. On Thursday 9 October 1823, a lantern was placed on top of the Arc de Triomphe in Paris and a temporary observation station established in a nearby suburb. Between 7:30 and 9:15 that evening, five changes were made in the period of the lantern's flash that observers were to note 'to the extent that they perceived them'.[23] The table recording their results indicated the time of night along with the scheduled duration of the phases: Appearance/Disappearance. As the rain and fog progressively became denser between the lantern and observation station, 'the flashes diminished to only three or four seconds, then to one or two seconds, and finally the light disappeared altogether at 8:45. It reappeared several minutes afterwards, but the flashes were still very short'. The lantern's signal, composed of telltale 'angles' of light and dark, became irregular and intermittent and eventually vanished. Given the clockwork timing of the experiment, Fresnel's commentary explains the unexpected gaps in the tabular record of what was actually observed. There was no place yet on the table for the state of the atmosphere; rather its movement produced gaps in the rubric of scheduled sightings. The Commission's attention to the materiality of communication was still limited to the workings of optics and light sources and the towers which were their pedestal. Indeed, among the arguments in support of the lenticular system was that the sea air did not diminish the prism's polish; one of the Commissioners commented as a matter of fact that 'it suffices to dust and clean it from time to time'.[24] Having previously recognized that it was inevitable, they only now began to explore interruption itself.

With an ordinance protecting its uninterrupted view to the Champs de Mars and the suburbs of Paris, the Dépôt des Phares, built on the heights of the Trocadero in 1848, succeeded Fresnel's *ad hoc* arrangement as the Commission's permanent laboratory of light.[25] Nominally the store and distribution centre for the equipment used in lighthouses — optics, lanterns, clockworks — here along the urban edge experiments could take place on the elements of the lighthouse system without interruption. Equipped with an instrument called a photometer, observers stationed at fixed distances from the Dépôt could measure the intensity and quality of light produced by a wide range of lens configurations, fuels, lighting elements, and so on. Invented the previous century by Pierre Bouguer, the photometer was essentially a black box, its front formed by a slotted screen, its back a plate of frosted glass.[26] The frosted glass served as an

Edward Eigen
Subject to circumstance: the landscape
of the French lighthouse system

abstract optical surface upon which to form comparisons of the intensity of two unequal sources of light. Employing the equation by which luminous intensity varies with the inverse square of distance, it was possible, based on the subjective judgement of precisely when the two lights achieved unity, to assign to the unknown source a relative intensity. Where Bouguer's fundamental *Treatise on Optics, on the Gradation of Light* (1760) guided painters in judging the relative distinctness and size of objects over distance and the effect of diaphanous media, the results of the Dépôt's experiments were expressed in formulas and tables.[27] These in turn were critical in helping to establish the optical scope of a given apparatus. Nonetheless, Reynaud adjudged that a 'graphic construction' was the most effective method for summarizing these facts.[28] It was on the surface of these graphs that could be traced the action of the one element which could not be standardized by the Commission: the atmosphere. This order of information constituted a user's manual for all the equipment exported from the Dépôt to the coast.

Before discussing the specifics of Reynaud's graphic construction, I will take a moment to note the visual means adopted to make the lighthouse system known. A remarkable 'Table of the general distribution of lights along the coast of France' published with Reynaud's *Mémoire sur l'Éclairage et le Balisage des Côtes de France* (1864) attempted to represent the very substance of light (Fig. 6.2). While, on the earliest maps of the Commission, symbols placed along the line of the coast, resembling a sequenced telegraphic code, indicated the placement of lights of different character, Reynaud's table is a figural taxonomy of luminous signals (Figs 6.3–6.6). Each figure described the distribution in time and space of a given intensity of light. It did not convey any information about location, but established the rate at which illumination took place. While the vaporous figures of the table are visually arresting, they should be read as so many budgets of luminous expenditure: at each given moment in time, a specific amount of light was available to the navigator. In vignettes placed throughout the volume on lighthouses in the series *Les Travaux Publics de la France* (1883), these same luminous figures, rendered in outline, were collaged onto the coastline, their distinct forms juxtaposed to the accidents of terrain they were meant to signal. In a map of the entire system, these 'fixed clouds', to use Ruskin's phrase, lose their geometric particularity and are rendered instead in a precise system of notation. Yet unlike a cloud, the perimeter of the overlapping circles is clear and distinct, the outline punctuated so as to indicate the character of each light, its intensity, the frequency of its flashes and eclipses. The black dot at the centre of each — a blind spot — represents the opaque mass of the tower, the luminous landscape's architectural prop.

92

These studies did not approach the question of what the light looked like, or did so only with regard to the varying optical scope of different characters of light. To this end, Reynaud commissioned an ambitious photographic survey of the towers that comprised the aforementioned volume. The images, produced by photographers such as Édouard Baldus, Alphonse Davanne and Hippolyte-Auguste Collard, not only documented the role lighthouses fulfilled as 'great paths of communication',[29] but also captured their considerable picturesque interest. One can see the tower's locality, but

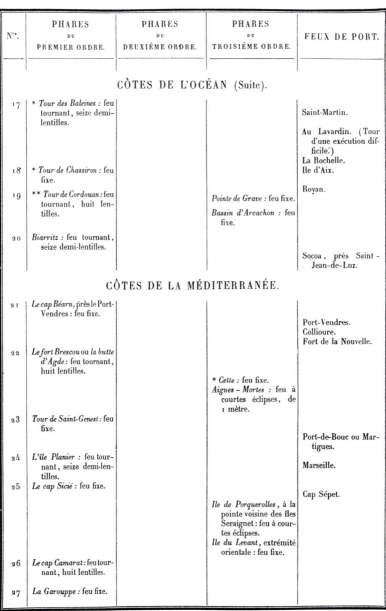

N°.	PHARES DU PREMIER ORDRE.	PHARES DU DEUXIÈME ORDRE.	PHARES DU TROISIÈME ORDRE.	FEUX DE PORT.
	CÔTES DE L'OCÉAN (Suite).			
17	* *Tour des Baleines :* feu tournant, seize demi-lentilles.			Saint-Martin.
				Au Lavardin. (Tour d'une exécution difficile.)
				La Rochelle.
18	* *Tour de Chassiron :* feu fixe.			Ile d'Aix.
19	** *Tour de Cordouan :* feu tournant, huit lentilles.		*Pointe de Grave :* feu fixe.	Royan.
			Bassin d'Arcachon : feu fixe.	
20	*Biarritz :* feu tournant, seize demi-lentilles.			
				Socoa, près Saint-Jean-de-Luz.
	CÔTES DE LA MÉDITERRANÉE.			
21	*Le cap Béarn,* près le Port-Vendres : feu fixe.			
				Port-Vendres.
				Collioure.
				Fort de la Nouvelle.
22	*Le fort Brescou* ou *la butte d'Agde :* feu tournant, huit lentilles.			
			* *Cette :* feu fixe.	
			Aigues-Mortes : feu à courtes éclipses, de 1 mètre.	
23	*Tour de Saint-Genest :* feu fixe.			
				Port-de-Bouc ou Martigues.
24	*L'île Planier :* feu tournant, seize demi-lentilles.			Marseille.
25	*Le cap Sicié :* feu fixe.			
				Cap Sépet.
			Ile de Porquerolles, à la pointe voisine des îles Seraignet : feu à courtes éclipses.	
			Ile du Levant, extrémité orientale : feu fixe.	
26	*Le cap Camarat :* feu tournant, huit lentilles.			
27	*La Garoupe :* feu fixe.			

6.2 'Table of the general distribution of lights along the coast of France', from Léonce Reynaud, *Mémoire sur l'Éclairage et le Balisage des Côtes de France* (Paris: Imprimerie Impériale, 1864), p. 357

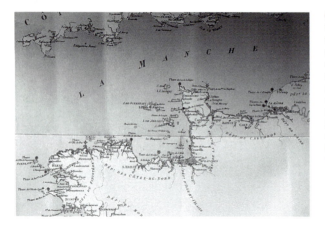

6.3 Detail, 'Map of the coast of France on which is indicated the position and nature of the different types of lights established or to be established along the coast in conformity with the general system proposed by the Commission des Phares,' (1826), from *Oeuvres Complètes d'Augustin Fresnel* (Paris: Imprimerie Impériale, 1870), III

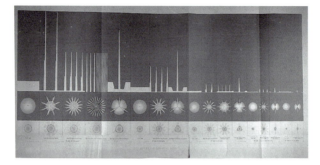

6.4 'Graphic table of luminous intensity and scope', from Léonce Reynaud, *Mémoire sur l'Éclairage et le Balisage des Côtes de France* (Paris: Imprimerie Impériale, 1864), p. 357

more particularly the point of attachment of its precise masonry construction to the unequal terrain (Fig. 6.7).[30] Of the towers' actual design, Reynaud wrote that it was necessary to regard as law the 'intelligent economy' that admits only what is useful, rejects the superfluous and 'manages' resources so as to multiply good results. 'Judicious distribution, rational forms, great stability, and perfect execution are the conditions judged to be fundamental.'[31] The tower was the very embodiment of a limited economy in which all such factors could be satisfactorily attended. The photographs might be said to fill in the rest, but by virtue of being pictures they can only serve as illustrations. Instead, the graph 'Progress in Coastal Illumination' printed in the volume's section on 'statistical information' acted as a sort of tableau of the towers — taken in sense of a tabulation (Fig. 6.8).[32] (Reynaud's *Mémoire* included examples of the blank registers and forms to be employed by lighthouse keepers to record every order of expense and aspect of their surveillance.) The graph shows how light itself was a commodity to be exchanged, its overall supply increasing at the same time that its price went down. Yet there was no place on the graph's curious dimensional scale — 1 millimetre = 1 year = five lighthouses = FF20 000 = 500 units of intensity — for the

6.5 'Graph of the scope of a 1st order scintillating light', from Emile Allard, *Les Travaux Publics de la France – V Phares et Balises* (Paris: J. Rothschild, 1883), fig. 148, p. 97

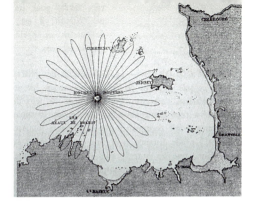

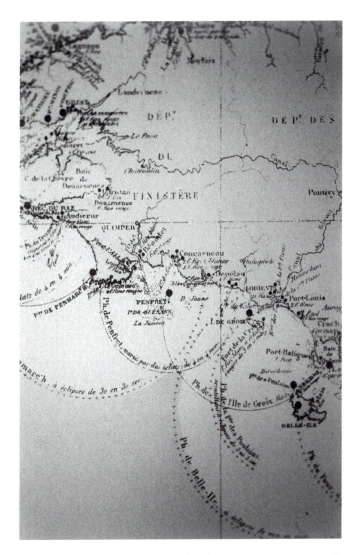

95

6.6 Detail, 'Map of the lighthouses of the coast of France' (1876), from Emile Allard, *Les Travaux Publics de la France – V Phares et Balises* (Paris: J. Rothschild, 1883)

role of circumstance. There was no accounting for the very set of conditions that could, for instance, have made photography of the towers impossible on any given day.

I will then identify the transparency of the atmosphere as the particularly optical nature of circumstance. The relative intensity of a light was not a sufficient measure of

6.7 'Phare du Petit Minou', from Emile Allard, *Les Travaux Publics de la France – V Phares et Balises* (Paris: J. Rothschild, 1883)

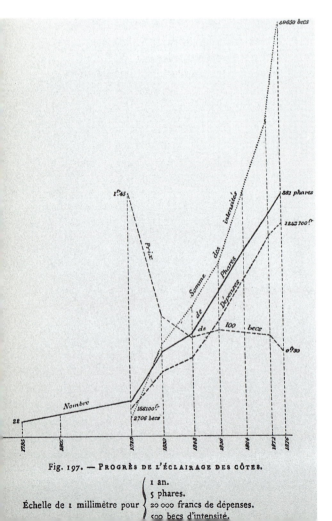

6.8 'Progress in the illumination of the Coasts', from Emile Allard, *Les Travaux Publics de la France – V Phares et Balises* (Paris: J. Rothschild, 1883), fig. 197, p. 121

Fig. 197. — PROGRÈS DE L'ÉCLAIRAGE DES CÔTES.

Échelle de 1 millimètre pour { 1 an.
5 phares.
20 000 francs de dépenses.
500 becs d'intensité.

its effectiveness along the coast. For the readings produced with a photometer were true only in 'an optical void' — that is, under specific and stable atmospheric conditions.[33] Given the two factors of human visual acuity and the 'more or less opaque body of the atmosphere', the optical scope of a given light varied widely.[34] As to human vision, it was assumed that the observer combines himself with the instrument and sees only what results from that combination. This could vary. Use of the photometer revealed unexpectedly that the near-sighted could detect a feebler source of light than the far-sighted in conditions of fog. In his log, Reynaud indicated which of his observers wore glasses and noted the likelihood of visual fatigue over the course of an evening's work. Yet the human body, like the tower, was an opaque entity, remaining separate from their investigations. Indeed, if there is a basis of comparison between eye-glasses and Fresnel's optics which corrected the path of the lantern's light, it can be found in Reynaud's comment that 'spectacles which so well assist under ordinary circumstances are but an insufficient palliative at sea, where the glasses soon become covered with moisture ... losing their clarity.'[35] For the purposes of their initial calculations, 'good sight, like that of mariners in general' was taken as a given, as was a median state of transparency, such as was the case on the clear Parisian nights when their experiments were conducted.

But for the Commission to understand the effectiveness of a signal, and how the eye registered it, it had to begin to account for the variable and unpredictable circumstances in which vision took place. Lighthouses themselves became stations of and for experimental observation. The scope and intensity of lights were recalculated according to a 'coefficient of transparency' that described the optical character of space itself. In the graphs that resulted from this step, the linear progress of light is seen to sag as if the opacity of the atmosphere were acting on it like a weight (Fig. 6.9). To determine the actual value of the coefficient, lighthouse keepers were instructed to go out on the high parapet of their towers three times an evening. There they were to take note whether the light of the neighbouring tower was visible, thereby establishing the mean level of local transparency. Reynaud's chief assistant, Emile Allard, wrote that the many thousands of observations logged by the lighthouse keepers, for which the Dépôt served as a centre of calculation, 'constituted information which would not be without interest to meteorologists'.[36] It may be remarked, however, that by this time meteorologists ceased to employ the naive empirical methods Allard adopted. Instead, meteorological stations were equipped with automatic photo-registration devices that flawlessly transcribed the movement of untiring measuring instruments that took the weather's 'pulse'.[37] Yet Allard was not interested in the weather as such, especially when consulting readouts that absented the observer from its midst. For Allard, and the Commission, and the navigators to whom their findings were communicated in suitable form, the visible state of the weather defined the very circumstance in which observation took place. Though safely sheltered in the light's very source, the lighthouse keeper shared the predicament of the mariner at sea anxiously searching for a signal.

The attempt graphically to express the distribution of circumstances can be seen in Allard's *Mémoire sur l'Intensité et la Portée des Phares* (1876) (Figs 6.10 and 6.11).

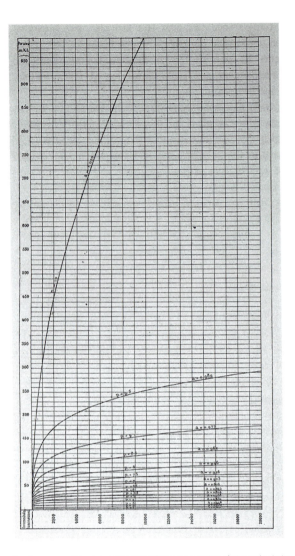

6.9 'Graph representing the scope of luminous intensities for various states of atmospheric transparency', from Emile Allard, *Les Travaux Publics de la France – V Phares et Balises* (Paris: J. Rothschild, 1883), fig. 112, p. 78

Where the Commission's earlier publication included calculation on the predictable diminishment of the luminous signal according to the varying coefficients of transparency, Allard redescribed the coast according to the likelihood of vision taking place in any particular maritime district, as indicated by the level of transparency recorded in the lighthouse keepers' logbooks. The range of any given light could thus be understood as distance from which there was as much probability of seeing the light as of not seeing it.[38] The coast was erased as a geographic entity; instead, space and time were expressed in terms of the functioning of vision. Each frame of the graph represented a statistical distribution of reported signal sightings. The series described the distribution of the state of transparency according to the changing of the seasons. Yet what were these points on the graph? They did not indicate the position of the

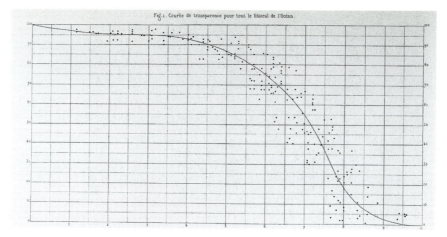

6.10 'Graph of transparency for the entirety of the Atlantic coast', from Emile Allard, *Mémoire sur l'Intensité et la Portée des Phares Comprenant la Description de quelques Appareils Nouveaux* (Paris: Imprimerie Nationale, 1876)

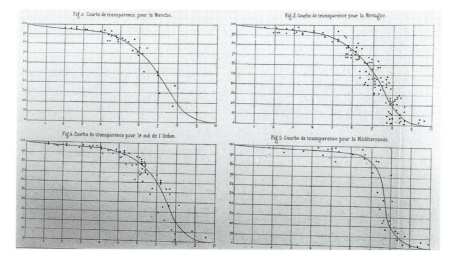

6.11 'Graph of transparency of the Channel, Brittany, the south Atlantic, the Mediterranean', from Emile Allard, *Mémoire sur l'Intensité et la Portée des Phares Comprenant la Description de quelques Appareils Nouveaux* (Paris: Imprimerie Nationale, 1876)

tower or of the eye, nor were they station points or even perspectively constructed vanishing points. Rather, each point represented a measure of chance — within each square, the erratic oscillation of circumstance was managed. What of the lines? In interpolating the points, Allard noted certain lighthouses consistently reported greater levels of visibility, from which he concluded that 'it was likely that the guardians of that lighthouse had more penetrating vision'.[39] In the terms of Reynaud's budget of light, one might now say: from this distance, at this time of year, in this region, the chance of finding a signal are one in ten.... The points mark out the path along which a signal decays into noise, and the channel of navigation is lost along with the light.

What can be gained from looking at the sky, especially when hoping to find a

Edward Eigen
Subject to circumstance: the landscape
of the French lighthouse system

clear signal? With this question one gets at the meaning, rather than the significance, of the luminous landscape. One's insistence on the question of circumstance hinges on the value of prevision (conjecture, forecast, estimate). A discourse distinguishing the foreseen and unforeseen serves as the structure for the emergence of maritime insurance. The apportioning of risk and profit in any complex exchange depended on taking stock of all relevant factors: season, the route taken, conditions of the ship, skill of the crew, good or bad news concerning storms.[40] Insurance was as much an experimental as an 'augural' science, or as one humorist wrote: the underwriter 'looks to the sky and thinks of a rate'.[41] By definition the premium, or rate, obeyed no rules and could not be fixed in advance. One nineteenth-century insurer and author of a work on the laws of chance wrote that even documents such as statistics of shipwrecks were of only limited use, for in the very time spent compiling them the circumstantial element would have destroyed their authority. Statistics were always 'late'[42] in coming to an understanding of things.

The documents here under discussion — budgets, graphs, tabulations, ultimately patterns of distribution — are so many means of reporting possible instances of seeing. The historian Matt Matsuda has discussed stock tables as a form of memory, recording how the market responded to daily or twice-daily reports in the press of the rising and falling fortune of politicians. The market thus served as a 'barometer' of events, an indicator of *les temps*. As one financial writer noted, 'the quotations of the Bourse are the numbered language of events as well as a sort of prediction, an anticipation of the future'.[43] If, to use a modern term, one can speak of the efficiency no less than the transparency of markets in circulating information and putting it to prudent use, the Commission's relentless efforts in calculating states of transparency, in running the odds as it were, speaks to how perishable such information was. The fear of mariners at sea described by Arago could be replaced with the modern anxiety of being up to the minute, in the hope of mastering the future course of events. The Commission, established to illuminate the coast, tried to give law to the circumstances outside of its control, to suspend time.

From the moment Perrault put down his telescope, desiring to get a closer look at Cordouan, he abandoned himself to the sea of optical subjectivity. His aborted voyage of observation was plagued by circumstance. Fortunately, there is another account of a visit to the tower in a small ship when Fresnel went to inspect its new optics. Observing from a point where his view of the tower itself was obscured by the large dunes near Royan, Fresnel saw at the moment of its flash 'a small aureole above the point on the horizon corresponding to the lighthouse, formed by the reverberations of the light in the air'.[44] The existence of the lighthouse is identified not as a material architectural entity, but rather as an atmospheric phenomenon. It would be years before the Commission addressed the other impression gathered by Fresnel during his inspection tour: mariners reported that the flash left an impression (afterimage) on the retina in the shape of the Cross of Malta. Afterimages, like the sound of the sea, can only be considered in the margins of experience of what was after all a highly rationalized system of communication. The very sound of the sea signalled to Perrault 200 years earlier the fact that plans made the night before were no longer possible given the circumstances to which one awoke. What was specific to the nineteenth century was the system of energetics, according to which boundaries of sound, light, heat, motion became fluid, forcing the recognition that 'we are once more on a pathless sea, starless, windless, and poleless'.[45] Vision takes places amid a cloud of sensation. There can be no fixed point of view, only a direction taken when the current circumstances are assessed from their very midst.

Edward Eigen
Subject to circumstance: the landscape
of the French lighthouse system

Notes

1   Jules Michelet, *La Mer* (Paris, 1861).

2   Claude Perrault, *Voyage à Bordeaux* [1669] (Paris: de la Renouard, 1909), pp. 174–175.

3   Bernard Forest de Bélidor, *Architecture Hydraulique* (1753), cited in Jean Guillaume, 'Le Phare de Cordouan, "Merveille du Monde", et Monument Monarchique', *Revue de l'Art*, 8 (1970), p. 42, n. 34. Léonce Reynaud wrote that the characteristic lack of ornamentation on lighthouses answered to the fact that they were situated in places where they were infrequently seen; L. Reynaud, *Mémoire sur l'Éclairage et le Balisage des Côtes de France* (Paris: Imprimerie Impériale, 1864), p. 158.

4   Michel Serres, *Hermes IV: Distribution* (Paris: Editions de Minuit, 1977), p. 228.

5   Léonor Fresnel, 'Introduction aux Mémoires Notes et Fragments sur les Phares', in *Oeuvres Complètes d'Augustin Fresnel* (Paris: Imprimerie Impériale, 1870), III, p. xxii.

6   François Arago, 'Éloge Historique d'Augustin Fresnel, lu 26 Juillet, 1830', in *Oeuvres Complètes d'Augustin Fresnel*, III, p. 520.

7   Antoine Picon, *French Architects and Engineers in the Age of Enlightenment*, trans. Martin Thom (Cambridge: Cambridge University Press, 1992), pp. 248–255.

8   'Fatality' and 'possibilism' are taken from the discourse of geography as it evolved in France during this period; Jean-Yves Guiomar, 'Vidal's geography of France' [trans. Arthur Goldhammer], in Pierre Nora (ed.), *Realms of Memory* (New York: Columbia University Press, 1997), pp. 187–209.

9   Arago, 'Éloge Historique d'Augustin Fresnel', p. 516.

10 Hans Blumenberg, *Shipwreck with Spectator, Paradigm for a Metaphor of Existence*, trans. Steven Rendall (Cambridge: MIT Press, 1997), p. 15.

11 Arago, 'Éloge Historique d'Augustin Fresnel', p. 518.

12 Serres, *Hermes IV: Distribution*, p. 37.

13 Josué Harari and David Bell, 'Introduction', in Michel Serres, *Hermes, Literature, Science, Philosophy* (Baltimore: Johns Hopkins University Press, 1982), p. xxxvi.

14 Serres, *Hermes IV: Distribution*, p. 228. The physicists Biot and Guy-Lussac ascended in a balloon from the Paris Observatory, then under Arago's direction, on 29 June 1850 to study the constitution and situation of the atmospheric cloud-cover; the Société Météorologique de France was founded two years later; Horace Chauvet, *François Arago et son Temps* (Perpignan: Imprimerie du Midi, 1954), p. 56.

15 On Howard and the 'morphological sciences', see Peter Galison, *Image and Logic* (Chicago: University of Chicago Press, 1997), pp. 73–88.

16 Luke Howard, 'On the modification of clouds', *Philosophical Magazine*, 16 (1803), p. 98.

17 '[D]ie Formung des Formlosen'; Johann Wolfgang von Goethe, 'Luke Howard to Goethe: a biographical sketch', in *Scientific Studies*, trans. Douglas Miller (New York: Suhrkamp, 1988), p. 143; for the original, see 'Luke Howard to Goethe, a biographical sketch', in *Johann Wolfgang von Goethe Werke: Hamburger Ausgabe* (Munich: Deutscher Taschenbuch, 1988), XIII, p. 304.

18 *Ibid.*, p. 143.

19 John Ruskin, *The Storm-Cloud of the Nineteenth Century* (New York: John Wiley & Sons, 1884), p. 1.

20 *Ibid.*, pp. 34–35.

21 *Ibid.*, p. 2.

22 On the evolution of this concept, see Georges Canguilhem, 'Le Vivant et son Milieu', in *La Connaissance de la Vie* (Paris: Vrin, 1992 [1965]), pp. 129–154.

23 Augustin Fresnel, 'Projet de Programme pour l'Expérience du jeudi 9 octobre 1823', in *Oeuvres Complètes d'Augustin Fresnel*, III, p. 184.

24 De Rossel, 'Rapport Contenant l'Exposition du Système Adopté par la Commission des Phares pour Éclairer les Côtes de France', in *Oeuvres Complètes d'Augustin Fresnel*, III, p. 248.

25 'Dépôt des Phares, à Paris', *Révue Générale de l'Architecture et des Travaux Public*, 29 (1872), pp. 201–203.

26 On the presence of instruments in visual discourse, see Lorraine Daston and Peter Galison, 'The image of objectivity', *Representations*, 40 (1992), pp. 81–128. On the use of instruments in the construction of modern subjectivity, see Jonathan Crary, *Techniques of the Observer* (Cambridge, MA: MIT Press, 1990).

27 Fernand de Dartein, *M. Léonce Reynaud, Sa Vie et ses Œuvres* (Paris: Vve. Ch. Dunot, 1885), p. 161. On Bouguer, see Martin Kemp, *The Science of Art* (New Haven and London: Yale University Press, 1990), p. 237.

28 Reynaud, *Mémoire sur l'Éclairage et le Balisage des Côtes de France*, p. 15, n. 2. On the emergence of graphs and tables as a universal language of communication, see Thomas Hankins and Robert Silverman, *Instruments and the Imagination* (Princeton: Princeton University Press, 1995), pp. 113–128.

29 Léonce Reynaud, 'Preface', in Emile Allard, *Les Travaux Publics de la France*, V: *Phares et Balises* (Paris: J. Rothschild, 1873).

30 A discussion of the visual codes of the photographs, though warranted, does not fall within the scope of the present essay; see Edward Eigen, 'From accident to incident: the graphs and photographic accounts of the Corps des Ponts et Chaussées' (forthcoming).

31 Reynaud, *Mémoire sur l'Écairage*, p. 159. By contrast, the lighthouse projects of 1851–52 produced by the student of the École des Beaux-Arts pushed the allegorical meanings of the lighthouse to almost absurd ends; Neil Levine, 'The romantic idea of architectural legibility: Henri Labrouste and the Neo-Grec', in *The Architecture of the École des Beaux-Arts*, ed. Arthur Drexler (New York: Museum of Modern Art, 1977), pp. 408–410.

32 On the relation of tableau and tabulation, see Michel Serres, *Hermes III: La Traduction* (Paris: de Minuit, 1974), p. 234.

33 Allard, *Phares et Balises*, p. 75.

34 Reynaud, *Mémoire sur l'Éclairage*, pp. 12–13.

35 *Ibid.*, p. 30, n.1.

36 Emile Allard, *Mémoire sur l'Intensité et la Portée des Phares Comprenant la Description de quelques Appareils Nouveaux* (Paris: Imprimerie Nationale, 1876), pp. 82–83. On the notion of centers of calculation, see Bruno Latour, *Science in Action* (Cambridge, MA: Harvard University Press, 1987), pp. 232ff.

37 Gaston Tissandier, *A History and Handbook of Photography* (Paris: Hachette, 1878), p. 282.

38 Allard, *Mémoire sur l'Intensité et la Portée des Phares*, p. 99.

39 *Ibid.*, p. 92.

Edward Eigen
Subject to circumstance: the landscape
of the French lighthouse system

40 Lorraine Daston, 'The domestication of risk', in *The Probabilistic Revolution*, eds Lorenz
    Krüger, Gerd Gigerenzer and Mary Morgan (Cambridge, MA: MIT Press, 1990), I, p. 254.

41 *Ibid.*, p. 254.

42 Alfred de Courcy, *Essai sur les Lois du Hasard* [1862], cited in L. A. Boiteux, *La Fortune de
    Mer* (Paris: École Pratique des Hautes Études, 1968), p. 176.

43 Cited in Matt Matsuda, *The Memory of the Modern* (New York: Oxford University Press,
    1996), p. 58.

44 Léonor Fresnel, 'Rapport adressé à M. Becquey, Directeur Général des Ponts et Chaussées
    sur le Renouvellement de l'Appareil d'Éclairage du Phare du Cordouan' (12 September
    1823), in *Oeuvres Complètes d'Augustin Fresnel*, III, p. 170.

45 Cited in Gillian Beer, 'Authentic tidings of invisible things', in *Vision in Context*, eds Teresa
    Brennan and Martin Jay (New York: Routledge, 1996), p. 88.

Section Three

Concepts of nature and body

Karen Lang

7   The body in the garden

'Nature', writes Raymond Williams, 'is perhaps the most complex word in the language.'[1] To tease out a few threads from what has become a rather dense conceptual carpet, this chapter will focus on eighteenth-century conceptions of nature as these relate to the garden. With the popularity of the garden, especially in England, came a flurry of writings that sought to define the garden as an aesthetic category.[2] Freshly conceived as the art of landscape, the garden was not set apart from the values of eighteenth-century society. Rather, to use the words of Ann Bermingham, 'the ostensible isolation of nature as a category and a value facilitated its being regularly appropriated by cultural subjects and social groups in a strategy of self-justification and self-preservation. Always desired for itself but always made to say something other than itself, nature never appeared except as part of a personal and social allegory.'[3] As an organising concept, nature – whether wild or cultivated – shaped and reflected the discourse of the eighteenth century.[4] In *Landscape and Ideology: The English Rustic Tradition, 1740–1860*, Ann Bermingham studies the chiasmatic relations between nature and culture, examining the means by which nature becomes culture and culture becomes second nature.[5]

This chapter will consider the transaction between nature and culture effected by the body in the garden. An exploration of the body in the garden implies several things. First, it signifies the human presence of makers and spectators in the garden. This body in the garden was often presumed to be male, and the act of viewing itself, which was assumed on the surface to be a straightforward, if not 'correct', engagement with nature, was in fact loaded with connotation. Second, the body in the garden refers to nature itself. By the eighteenth century nature had long been gendered feminine. In this sense the body in the garden is a female body, while personifications of nature were just as assuredly female. The Vale of Venus at Rousham in Oxfordshire, the Temple of Venus and the Queen's Valley at Stowe in Buckinghamshire, as well as the statue of the Venus de' Medici at The Leasowes in Shropshire, indicate the femininity, if not to say sexuality, of the eighteenth-century English landscape.[6]

As eighteenth-century writings discourse on the nature of the garden, so they reveal the ways in which 'nature', a deeply gendered and valuative term, could service the conceptual schemata of eighteenth-century society. In 'The Moralists' (1709), for example, the 3rd Earl of Shaftesbury mounted a spirited defence of the '*primitive state*' of nature:

> I shall no longer resist the Passion growing in me for Things of a *natural* kind; where neither *Art*, nor the *Conceit* or *Caprice* of Man has spoil'd their *genuine order*, by breaking in upon *that primitive state*. Even the rude *Rocks*, the mossy *Caverns*, the irregular unwrought *Grotto's*, and broken *Falls* of Waters, with all the horrid Graces of the *Wilderness* it-self, as representing NATURE more, will be more engaging, and appear with a Magnificence beyond the formal Mockery of Princely Gardens.[7]

'Princely gardens' refers especially to the highly structured French gardens that had exerted an influence on English taste. In an essay for *The Guardian* of 1713, Alexander Pope echoed Shaftesbury when he urged a return to 'the amiable Simplicity of unadorned Nature, that spreads over the Mind a more noble Sort of Tranquility, and a loftier Sensation of Pleasure, than can be raised from the nicer Scenes of Art'.[8] Advocating the 'genuine order' of nature over the 'formal mockery' of the French garden, Shaftesbury and Pope herald a transition in the style of the English garden. This new art of landscape, soon to become a national style of gardening, would aim to engage the spectator with a more accurate appearance of nature, including the caverns, grottoes, and waterfalls that figure in Shaftesbury's description of 'NATURE'.[9]

Contemporary ideas on nature did more than fortify English national identity. When, in the eighteenth century, mind and nature came to be defined as equivalent, this conceptual move brought the body and nature into proximity. At the same time, however, an understanding of the equivalence of mind and nature solidified a hierarchical relation between form and matter — between humankind and the realm of nature — which reverberated in the contemporary political and social order. The spectator's body in the garden, now bound to nature through conceptual equivalence, is nevertheless superior to the nature it forms: if, at this time, the body in the garden was generally male, and nature was characterised as female, then the subordinate status of nature echoed the gender inequality of eighteenth-century British society. To this end, the relation of the spectator to the garden 'possesses more than metaphorical significance'.[10] In short, the garden is never innocent: studying how the body of nature is formed and consumed by the body in the garden, this chapter will discuss Pope's garden at Twickenham in Surrey as an appearance of nature and as a site for culture.

Matter and form, nature and mind

If, in one sense, the body in the garden refers to nature as feminine matter, gardening implies an improvement of nature, an active process of transforming the matter of nature into specific form. The conceptual pairing of form and matter found in the garden has been integral to the concept of nature since classical times, though form and matter, and the nature of their interrelation, have been variously defined.[11] Whether considered as an uncontrollable force, as a fruitful mother, or, the result of a Christian retouching in the Middle Ages, as a modest maiden, Natura participated in an organicist model of the world, one in which microcosm and macrocosm reflected each other and were bound together.[12] Something of this viewpoint can be seen in an illustration to an encyclopedic work published in 1617 by the English Rosicrucian, Robert Fludd.

Serving as the frontispiece for Fludd's *Utriusque Cosmi Historia* is an etching by Matthäus Merian entitled 'Mirror of all of Nature and Picture of the Arts' (Fig. 1).[13] The idea of the microcosm contained within the macrocosm is here defined through an arrangement of concentric circles representing the realms of man, nature and Heaven. At the centre, an ape sits on a terrestrial globe. Its left hand is chained to a personification of nature while the right hand of Natura is bound to the hand of God, indicated by the Hebrew inscription 'Yahweh', which appears in the cloud above her. Standing between the realms of Heaven and earth, the personification of Nature encompasses the mineral, vegetable and animal realms, including the elements of earth, air, fire and water, as well as the spheres of the planets and fixed stars. The ape is shown enclosed within the spheres of the Liberal Arts, which include Alchemy, Agriculture, Animal Husbandry and Medicine. As the accompanying text explains, 'Nature, not Divine, but the closest handmaid of God, has under her a servant or attendant who by imitating her mistress, impressing upon herself in agreement the likenesses of things produced by Nature, marvellously follows and imitates Nature's vestiges and delineations.'[14] If Natura is here given the more lofty position and creative power, the ape of nature — though clearly dependent on nature — is given the formative capacity to rival nature's productions.

In Fludd's conception the ape of nature, who 'emulates man, as human skill emulates nature', is a symbol of the artist.[15] Fludd presents the '*ars simia naturae* as an occultist metaphor', one which 'also had its echoes among the writings of his colleagues'.[16] Rather than pursue the occultist connotations of the frontispiece, I would like to draw attention to the ape's labour. Chained to nature by his left hand, in his right hand the ape holds a small globe which he measures with a compass. The ape's gesture is reminiscent of the *deus geometer*; the globe he measures is one he has fashioned himself. The ape's activities, both implicit (the forming of the globe) and explicit (the measuring of the globe), highlight the problem of form and matter.

A preoccupation with form and matter has precipitated extended philosophical commentary. Briefly, for our purposes, Plato and Aristotle define matter as inferior to form: matter is feminine, form is masculine.[17] According to Aristotle, whose theory proved most influential in the eighteenth century, form is an active male principle that gives shape to passive, feminine matter, an activity that creates the world of existing things.[18] In the frontispiece for Fludd's treatise the larger figure of Natura, along with occultist notions of the mysteries of nature associated with her, make her the prominent figure. In spite of his dependence on nature, the ape nevertheless plays an important role in Fludd's conception. For it is the ape, emblem of the Liberal Arts, who forms the human world through his labour. In Merian's engraving is therefore found the gendering of nature and the division of form and matter that had comprised the concept of nature

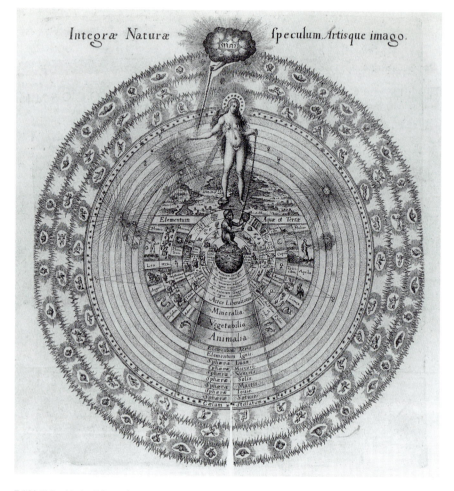

7.1 Matthäus Merian, 'Mirror of all of Nature and Picture of the Arts', etching, from Robert Fludd, *Utriusque cosmi … historia*, Oppenheim, 1617. (Photograph: Getty Research Institute for the History of Art and the Humanities)

110

since classical times. On the other hand, the occultist connotations of Fludd's scheme, which lend the figure of Natura an especial importance, were somewhat anomalous in 1617. By this time, form was acceding to dominance over matter, a conceptual move in tune with the hierarchical relation of form and matter in Aristotle's philosophy.

During the course of the scientific revolution of the seventeenth century, the organicist view of the world found in Fludd's treatise was gradually overcome by a mechanical conception of nature. Whereas the organicist model of nature esteemed and sanctified nature as a cosmic or divine power, the mechanistic view stressed the discovery of nature's laws and secrets.[19] Nature was thereby rendered vulnerable to the probings of humankind, while stress was placed on the actions and analysis of the researcher. Through a gradual process of equivalence, nature's laws were compared with the laws of the human mind, while nature, which contained form within itself, was likened to the ability of the mind to create form from itself. By the early eighteenth century, the concept of nature would thus include the world of natural forms as well as the world of the human mind. When Ernst Cassirer writes that '"[n]ature" therefore does not so much signify a given group of objects as a certain "horizon" of knowledge, of the comprehension of reality',[20] he records the expanded scope of the concept of nature as well as the position of the mind over nature. Indeed, the 'true essence of nature is [now] not to be found in the realm of the created (*natura naturata*), but in that of the creative process (*natura naturans*)'.[21]

In a brief discussion of form and the formative process, Shaftesbury, in his 1709 essay 'The Moralists', underscored the new outlook in a dialogue between Theocles and Philocles:

> But in Medals, Coins, Imbost-work, Statues, and well-fabricated pieces, of whatever sort, you can discover the *Beauty* ... but not for the *Metal's* sake. 'Tis not then the *Metal* or *Matter* which is beautiful with you No. But *the Art*. Certainly. *The Art* then is the Beauty. Right. And *the Art* is that which beautifies. The same. So that the Beautifying, not the Beautify'd, is really Beautiful. It seems so. For that which is beautify'd, is beautiful only by the accession of something beautifying: and by the recess or withdrawing of the same, it ceases to be beautiful. Be it. In respect of Bodys therefore, *Beauty* comes and goes. So we see.
>
> Here, then, said he, is all I wou'd have explain'd to you before: '*That the Beautiful, the Fair, the Comely*, were never in the *Matter*, but in the *Art* and *Design*; never in *Body* it-self, but in the *Form* or *Forming Power*'.... What is it you admire but Mind, or the Effect of *Mind*? 'Tis *Mind* alone which forms. All which is void of *Mind* is horrid: and Matter formless is *Deformity it-self*.[22]

As Shaftesbury neglects to cite Aristotle for his ideas, so he does not indicate of whose mind he speaks. Judging his intended audience, however, one may infer a selected readership of men like Shaftesbury himself: Augustan men of property and good breeding, most likely aristocrats with an education in the classics. For these 'earls of creation', taste was second nature and nature, in the form of the landscape garden, became a preferred site upon which to exercise taste and judgement.[23]

John Dixon Hunt suggests that '[t]his stress upon *how* the mind reads the "pleasing scenes the landscape wide displays" and how it makes those images its own ... could not have been possible without the new art of landscape gardening'.[24] John Locke and Joseph Addison's theories of mental processing are certainly central to an understanding of what Hunt has felicitously termed 'the figure in the landscape', and the 'close connection between the eighteenth-century English landscape garden and current developments in philosophy has long been acknowledged'.[25] Instead of concentrating on the specific manner in which the mind reads the landscape, in what follows I would like to address the implications of *natura naturans* for the body in the garden.

The equivalence of nature and mind is manifest in the following lines by Alexander Pope: 'First follow Nature, and your judgment frame/ By her just standard, which is still the same'.[26] If Nature was to be followed, she was not made to be left alone. Read in one way, Pope's lines indicate how judgement frames. That the mind makes nature, as nature reflects the mind, can be seen in the formation of Pope's garden at Twickenham. By the time Pope was fashioning his garden, the distinction between form and matter had taken on the impress of Aristotle's philosophy. In fact, Aristotle's gendering of form and matter, as well as his understanding of form as superior to matter, had become so imbedded in the conceptual schemata of eighteenth-century culture that Aristotle no longer needed to be invoked directly. In the manner of all successful intellectual inheritances, overt reference to Artistotle faded as his theories took on a life of their own, as they became, that is, more established and commonplace.

Inhabitants of the grotto

By the time Pope moved to his villa at Twickenham in 1719, gardening was recognized as an art form. Horace Walpole, who did much to establish the garden as an aesthetic category, declared the garden one of the sister arts: 'Poetry, Painting and Gardening, or the science of Landscape, will forever by men of Taste be deemed Three Sisters, or the Three New Graces who dress and adorn Nature.'[27] Though nature had long been compared with the feminine, she now found her adornment in the guise of the English garden. In addition to equating the garden with the Liberal Arts of Poetry and Painting, Walpole's statement points to the role of the man of taste in making such a judgement. One can safely infer that it was the man of taste who typically 'dress[ed] and adorn[ed] Nature', since, in the eighteenth century, it is he who participated most prominently in the 'three sister' arts.

In his 1731 *An Epistle to Lord Burlington*, Pope conveys his own thoughts on gardening, including his alliance of the garden with the feminine. Satirising the regularity of the formal garden, Pope here supports the transition to a less cultivated appearance of formed nature:

> In all, let Nature never be forgot.
> But treat the Goddess like a modest fair,
> Nor over-dress, nor leave her wholly bare;
> Let not each beauty ev'ry where be spy'd,
> Where half the skill is decently to hide.
> He gains all points, who pleasingly confounds,
> Surprises, varies, and conceals the Bounds.[28]

Following a commonplace of eighteenth-century poetry, here Pope shifts between the actual and the moral landscape. Treating the goddess 'like a modest fair' thus signifies the aesthetic and moral registers: the improvement of nature, when carried out properly, becomes an exercise in freedom and restraint. As nature's body reveals and conceals — as the body in the garden preambles along straight and curved paths, as it meets with prospects and dense woods — so the spectator's view of the garden is positioned, simultaneously tantalised and held in check.[29] In all, the landscape remained 'remote from the observer', who derived pleasure or denoted measure in what he saw.[30]

Considerable variety through contrast — whether of flora, prospect, or landscape architecture — provided delight for the eye and entertainment for the mind. Variety, however, had its conceptual limits. Remarking on the current, though fading, fashion for topiary in the garden, Pope notes how excessive cultivation caused only suffering for the eye.[31] The use of topiary in a formally patterned garden did not so much 'pleasingly confound' the boundary as downright invert the relation of nature and culture. The point was not to subsume matter into form, or form into matter, but carefully to plot the relation between them. Like the ape that patterns human skill, the gardener should use his skill in emulation of nature. In this way nature could variously appear, neither 'overdress['d]' nor 'wholly bare'.

If the garden was fashioned by the man of taste, it reflected his taste, and in this way, the garden was equated with its owner. Hence, Walpole, in his *The History of the Modern Taste in Gardening*, celebrates Pope's garden as a 'singular effort of art and taste', one that revealed his 'exquisite judgment'.[32] Walpole found Pope's achievement all the more remarkable since his garden consisted of five acres, a quite modest plot of land when compared with the vast acreage of the landscape garden at Stourhead in Wiltshire, or of Pope's friend Lord Bathurst's forested acres at Cirencester in Gloucestershire, for example.[33] Pope was well aware of the limitations of his rented plot, yet he continued to transform his garden until his death in 1744.[34] Writing to Bishop Atterbury in 1725, Pope indicated the nature and extent of his activity with vivid metaphor: 'I am as busy in three inches of gardening as any man can be in threescore acres. I fancy myself like the fellow that spent his life in cutting ye twelve apostles in one cherry stone.'[35] Carving 'twelve apostles in one cherry stone' is not only a felicitous metaphor for Pope's endeavours; the phrase likewise hints at the relation between variety and unity which Pope strove for in the general layout and individual features of his garden. Within a unified conception of nature, Pope created a garden with sufficient variety to appeal to the mind and imagination of the spectator.[36]

Located fifteen miles west of London on the Hampton Court Road, Twickenham, neither town nor country, offered Pope an ideal spot in which to live out a classically inspired rural retirement.[37] The famed poet clearly desired a residence outside the hurly-burly of London; yet his decision to move to the village of Twickenham may have also been influenced by the ten-mile rule, which forbade Roman Catholics like Pope from living within ten miles of Westminster Abbey. The sketches in Pope's 'Homer' manuscript in the British Museum, as well as the plan of his actual garden, rely on the elements of variety through contrast and surprise which the poet had written of in his 1731 *An Epistle to Lord Burlington*. Throughout the garden, the spectator was shielded from the exterior world by the clever use of 'assembling shades'.[38] The secluded space of the garden fit in with the contemporary politics of enclosure, which appealed to the newly emergent agrarian capitalist class.[39] As Carole Fabricant suggests, in the private world of the garden 'the spectator-owner was encouraged to create his own private spaces capable of protecting *him* from exposure to the view of *others*, [while] his *own* possessions were to remain wholly exposed to *his* view'.[40]

John Searle's 1745 plan of Pope's garden indicates the placement of his classicising villa on the waterfront, with the garden extending back from the banks of the Thames (Fig. 7.2).[41] Pope's garden included a garden house, orangerie, grotto, shell temple, several urns and an obelisk in memory of his mother.[42] This garden furniture was arranged within a plan of straight and curved paths marked by occasional large or small mounts, which offered the spectator extensive prospects, and edged by groups of 'solitary groves', some quincunxes, a bowling green, vineyard and kitchen garden. The classical lines of Pope's villa, which put the viewer in mind of eternally valid truths, appear as a foil to the variety of nature's appearance in the garden. Yet, the classical and what is now termed the more picturesque were conceived within a unified conception of nature. Mind and nature, it will be remembered, were equated at this time through an emphasis on the formative capacity. As the classicising villa, the garden statuary, urns and inscriptions supplied a contrast to the associations occasioned by the varied elements of the garden, so villa and garden, when considered as an ensemble, offered a richer display of *natura naturans* — of the creative capacity of nature — for the mind of the spectator.[43]

In this sense, Pope's famous grotto might be considered a microcosm within the macrocosm of his garden. The grotto began *c.*1720 as an underground passage between villa and landscape — a useful means of avoiding the traffic on the Hampton Court Road. By 1745, however, the grotto had expanded into a sixty-four-foot-long, multi-chambered *museum*, complete with a tunnel from house to garden, two galleries, one at either end of the tunnel, five rooms and a lateral connecting passage (Fig. 7.3).[44]

'An Account of the MATERIALS which compose the GROTTO', published with Searle's plan of 1745 (pp. 5–10), indicate a treasure-trove of mineral and marble. The variety of rockwork, flint, oar, spar, crystal, gems and fossils that lined the passageway and the various caverns surely provided more than adequate stimuli for the imagination.

114

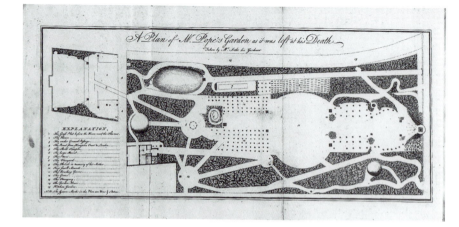

7.2 Plan of Alexander Pope's garden, from John Searle, *A Plan of Mr. Pope's Garden* (London, 1745), frontispiece. (Reproduced by permission of the Huntington Library, San Marino, California)

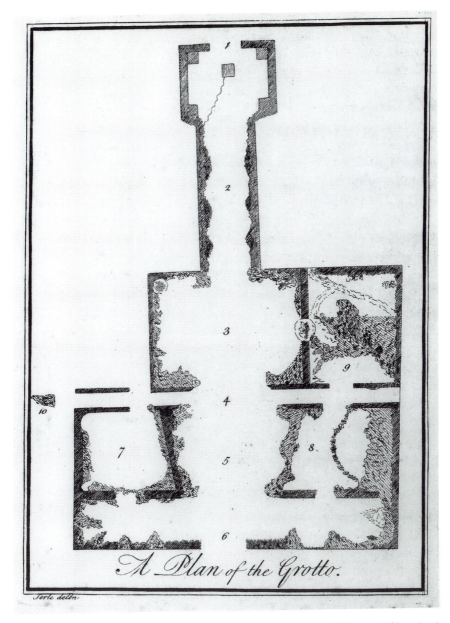

7.3 'A Plan of the Grotto', from John Searle, *A Plan of Mr. Pope's Garden* (London, 1745), opp. p. 5. (Reproduced by permission of the Huntington Library, San Marino, California)

Much of the grotto ornament came from friends, who either gave minerals from their own mines or procured specimens during travels abroad, including marble from the grotto of Egeria near Rome, gold and silver from Mexico and Peru. The building history of the grotto demonstrates Pope's affinity for collecting. Satisfied with his labours, the poet, in a letter to Lord Bolingbroke, declared the grotto — on account of 'all the

7.4 'A Perspective View of the Grotto', from John Searle, *A Plan of Mr. Pope's Garden* (London, 1745), opp. p.10. (Reproduced by permission of the Huntington Library, San Marino, California)

varieties of nature under ground' – 'a study for virtuosi, and a scene for contemplation'.[45] In this 'hidden retreat closed to the public, invulnerable to the intrusion of pro-Ministry Whigs, Grub Street hacks, middle-class tradesmen and others outside Pope's élite circle', the poet could entertain an 'ideal Augustan community'.[46]

In Pope's own estimation, the grotto was a place for inspiration and investigation, for flights of fancy and controlled reflection. While the internal caverns provided refuge from the world, the tunnel brought in the world at entrance and exit. Searle's 'perspective view' indicates a series of archways along the tunnel, culminating in a framed view of the garden (Fig. 7.4).[47] A drawing by Kent provides a view of the grotto entrance from the garden (Fig. 7.5). The profusion of detail in Kent's drawing, including Venus surrounded by a group of river gods at the left-hand side, as well as the pen strokes marking out a rainbow, indicate a fantasy. The Shell Temple in the centre of the drawing, however, resembles Pope's description. On the right-hand side, Pope and Kent stand near a bust of Homer. Kent holds a palette and brush, while Pope demonstrates the use of a perspective glass to capture the view of the river on the opposite end of the tunnel. Variety and surprise, those elements Pope deemed most worthy in the experience of a garden, are here revealed as the outcome of nature and artifice.

Imagining the space of the garden and the tunnel together, one can trace a passage from uncultivated to formed nature (Figs 7.4 and 7.5). In doing so, the Shell Temple operates as a hinge between nature and culture in two senses: in manner of construction it lies between the nature of the garden and the highly contrived, ornate grotto; for the ambulatory body in the garden, the series of framed prospects offered

7.5 *A 'Fantasy' of Pope's Garden*, by William Kent. (Drawing © The British Museum)

through the Shell Temple resides between the freer spaces of the garden and the directed passageway throughout the grotto. Nevertheless, in its lavish display of the wonders of nature, the subterranean grotto, the most cultivated space of the garden, connotes the natural,[48] while the garden, which strikes a measure between the unformed and the formed, is a terrain for culture, for the activities of *homo ludens*.

Moving underground, the transaction between nature and culture is best seen in the grotto cavern Pope designed as a place for his own poetic inspiration (Fig. 7.3, no. 3). Fitted out with a panoply of minerals, shells, shards of glass and an alabaster lamp, this chamber alternated between a *camera obscura* and an illuminated museum. When the doors of the grotto were shut, glints and reflections from the encrustations on the interior and the boats sailing along the Thames on the exterior danced across the walls. In a seeming prolepsis, Addison, writing in a 1712 issue of *The Spectator*, describes a *camera obscura* likewise located between river and park. Indicating how the contrived resembles nature, Addison explains the effect of the flitting images on the beholder: 'I must confess, the novelty of such a sight may be one occasion of its pleasantness to the imagination, but certainly the chief reason is its near resemblance to nature, as it does not only, like other pictures, give the colour and figure, but the motion of the things it represents.'[49]

A second drawing by Kent provides a view into the illuminated chamber, where the poet contemplates by lamplight, and dragonflies, symbols of the psyche, flutter above (Fig. 7.6).[50] During his 'grottofying' Pope had discovered a spring.[51] The murmur

117

of the water, which fell 'in a perpetual Rill' and echoed through this 'Cavern day and night', served as an aid to meditation.[52] Writing to Edward Blount in 1725, Pope concludes that his grotto 'wants nothing to compleat it but a good Statue with an Inscription, like that beautiful antique one which you know I am so fond of …'.[53] The garden grotto at Stourhead, created in the 1740s by Pope's friend Henry Hoare, contains a statue of the sleeping nymph the poet had in mind (Fig. 7.7).[54] Pope's translation of the Latin inscription is engraved on the marble basin.

> Nymph of the Grot, these sacred Springs I keep,
> And to the Murmer of these Waters sleep;
> Ah, spare my Slumbers, gently tread the Cave!
> And drink in silence, or in silence lave!

The Stourhead sleeping nymph is located at the source of a spring. 'Ancient traditions linked nymphs with Muses, and they too were associated with springs and grottoes.'[55] The statue of the sleeping nymph desired by Pope would have referred to his grotto spring and to the muse of his contemplative life.

Whereas the quiescent nymph, guardian of the grotto, slumbers to the murmur of the waters, Pope found that the 'perpetual Rill' of the water facilitated poetic meditation. Indeed, for Pope, the creation of poetry, as well as the whole range of effects of his *camera obscura*, were possible only when one had 'a mind to light it up'.[56] In the construction and experience of Pope's grotto one finds the eighteenth-century principle of *natura naturans*. If, as Cassirer writes, the 'true essence of nature' is found in 'the creative process', then the concept of nature may encompass mind, but mind is clearly over matter. For the ambulatory spectator of Pope's garden, as for the seated poet in his cavern, nature provided scenes for contemplation and inspiration, views made all the more expansive when the mind could bring them to life.

Nature slain and nature seen

Pope summed up his ambitions for the grotto when he wrote: 'I would be glad to make the place resemble nature in all her workings, & entertain a sensible, as well as dazzle a gazing spectator.'[57] In creating a grotto that resembled nature, Pope followed a long tradition. While Ovid in the *Metamorphoses* described how 'Nature by her own cunning had imitated art' in the creation of a 'secret nook',[58] Pope used the riches of nature to fashion a grotto that imitated nature. Pope's dependence on nature is, in this sense, similar to that of the ape of nature on the frontispiece for Fludd's treatise. The poet, depicted in Kent's drawing ruminating in his subterranean enclosure, is, moreover, like the ape contained within, and surrounded by, a macrocosm of the natural world. Yet, in Pope's manufactured grotto nature is slain before it is seen: the formative capacity of the mind, first hinted at with the ape of nature, here dominates the matter that likewise serves as its inspiration.

Pope's contrivance of nature, however natural in effect, is placed in the service of the spectator. The eighteenth-century transition in the English garden from a highly

7.6 William Kent, *Alexander Pope in his Grotto*, c.1723–30. Pen, ink and wash drawing. (Courtesy Devonshire Collection, Chatsworth. Trustees of the Chatsworth Settlement. Photograph: Photographic Survey, Courtauld Institute of Art)

patterned to a less formal style, which traded on variety and surprise, opened up a compass of associations for the viewing subject. To capture the full effects of the natural and the artificial, Pope's garden and grotto necessitated a physical and mental engagement on the part of the body in the garden. Entering this aestheticised landscape – or one might even say heterotopia – the observer stepped outside society and history and into an artificial nature.[59] As the formed nature of the garden, and especially Pope's grotto, connotes the natural, so the artificial is made natural again by

7.7 Sleeping Nymph in the main niche of the grotto at Stourhead in Wiltshire, from Osvald Sirén, *China and Gardens of Europe of the Eighteenth Century* (New York, 1950), pl. 51

the associations or judgement of a spectator who remained engaged with, yet separate from, the landscape.[60]

Underscoring the need for a 'mind to light it up', Pope translates the experience of the ambulatory spectator into an occasion for the mind. At the time he was fashioning his garden, the formative capacity of the mind, akin to nature and hence deemed natural, was not considered separate from nature so much as necessary to nature. Indeed, the nature of the garden required the mind in the body in the garden to turn matter into form. To return to the words of Shaftesbury, 'never in *Body* it-self, but in the *Form* or *Forming Power*'. Form over matter and mind over body. Whether nature slain or nature seen, Pope's garden and grotto at Twickenham exemplify a wider cultural relation of mind and body and landscape, a problematic that gained expression through the eighteenth-century conception of *natura naturans*.

Acknowledgements

My thanks to Jan Birksted for his encouragement, and for his valuable editorial comments. My understanding of the relations between macrocosm and microcosm, and how these relate to the production of knowledge, was sharpened during my residency as a Fellow at the University of California Humanities Center in 1999, where I participated in a working group on 'Microcosms: Objects of Knowledge'. I thank Mark Meadow and Bruce Robertson, who conceived of the group, for inviting me to participate. Finally, thanks to the staff of the Huntington Library, San Marino, California.

121

1   Raymond Williams, *Keywords: A Vocabulary of Culture and Society* (London: Croom Helm, 1976), p. 184. Cf. the entries on nature in Otto Brunner, Werner Conze and Reinhard Koselleck (eds), *Geschichtliche Grundbegriffe: Historisches Lexikon zur politisch-sozialen Sprache in Deutschland* (Stuttgart: Kletta-Cotta, 1978), IV, pp. 215–240; and Joachim Ritter and Karlfried Gründer (eds), *Historisches Wörterbuch der Philosophie* (Basle: Schwabe & Co. 1971), VI, cols 421–478. Also R. G. Collingwood, *The Idea of Nature* (London: Oxford University Press, 1978); Clarence Glacken, *Traces on the Rhodian Shore: Nature and Culture in Western Thought from Ancient Times to the End of the Eighteenth Century* (Berkeley: University of California Press, 1967); and the essays on nature in Arthur O. Lovejoy, *Essays in the History of Ideas* (New York: G. P. Putnam's Sons, 1960).

2   The most important of these are reprinted in the anthology by John Dixon Hunt and Peter Willis (eds), *The Genius of the Place: The English Landscape Garden 1620–1820* (Cambridge, MA: MIT Press, 1993).

3   Ann Bermingham, *Landscape and Ideology: The English Rustic Tradition, 1740–1860* (Berkeley: University of California Press, 1986), p. 155.

4   On nature as a 'controlling idea' in the eighteenth century, see Basil Willey, *The Eighteenth Century Background: Studies on the Idea of Nature in the Thought of the Period* (Boston: Beacon, 1961); Ernst Cassirer, *The Philosophy of Enlightenment* (Princeton: Princeton University Press, 1951), pp. 37–92; and Martin Warnke, *Political Landscape: The Art History of Nature* (Cambridge, MA: Harvard University Press, 1995). On the location of the garden along an eighteenth-century divide separating the classification of the wild and the tame, see Harriet Ritvo, 'At the edge of the garden: nature and domestication in eighteenth- and nineteenth-century Britain', *Huntington Library Quarterly*, 55/3 (1992), pp. 363–378.

5   See also Ann Bermingham, 'The Picturesque and ready-to-wear femininity', in *The Politics of the Picturesque*, eds Stephen Copley and Peter Gartside (Cambridge: Cambridge University Press, 1992), pp. 81–119.

6   The characterization of nature as feminine reveals itself etymologically. When one considers the body in the garden in terms of nature, one is referring to the matrix or the matter of the garden. Not surprisingly, both matrix and matter are related to *mater*, Greek for 'mother'. On this, see *A Greek–English Lexicon*, compiled by George Liddell and Robert Scott (Oxford, 1996). The word 'nature' is feminine in Greek, Latin, French, Italian, Spanish and German. Of course, as Friedrich Nietzsche pointed out in 1873, the gendering of objects and concepts does not reveal inherent truths so much as the arbitrary nature of metaphor, 'far flown beyond the canon of certainty'; F. Nietzsche, 'On truth and falsity in their ultramoral sense', in *The Complete Works of Friedrich Nietzsche*, ed. Oscar Levy (New York: Gordon, 1974), II, pp. 171–192.

7   Anthony Ashley Cooper, 3rd Earl of Shaftesbury, 'The moralists, a philosophical rhapsody', in *idem, Characteristicks of Men, Opinions, Times*, ed. Philip Ayres (Oxford: Clarendon, 1999), II, p. 101. Shaftesbury's lines are often quoted in the literature on the eighteenth-century English garden. Also David Leatherbarrow, 'Character, geometry and perspective: the Third Earl of Shaftesbury's principles of garden design', *Journal of Garden History*, 4/4 (1984), pp. 332–358.

8   Alexander Pope, essay from *The Guardian* (1713), in Hunt and Willis, *Genius of the Place*, p. 205. In his promotion of the 'amiable simplicity of unadorned nature', Pope followed the ancients. While classical gardens had not survived, literary description of them had. In his essay Pope provides the first English translation of Homer's description of the gardens of Alcinous.

9   Rudolf Wittkower, 'English Neo-Palladianism, the landscape garden, China and the Enlightenment', in *idem, Palladio and English Palladianism* (New York: Thames & Hudson, 1983), pp. 170–190, 217–219, shows the interdependence in England, 'current from Shaftesbury's days onwards, of the complementary relationship between political freedom, moral conduct, the formation of taste and the love of the landscape garden' (p. 190). In terms of the garden, then, the natural state of nature connoted the natural estate of English

politics, while the highly patterned garden signified the yoke of the French citizen under absolutism.

10 Carole Fabricant, 'Binding and dressing Nature's loose tresses: the ideology of Augustan landscape design', *Studies in Eighteenth-Century Culture*, 8 (1979), p. 109: 'Throughout eighteenth-century treatises on landscape, Nature was given her due, allowed to assert – indeed, *flaunt* – her superiority over the quaint and rigidly confining forms of art, before she was, as it were, put in her place, subordinated to the spectator's critical eye and the recreator's shaping hand.' Fabricant demonstrates how statements on nature in these treatises, though they may have come to be 'commonplaces or figures of speech', are nevertheless 'statements about how power was conceived and wielded during this period' (p. 113). Also *idem*, 'The aesthetics and politics of landscape in the eighteenth century', *Studies in Eighteenth-Century British Art and Aesthetics*, ed. Ralph Cohen (Berkeley: University of California Press, 1985), pp. 49–81.

11 H. J. Johnson, 'Changing concepts of matter from antiquity to Newton', in *Dictionary of the History of Ideas*, ed. P. P. Wiener (New York, 1973), III, pp. 185–196; E. McMullin (ed.), *The Concept of Matter in Greek and Medieval Philosophy* (Notre Dame: University of Indiana Press, 1965).

12 For an account of the literary uses of 'the Goddess Natura' in the Middle Ages, see Ernst R. Curtius, *European Literature and the Latin Middle Ages*, trans. Willard R. Trask (Princeton: Princeton University Press, 1973), pp. 106–127. Also Robin Attfield, 'Christian attitudes to nature', *Journal of the History of Ideas*, 44/3 (1983), pp. 369–386.

13 The complete title of Fludd's text is *Utriusque cosmi, majoris scilicet et minoris, metaphysica atque technica historia* (Oppenheim, 1617). Only the first two volumes of Fludd's treatise – those on the macrocosm – were published. The first, subsequently entitled *Historia technica*, contains the frontispiece illustrated here as Fig. 1. As H. W. Janson notes, 'Ars Simia Naturae', in *Apes and Ape Lore in the Middle Ages and the Renaissance* (London: The Warburg Institute, University of London, 1952), p. 305, Merian's engraving is 'an outline of the entire project in both verbal and pictorial form'. Also Horst Bredekamp, *The Lure of Antiquity and the Cult of the Machine: The Kunstkammer and the Evolution of Nature, Art and Technology*, trans. Allison Brown (Princeton: Markus Wiener, 1995), pp. 70–71; Wolfgang Kemp, 'Natura: Ikonographische Studien zur Geschichte und Verbreitung einer Allegorie', dissertation, University of Tübingen, pp. 88–103, *passim*; and Carolyn Merchant, *The Death of Nature: Women, Ecology and the Scientific Revolution* (New York: HarperCollins, 1980), pp. 11–12.

14 Janson, 'Ars Simia Naturae', p. 305, which provides the Latin original. More specifically, this Natura is 'modelled upon Apuleius' description of Isis, as evidenced by such details as the crescent on her womb and her strange way of standing, with one foot on water the other on dry land'. She is then 'the Moon Goddess Supreme, the Female Principle, the Fount of Fertility, from which the ape "depends" as the male "artifex"' (pp. 305–306).

15 Bredekamp, *Lure of Antiquity and the Cult of the Machine*, p. 70.

16 Janson, 'Ars Simia Naturae', p. 307.

17 Plato, *Timaeus*, trans. Benjamin Jowett, in *The Collected Dialogues of Plato*, eds Edith Hamilton and Huntington Cairns (Princeton: Princeton University Press, 1961), pp. 1177ff; Aristotle, *Metaphysics*, 1032a–1038b, in *The Basic Works of Aristotle*, ed. Richard McKeon (New York: Random House, 1941), pp. 792–804; *Generation of Animals*, trans. A. L. Peck (Cambridge, MA: Harvard University Press, 1963), p. 732a. Also M. Cline Horowitz, 'Aristotle and woman', *Journal of the History of Biology*, 9/2 (1976), pp. 183–213.

18 For this, see David Summers, 'Form and gender', in *Visual Culture: Images and Interpretations*, eds Norman Bryson, Michael Ann Holly and Keith Moxey (Hanover: University Press of New England, 1994), pp. 384–411. In addition to demonstrating that the relation between form and matter 'has, for two and a half millennia and in countless contexts of use, been a deeply gendered distinction' (p. 393), Summers, in the manner of a disciplinary archaeology, relates classical and Renaissance notions of form and gender to the history of art. In so doing, he provides a more fundamental reason for the exclusion of women artists from the discipline than has been noted previously. On the broader implications of form for art history, see *idem*,

'Form, nineteenth-century metaphysics, and the problem of art historical description', *Critical Inquiry*, 15/2 (1989), pp. 372–406. Patricia L. Reilly, 'The taming of the blue. Writing out color in Italian Renaissance theory', in *The Expanding Discourse: Feminism and Art History*, eds Norma Broude and Mary D. Garrard (Boulder: Westview, 1992), pp. 87–99, analyses the ways in which Aristotle's hierarchical positioning and gender coding of form and matter permeate the treatises of the *disegno/colore* controversy in Italian Renaissance art theory. I thank my colleague Todd Olson for bringing this essay to my attention.

19 On the shift from an organicist to a mechanistic view of nature, see Merchant, *Death of Nature*.

20 Cassirer, *Philosophy of Enlightenment*, p. 39.

21 *Ibid.*, p. 38. In his Seventh Discourse, delivered on 10 December 1776, Joshua Reynolds exemplified this idea: 'My notion of Nature comprehends not only the forms which Nature produces, but also the nature and internal fabric and organization, as I may call it, of the human mind and imagination'; J. Reynolds, *Discourses*, with an Introduction and Notes by Roger Fry (New York: E. P. Dutton & Co., 1905), p. 193.

22 Lord Shaftesbury, 'The moralists', p. 106. Also Jerome Stolnitz, 'On the significance of Lord Shaftesbury in modern aesthetic theory', *Philosophical Quarterly*, 11/43 (April 1961), p. 103.

23 'Earls of creation' is from James Lees-Milne, *The Earls of Creation: Five Great Patrons of Eighteenth-Century Art* (London: Hamish Hamilton, 1962). In his 'The public prospect and the private view: the politics of taste in eighteenth-century Britain', in *Landscape, Natural Beauty and the Arts*, eds Salim Kemal and Ivan Gaskell (Cambridge: Cambridge University Press, 1993), p. 81, John Barrell demonstrates how the 'prospective' view, which requires the ability to abstract, and to bring particulars into an ordered form, could legitimate contemporary political authority, since only the man of independent means was considered capable of generalizing, and so of producing truly abstract ideas.

24 John Dixon Hunt, *The Figure in the Landscape: Poetry, Painting, and Gardening during the Eighteenth Century* (Baltimore: Johns Hopkins University Press, 1976), p. xiii.

25 Charles H. Hinnant, 'A philosophical origin of the English landscape garden', *Bulletin of Research in the Humanities*, 83/2 (1980), pp. 292–306; also H. Frank Clark, 'Eighteenth-century Elysiums: the role of "Associationism" in the landscape movement', *Journal of the Warburg and Courtauld Institutes*, 6 (1943), pp. 165–188. Taking a critical step forward, Peter de Bolla recently demonstrated how 'eighteenth-century models of vision and visuality … figure the facts of vision'; P. de Bolla, 'The charm'd eye', in *Body & Text in the Eighteenth Century*, eds Veronica Kelly and Dorothea von Mücke (Stanford: Stanford University Press, 1994), pp. 89–111, 307–313.

26 Cited in Willey, *Eighteenth Century Background*, p. 18.

27 Cited in Hunt and Willis, *Genius of the Place*, p. 11. On Walpole's 'sister arts', see Hunt, *Figure in the Landscape*; and Stephanie Ross, *What Gardens Mean* (Chicago: University of Chicago Press, 1998), chs 3, 4.

28 Alexander Pope, *An Epistle to Lord Burlington*, lines 51–56, in *The Twickenham Edition of the Poems of Alexander Pope*, ed. John Butt (New Haven and London: Yale University Press, 1939–61), III/ii, 138. The principles of gardening indicated in Pope's lines would remain foremost for him. For instance, Joseph Spence, *Observations, Anecdotes, and Characters of Books and Men*, ed. James M. Osborn (Oxford: Clarendon Press, 1966), I, p. 612. In terms of taste in gardening, Pope was ahead of his time as these principles would find full expression only later in the century with the rise of the Picturesque style in gardening. Rather than weigh in on whether Pope's garden was solely classical in inspiration or purely picturesque in conception, I prefer to steer clear of such an attenuated estimation. As I hope to show in what follows, Pope was certainly inspired by the ancients as well as by his contemporaries.

29 On the paradox of a staging of nature, see Helmut Schneider, 'The staging of the gaze: aesthetic illusion and the scene of nature in the eighteenth century', in *Reflecting Senses: Perception and Appearance in Literature, Culture, and the Arts*, eds Walter Pape and

Frederick Burwick (Berlin: Walter de Gruyter, 1995), pp. 77–95. The positioning of views in the early eighteenth-century English garden and the different viewpoints onto these scenes is examined by Ronald Paulson, 'The poetic garden', in *idem, Emblem and Expression: Meaning in English Art of the Eighteenth Century* (Cambridge, MA: Harvard University Press, 1975), pp. 19–34, 233–234. Also *idem*, 'The pictorial circuit & related structures in 18th-century England', in *The Varied Pattern: Studies in the 18th Century*, eds Peter Hughes and David Williams (Toronto: A.M. Hakkert 1971), pp. 165–187.

30 John Barrell, *The Idea of Landscape and the Sense of Place 1730–1840* (Cambridge: Cambridge University Press, 1972), p. 48, discusses the implications of the separation of the observer from the landscape.

31 In the satire on Timon's Villa in his *An Epistle to Lord Burlington* (lines 117–122), Pope notes the tedious and unwholesome effect on the spectator when 'Grove nods at grove, each Alley has a brother,/ And half the Platform just reflects the other. The suff'ring eye inverted Nature sees,/ Trees cut to Statues, Statues thick as trees,/ With here a Fountain, never to be play'd,/ And there a Summer-house, that knows no Shade'. Cf. Pope's essay of 1713 for *The Guardian*, in Hunt and Willis, *Genius of the Place*, pp. 204–208; and Joseph Addison's remarks in *The Spectator*, no. 414 (25 June 1712), in *The Spectator*, ed. Gregory Smith (London: Dent, 1963), III, p. 286.

32 Horace Walpole, *The History of the Modern Taste in Gardening* [1771/80], in Hunt and Willis, *Genius of the Place*, p. 315.

33 For the significance of the increasing size of country estates and their gardens, see Joan Bassim, 'The English landscape garden in the eighteenth century: the cultural importance of an English institution', *Albion*, 11 (Spring 1979), pp. 15–33.

34 Contemporary accounts of Pope's garden include the poet's description of his grotto in a letter to Edward Blount, 1725; John Searle, *A Plan of Mr. Pope's Garden* (1745); and an 'Epistolary description' by the correspondent of *The Newcastle General Magazine* (January 1748). Malcolm Andrews, 'A new description of Pope's garden', *Journal of Garden History*, 1/1 (1981), pp. 35–36, quotes from a short description of the garden, penned in 1742, which he discovered in the British Library. Extended studies of the garden include Maynard Mack, *The Garden and the City: Retirement and Politics in the Later Poetry of Pope 1731–1743* (Toronto: University of Toronto Press, 1969); Hunt, *Figure in the Landscape*, pp. 58–104; Morris R. Brownell, *Alexander Pope & the Arts of Georgian England* (Oxford: Clarendon, 1978); Peter Martin, *Pursuing Innocent Pleasures: The Gardening World of Alexander Pope* (Hamden: Archon, 1984); and Helen Deutsch, 'Twickenham and the landscape of true character', in *idem, Resemblance & Disgrace: Alexander Pope and the Deformation of Culture* (Cambridge, MA: Harvard University Press, 1996), pp. 83–135, 241–255.

35 *The Works of Alexander Pope*, vol. X, p. 183, cited in Frederick Bracher, 'Pope's grotto: the maze of fancy', in *Essential Articles for the Study of Alexander Pope*, ed. Maynard Mack (Hamden: Archon, 1968), p. 115. Bracher's essay originally appeared in the *Huntington Library Quarterly*, 12 (1949), pp. 140–162.

36 The idea of variety within unity is well expressed in a couplet from Pope's poem *Windsor Forest*, which was composed in 1704: 'Where Order in Variety we see,/ And where, tho' all things differ, all agree'; Butt, *Twickenham Edition of the Poems of Alexander Pope*, I, pp. 140–150, lines 15–16.

37 This theme is explored in the erudite study by Mack, *Garden and the City*; and Maren-Sofie Røstvig, *The Happy Man: Studies in the Metamorphosis of a Classical Ideal* (New York: Humanities Press, 1971), II, pp. 11–111, 422–439. Deutsche (1996) discusses Pope's retirement as 'an escape from both physical deformity and social distemper into self-possession' (p. 32).

38 Horace Walpole, *A History of the Modern Taste in Gardening*, cited in Mack, *Garden and the City*, p. 26.

39 On the politics of enclosure, see John Barrell, *The Dark Side of Landscape: The Rural Poor in English Painting, 1730–1840* (Cambridge: Cambridge University Press, 1980);

Bermingham, *Landscape and Ideology*; and Raymond Williams, *The Country and the City* (London: Chatto & Windus, 1973).

40 Fabricant, 'Binding and dressing Nature's loose tresses', p. 120. Cf. Deutsche: 'In the garden and the grotto, femininity in all its natural aberration and social appropriability becomes the background against which masculine integrity makes itself visible' (p. 85).

41 John Searle, *A Plan of Mr. Pope's Garden As it was left at his Death: with a Plan and Perspective View of the Grotto* (London, 1745); repr. with an Introduction by Morris R. Brownell. No. 211 (Los Angeles: Augustan Reprint Society, 1982); James Sambrook, 'The size and shape of Pope's garden', *Eighteenth-Century Studies*, 5 (Spring 1972), pp. 450–455, gives corrections in the orientation of Searle's plan.

42 The Shell Temple is by William Kent; John Dixon Hunt, *William Kent, Landscape Garden Designer: An Assessment and Catalogue of His Designs* (London: A. Zwemmer, 1987), cat. 66. As Walpole noted, and as Searle's plan indicates, the obelisk to Pope's deceased mother is the visual and emotional climax of the garden.

43 The juxtaposition of classicising architecture with less formal gardens marks the shift to a national style of landscape gardening in England. Lord Burlington, inspired by the Palladian architecture and the less formal style of the Renaissance gardens he saw in Italy on his Grand Tour, promoted these features in his house and gardens at Chiswick. Visiting Lord Burlington in 1716, Pope was inspired by what he saw. It would not be until the 1730s, however, when William Kent altered Burlington's gardens, that a more naturalised style in gardening would find its definitive expression.

44 For Pope's own plans of his grotto, dated 14 January and 29 December 1740 respectively, see Mack, *Garden and the City*, pp. 58–59. In addition to the discussions of the grotto in Mack, Brownell, *Alexander Pope & the Arts of Georgian England*, and Martin, *Pursuing Innocent Pleasures*, see Richard D. Altick, 'Mr. Pope expands his grotto', *Philological Quarterly*, 21/4 (1942), pp. 427–430; R. W. Babcock, 'Pope's grotto today', *South Atlantic Quarterly*, 42/3 (1943), pp. 289–295; Benjamin Boyce, 'Mr. Pope, in Bath, improves his grotto', in *Restoration and Eighteenth-Century Literature: Essays in Honor of A. D. McKillop*, ed. Carroll Camden (Chicago: University of Chicago Press, 1963), pp. 143–53; and Bracher, 'Pope's grotto: the maze of fancy'. For a sample of poetry inspired by Pope's grotto, see Mack, *Garden and the City*, appendix E, pp. 266–271. On grottoes in general, see Robert A. Aubin, 'Grottoes, geology, and the Gothic Revival', *Studies in Philology*, 31/3 (1934), pp. 408–416, who supposes that the popularity of grottoes in the first decades of the eighteenth century 'may have been instrumental in inspiring the Gothic revival (p. 414)'. For a thorough and fascinating history of the grotto, see Naomi Miller, *Heavenly Caves: Reflections on the Garden Grotto* (New York: George Braziller, 1982).

45 Letter to Lord Bolingbroke, 3 September 1740, in *The Correspondence of Alexander Pope*, ed. George Sherburn (Oxford: Clarendon, 1956), IV, pp. 261–262.

46 Fabricant, 'Binding and dressing Nature's loose tresses', p. 119; Mack, *Garden and the City*, pp. 66ff. A phrase from Horace's Epistle I.18, inscribed over the entrance to the grotto, 'Secretum iter et fallentis semita vitae' (Secret passage and the path of an unnoticed life), announces the theme of withdrawal and seclusion. According to Deutsch, 'fallentis' [unnoticed] has a primary meaning of deceiving, and the grotto seen from this perspective is less a secret passsage to a classically inherited privacy than a paradoxically public display of the deformity that barred Pope from public life and physical exertion, and made retirement less volitional than compulsory' (p. 131).

47 A later 'perspective view' of the grotto includes statues in the niches on either side of the tunnel. For an illustration, see Edward Ironside, *History and Antiquities of Twickenham*, opp. p. 81; and Mack, *Garden and the City*, p. 82.

48 'I wish you were here to bear Testimony how little it [the grotto] owes to Art, either the Place itself, or the Image I give of it'; Alexander Pope, letter to Edward Blount, 2 June 1725, cited in Brownell, *Alexander Pope & the Arts of Georgian England*, p. 257.

49 Joseph Addison, *The Spectator*, no. 414 (25 June 1712), in Smith, *The Spectator*, Volume III p. 285. Mack, *Garden and the City*, p. 47, finds analogies in Pope's *camera obscura* to

Plato's cave, Locke's 'dark room' of the understanding and 'Plotinus's notion that the mind is a power … giving a "radiance out of its own store".' On 'the *camera obscura* and its subject', see Jonathan Crary, *Techniques of the Observer: On Vision and Modernity in the Nineteenth Century* (Cambridge, MA: MIT Press, 1990), pp. 25–66.

50 Another drawing by Kent or Dorothy Boyle of Pope at work in the grotto is in the collections of the Trustees of the Chatsworth Settlement; for a reproduction, see Mack, *Garden and the City*, p. 43.

51 'Grottofying' is a verb of Pope's invention; Grace Haber, 'A. Pope — "imployed in Grottofying"', *Texas Studies in Language and Literature*, 10 (Fall 1968), p. 386.

52 Alexander Pope, letter to Edward Blount, 2 June 1725, cited in Brownell, *Alexander Pope & the Arts of Georgian England*, p. 255. The sensation and diversity of the waterworks is described in the 'Epistolary description', *Newcastle General Magazine* (January 1748), repr. Mack, *Garden and the City*, appendix A.

53 Letter to Blount, 2 June 1725, cited in Brownell, *Alexander Pope & the Arts of Georgian England*, p. 257.

54 On the iconography of the statue and the origin of the inscription, see Otto Kurz, '*Huius Nympha Loci*', *Journal of the Warburg and Courtauld Institutes*, 16 (1953), pp. 171–177; Elisabeth B. MacDougall, 'The sleeping nymph: origins of a humanist fountain type', *Art Bulletin*, 57/3 (1975), pp. 357–365; and Miller, *Heavenly Caves*, pp. 77–85. On the grotto at Stourhead, see Kenneth Woodbridge, *Landscape and Antiquity: Aspects of English Culture at Stourhead, 1718 to 1838* (Oxford: Clarendon, 1970), *passim*. A bust of Pope is included in Kent's Temple of British Worthies of 1733 at Stowe.

55 MacDougall, 'Sleeping nymph', p. 362.

56 Letter to Blount, 2 June 1725, cited in Brownell, *Alexander Pope & the Arts of Georgian England*, p. 255.

57 Sherburn, *Correspondence of Alexander Pope*, IV, p. 228.

58 Ovid, *Metamorphoses*, III, lines 157–161, quoted in Mack, *Garden and the City*, p. 58.

59 On the garden as a heterotopia, see Michel Foucault, 'Of other spaces', *Diacritics*, 16/1 (1986), pp. 22–27.

60 Cf. Dabney Townsend, 'The Picturesque', *Journal of Aesthetics and Art Criticism*, 55/4 (1997), p. 368, who argues that 'the picturesque introduces both a temporal and a physical distance that influences the formulation of "distance" as an aesthetic term'.

Stanislaus Fung

8 Self, scene and action: the final chapter of *Yuan ye*

The seventeenth-century Chinese treatise on gardens, *Yuan ye*, is well known as a text full of literary allusions.[1] Ever since the late Professor Chen Zhi published his annotated edition of this treatise in 1979, students of Chinese gardens have appreciated the allusive nature of the text.[2] The recent translation of *Yuan ye* into French by Che Bing Chiu has made a similar contribution in highlighting and explicating the literary allusions of the treatise for Western readers.[3] It remains very much the case, however, that very little has been said about the conceptual significance of literary allusions in this Chinese treatise on gardens. Scholars have been inclined to acknowledge the literary aspects of the treatise while simultaneously dismissing them as crucial considerations in understanding the importance of *Yuan ye* as a treatise. Students of Chinese gardens are therefore confronted with a puzzle: scholars seem to have devoted a good deal of effort to explicate features of the treatise, even though these seem largely 'ornamental' and inconsequential.

In recent years, new analyses of *Yuan ye* have appeared that attempt to construe the literary aspects of this treatise in new ways. Careful reading of the treatise has shown how the rhetorical features of the text might be related to issues such as the dichotomy of subject and object, and to the status of the garden designer.[4] This chapter is an attempt to develop a similar approach that throws new light on the final chapter of *Yuan ye* which is devoted to a discussion of the notion of 'borrowing views', and is the first of its kind in Chinese writings on gardens. In modern scholarship, 'borrowing views' is often understood as the fixed relationship between a distant scenic object and viewing subject. Recent work has shown that there are some reasons for believing that this common understanding of 'borrowing views' is not supported by the text of *Yuan ye*.[5] My first objective here is to argue that 'borrowing views' has to do with a specific kind of *design thinking* rather than specific *designed vistas* in gardens. My second objective is to suggest a line of thinking that would explain why in *Yuan ye* 'borrowing views' is said to be the most important aspect of garden design.

In pursuing these two objectives, two general premises will be followed: (1) it is important to locate interpretative keys that help open up the treatise to new readings; it

Stanislaus Fung
Self, scene and action: the final
chapter of *Yuan ye*

is not sufficient to read the text by itself. In what follows, I will consider the recent work of the comparative philosopher, Wu Kuang-ming, in relation to some sections on 'borrowing views' in *Yuan ye*.[6] (2) It is important that one does not take for granted the status of this treatise as a classic, which by definition must address the present time as if it was written specifically to do so, and is not merely a seventeenth-century text addressing seventeenth-century readers. I hope to evoke a sense of how the treatise might be related to some of the concerns and possibilities of our time.

The chapter on 'borrowing views' has four central sections, one for each of the four seasons. The whole text is often considered 'poetic': there is no logical argumentation, the topic of discussion seems to change frequently, and the text is full of literary allusions.

Drift and gist

As I examined the text, I discovered a pattern. As one follows the drift of the text, one gets the sense that the gist of the text revolves around three hubs of consideration: self, scene and action. These can be seen clearly in the section on Spring:

> Extending to the utmost one's gaze upon a lofty field,
>> distant peaks form an encircling screen.
> Halls are open so that congenial air wafts over oneself,
>> before the door, Spring waters flow into a marsh.
>
> Amidst enchanting reds and beautiful purples,
>> one delightedly encounters immortals among the flowers.
> There are happy sages and acclaimed worthies
>> who are comparable to the 'prime minister in the mountain'.
>
> The life of leisure has been the subject of a *fu* poem;
>> fragrant plants respond to one's sympathy.

> Sweep the paths and protect the young orchids
>> so that secluded rooms may share in their fragrance.
> Roll up the bamboo blinds
>> and invite the swallows to occasionally cut the light breeze.
>
> Piece by piece fly the petals,
>> thread by thread sleep the willows.
> When coldness produces a slight chill,
>> set up swings high above.
> One's interests would be in accord with the pure and the remote,
>> and one can find pleasure amongst hills and ravines.
> Suddenly thoughts beyond the dusty world come
>> and one seems to be walking in a painting.[7]

This passage begins with four lines about scenes, moving from the 'there' of the lofty field and distant peaks to a 'here' of the open halls and the door. These lines are followed by four lines about self and experience, moving from the present scenes of the previous lines to considerations of an exemplary past. Encountering immortals among flowers is related to a story from Feng Menglong's writing about Qiuxian whose love for flowers so moved the spirits that he was granted a meeting with a fairy one evening. The prime minister in the mountains is Tao Hongjing (c.456–536 CE), a recluse who was consulted by Emperor Wu of the Liang dynasty. The self is analogised with historical figures.

The passage continues with two lines relating passive action and active response, something written about and something responding to us. The allusion is to Pan Yu (247–300)'s rhapsody 'On Living in Idleness' in the *Anthology of Refined Literature*, a collection that all literate Chinese used to memorise. The fragrant flowers are referring to the equally famous *Li sao* by Qu Yuan (c.340–287 BCE), where one reads that the plants are in poor condition for lack of their human companions. The 'life of leisure' and 'fragrant plants' can refer both to the present and also play their parts in the allusions. The lines engage the reader in shuttling between here-and-now and then-and-there.

The passage then continues with four lines about actions in what seems to be a near-by scene: sweeping paths and rolling up blinds.

Next, the reader encounters more lines of scenes, with a bit of action at the end: setting up swings. The words for 'slight chill' are seasonally specific; they refer to the chill that one gets in spring, and this echoes the idea of the returning swallows that the previous line said would 'cut the light breeze'. The setting up of swings is figured as a response to circumstance. The final lines of the passage take this up further. These lines are about the inner sentiments of a self, but unlike the emphasis on allusive analogies of self with the 'prime minister in the mountains' and the like, these lines refer both to the many discussions of the dusty world, hills and ravines and walking in paintings in Chinese literature, and to experiences that are yet-to-come.

It should be clear, therefore, that one performs and undergoes a shuttling between scene, self, action, scene and self in the reading of this passage, between here-and-now and there-and-then. In the other parts of this chapter, the text does not follow this sequence rigidly, so that there is a pattern to be discerned but not a systematic and mechanical thinking to be formularised.

This pattern of the text corresponds to what Wu Kuang-ming calls 'performative thinking', which, he says

> is peripatetic and ambi-guous, thinking 'driving' itself 'around'; at each step the scene changes and develops.... The locus of the dynamic peripatetic I (a demonstrative) is evoked by the situation, where the I is situated. And the I begins to tell a story, by confirming what is the case.... It is thus that thinking goes, experiencing and taking in the unfamiliar that as the new familiar this, and in this taking-as is Chinese metaphor.[8]

The text of *Yuan ye* does not inspect an object (borrowing views) in a thorough way,

Stanislaus Fung
Self, scene and action: the final
chapter of *Yuan ye*

defining and refining, telling us in an unequivocal manner what it is. Rather, it is peripatetic and meandering, the reader undergoes an experience of reading and thinking peripatetically. By following the drift of the text, the reader catches the gist of 'borrowing views'.

The fresh and the new

One should remember that *Yuan ye* is the first Chinese text to treat the notion of 'borrowing views' in detail. It is therefore striking that it does not emphasise novelty or newness of its ideas. Instead, one finds this instaurational text dealing mainly with common experiences (facing an encircling mountain range) and gnomic phrases (stories abbreviated into a phrase, e.g. 'the prime minister in the mountain'). The emphasis is on rhetorical commonplaces. To borrow two terms from Wu Kuang-ming's work, I would suggest that the treatise eschews an emphasis on the unfamiliar that leads to an appreciation of novelty, and stays instead with the familiar, renewed through a sense of the fresh. How does the familiar not fall into the banal? How can it be renewed through a sense of the fresh? Here I would point to two features of the meandering thinking in *Yuan ye*'s discussion of 'borrowing views'.

First, there is the problem of the four sections of the chapter, each focussing on one of the four seasons. The modern scholar Zhang Jiaji has promoted a view that there are four distinct sections, corresponding to four separate categories of seasonal phenomena.[9] The problem here is that the typicality and predictability of seasonal phenomena might lead to an emphasis on familiar annual experiences, to the detriment of the freshness of experience that refreshes us. The modern scholar Zhao Yihe has called attention to the fact that the four sections are not clearly disjunct but are linked by transitional passages.[10] For instance, for summer–autumn

> Linen garments [for summer] cannot withstand new coolness,
>> the fragrance of lotus in the pool lingers.
> The leaves of the *wutong* tree fall suddenly startled by autumn,
>> while insects cry desolately amidst grasses.[11]

For autumn–winter: 'just when one feels that the bamboo fences are decrepit and chrysanthemums are advanced in life, one should explore the warm parts of mountain ranges for the early plum blossoms'.[12]

The text consistently indicates phenomena that arise from the change of seasons and does not emphasise the integrity of each season as a distinctive category. It is the emphasis on the experience of seasonal flux rather than on fixed seasonal features that indicates the road to freshness. Again, this is consonant with performative thinking. As Wu Kuang-ming puts it, 'life is a living through, an embodying through undergoing'.[13] The emphasis is on the concrete time of lived experience and not on an abstract sense of temporal regularity.

Second, focussing now on each of the four parts of the chapter, one can return to the earlier observation that the shuttling between self, scene and action is a discernible pattern but it is neither systematic nor mechanically repetitive. There, too, what is highlighted is the relationship between the character of this shuttling and the freshness of a peripatetic thinking.

At the end of the chapter, the text reads:

> Now the borrowing of views is the most important factor in gardens. Such are borrowing from afar, borrowing from nearby, borrowing from above, borrowing from below, and borrowing in response to the seasons. Yet attracted by the nature of things, as one's eyes perceive, one's heart anticipates, just as [in painting] the idea precedes the brush, and only then can one depict exhaustively.[14]

Here one is taken in a strange way to the heart of garden design, to the moment of design conception. The puzzle here is: what would the wandering between here-and-now and there-and-then have to do with the immediate and interior scene of creativity and its relationship to elsewheres?

Wu Kuang-ming's idea of Chinese thinking as metaphorical and historical thinking is of help here. 'History', he says,

> is my understanding of other times. This means that history is my metaphorical reach-out in time. For metaphor is an activity of my understanding the there-then from the now-here — my present situation, my self. The then can be the future as much as the past. The future has, in its metaphorical relation to the now, as much historical connection to the now as the past does. The past is historical; the future is a proleptive, prevenient, history.[15]

In the light of these remarks, one can consider the shuttling between self, scene and action, between the self analogised with historical figures and the self of immediate and possible future experiences, that have been noted in *Yuan ye* as metaphorical and historical thinking in this sense. Wherever a new or possible scene is figured in terms of something familiar and remembered, there seems to be a resonance with Wu Kuang-ming's discussion of freshness:

133

> Even if we are made new, our hearts are still with the comfortable old where everything is familiar, where even imperfections are our home. And so we like the fresh and dislike the new. . . . We can break through the threatening new into the fresh via the familiar; we then start anew in the secure old. And this is what metaphor brings us. Metaphor is thus a logic of disclosing the new and assimilating it into the fresh.[16]

In sum, *Yuan ye* asks designers to take on reinterpretation as the process of creation. It offers not a method of borrowing views, but a way of designing a process of thinking. It does not provide historical knowledge but rather continuity of culture; this implies both

Stanislaus Fung
Self, scene and action: the final
chapter of *Yuan ye*

losses and transformation. The literary allusions or gnomic phrases and stories involved
in *Yuan ye*'s account of borrowing views are the vehicle of cultural continuity and not
mere rhetorical ornament. This usage of allusions makes the treatise self-referentiality
consistent: it is a text on borrowing that borrows from other texts, so that there is no
separation between topic and mode of operation. The implied contract with the readers
is that they too will metaphorically extend it to other situations. The Chinese text
configures gnomic phrases and common or likely experiences and this configurative
thinking, sticking very much to concrete particulars, avoids the abstraction commonly
involved in logical argumentation. So how are the particulars related to a general
understanding without recourse to abstraction? Generality here connotes mutuality. 'My
solicitous concern about this particular elder of mine, once mentioned, calls forth its
generalising into our respective, then common, concern about our elders, then the kindly
concern in general for the elderly in general.'[17] The particular situation of the hermit in
the mountain evokes a generalised perspective on the interpenetration of active
governance and passive reclusion.

The master's voice and the meandering thought

It is well known that the author of *Yuan Ye*, Ji Cheng (b.1582), was someone who
designed gardens for others,[18] whereas owners and visitors wrote the vast majority of
Chinese writings on gardens. For this reason, *Yuan ye* has often been valued as
embodying the voice of the traditional master designer, conveying to readers his
intentions and inner sentiments. This view has not been borne out by the foregoing
reading of the final chapter. If there is an implied subject of the text, an actor who
designs and borrows views, it is ambiguous whether it is 'designer' or 'client/visitor'. This
fractured identity (designer/client) of the implied subject of the text means that there is
no voice of final authority. In this sense, *Yuan ye* is not a professional text in which the
voice of authority belongs unequivocally to the designer. In effect, the text continues the
equivocation of *zhuren*, owner and he-who-can-direct introduced in the first chapter of
Yuan ye. One has to understand here the mutuality of agent and act, designer and
designing.[19] The designer does the designing, but the designing also 'does' the
designer, i.e. the designer is 'actualised' as designer in the making of a particular
garden. Becoming a designer occurs *pari passu* with the act of designing. It is not a
question of *being* a designer by virtue of a pre-established capacity to design, derived
from a text such as *Yuan ye*.

It might now be more easy to understand why *Yuan ye* tells us that 'borrowing
views' is the most important aspect of garden design. The final chapter shows that it
pertains to the heart of the creative moment in garden design. It involves a meandering
thinking that binds here and there, far and near, then and now, inner sentiment and
external scene, which one undergoes more than understands. This is not a thinking that
deals with univocal concepts, logical argumentation and the application of principles, but
a metaphorical and historical thinking that eschews theoretical abstraction in favour of
the allusive language of concrete particulars.

Concluding remarks

It is apparent from the foregoing discussion that the final chapter of *Yuan ye* raises issues such as the parity between garden designer and visitor, the role of poetic language and memory in the construction of landscape experiences, the shock of the new versus the refreshing freshness, and so on. To the extent that these themes can be recognised as cognate with many aspects of contemporary thinking in architecture and landscape architecture, I would argue that *Yuan ye* might have a role to play in enriching contemporary design culture.

However, it would be a mistake to imagine that, in matters of cross-cultural exchange, Chinese writings on gardens represent a simple plenitude of insights for appropriation. Rather, the Chinese tradition faces a danger, and cross-cultural exchange can provide much needed stimulation in confronting a serious problem: the peripatetic thinking that I have highlighted in the final chapter of *Yuan ye* has the danger of falling from the fresh to the banal, from subtlety to clichés as it attempts to renovate the old and familiar through the fresh. The atrophy of thought here takes the form of the repetition of clichés and the enumeration of facts, staying on the immediate level of information. A new burst of scholarly writings on *Yuan ye* appeared in the 1980s. There has been a tendency to focus on a few selected phrases and ideas in the treatise, and to discuss their importance by repeating the original framework of discussion.[20] Over time, there has been a tendency to focus on content at the expense of an awareness of the meandering thinking that animates it, so that the consonance of topic and mode of operation that has been foregrounded above has often been overlooked. It is here that the conceptual resources of the Western tradition has a special pertinence, for it offers a language that allows us some distance from the Chinese performative thinking and can stimulate new readings that refresh one's sensitivity for yet other new readings.

Acknowledgements

The ideas of this chapter were first explored in conversation with Michel Conan and David L. Hall, and with students in my course on Chinese gardens at the University of Pennsylvania, Philadelphia, in 1998. I owe much to the insights and advice that I received from them. I am indebted to Jan Birksted for providing the opportunity to present the first draft of this chapter at the conference of the Association of Art Historians (UK) in the University of Exeter in April 1998. A second draft was presented at a seminar in the Direction de l'Architecture in Paris in June 1998. For valuable comments and discussion, I am grateful to Françoise Ged, Observatoire de l'Architecture de la Chine contemporaine, who organised the seminar, and to the discussants that she invited: Che Bing Chiu, Yolande Escande and Antoine Gournay.

Stanislaus Fung
Self, scene and action: the final
chapter of *Yuan ye*

Notes

1 Knowledge of *Yuan ye* relies principally on the Ming printed edition now in the collection of the Naikaku Bunko, Tokyo.

2 *Yuan ye zhu shi*, annotated edn by Chen Zhi (Beijing: Zhongguo jianzhu gongye chubanshe, 1979; revd edn 1988). Also Zhang Jiaji, *Yuan ye quan shi* (Taiyuan: Shanxi renmin chubanshe, 1993).

3 Ji Cheng, *Yuanye: Le traité du jardin*, trans. Che Bing Chiu [Qiu Zhiping]. Collections jardins et paysages (Besançon: Les Éditions de l'Imprimeur, 1997).

4 Stanislaus Fung, 'Body and appropriateness in *Yuan ye*', *Intersight*, 4 (1997), pp. 84–91.

5 Stanislaus Fung, 'Here and there in *Yuan ye*', *Studies in the History of Gardens & Designed Landscapes*, 19/1 (1999), 36–45.

6 Wu Kuang-ming, *On Chinese Body Thinking: A Cultural Hermeneutic* (Leiden: E. J. Brill, 1997); *idem*, 'Spatiotemporal interpenetration in Chinese thinking', in *Time and Space in Chinese Culture*, ed. Huang Chun-Chieh and Erik Zürcher (Leiden: E. J. Brill, 1995), pp. 17–44.

7 Zhang, *Yuan ye quan shi*, p. 325.

8 Wu, *On Chinese Body Thinking*, p. 196.

9 Zhang, *Yuan ye quan shi*, pp. 133–134. See also Zhao Guangchao, *Bu zhi Zhongguo mu jianzhu* (Xianggang: Sanlian shudian, 2000), p. 171.

10 Zhao Yihe, "Yuan ye, jiejing' shizhi', in *Zhonghua gu jianzhu*, ed. Zhongguo kexue-yuan. Zhonghua gu jianzhu yanjiushe, 13–18 (Beijing: Zhongguo kexue jishu chubanshe, 1990).

11 Zhao, "Yuan ye, jiejing' shizhi', p. 14.

12 *Ibid.*, 15.

13 Wu, *On Chinese Body Thinking*, p. 197.

14 Zhang, *Yuan ye quan shi*, p. 326.

15 Wu, 'Spatiotemporal interpenetration in Chinese thinking', p. 19.

16 *Ibid.*, p. 21.

17 Wu, *On Chinese Body Thinking*, p. 321.

18 Cao Xun, 'Ji Cheng yanjiu', *Jianzhushi*, 13 (December 1982), pp. 1–16.

19 Fung, 'Body and appropriateness in *Yuan ye*'.

20 For example, Yu Weiguo, 'Chong du *Yuan ye* sui bi', *Jianzhushi*, 13 (December 1982), pp. 17–22.

Alessandra Ponte

9   The house of light and entropy: inhabiting the American desert

I know the deserts, their deserts, better than they do, since they turn their backs on their own space as the Greeks turned their backs on the sea, and I get to know more about the concrete, social life of America from the desert than I ever would from official or intellectual gatherings. American culture is heir to the deserts .... (Jean Baudrillard, 1988)[1]

It was not only Jean Baudrillard. It is, rather, a short circuit. Baudrillard and Umberto Eco and then an article in *Art Forum*, and this time written by an American, Jane Tompkins (the article later became a chapter in a best seller on the genre of the western in literature and cinema). Tompkins considered why the western privileged the desert: 'It chooses the desert because its clean, spare lines, lucid spaces, and absence of ornament bring it closer to the abstract austerities of modern architectural design than any other kind of landscape would.'[2] It is not so much the meaning of the phrase that is surprising, but rather finding the concepts of western, desert, architecture and modern side by side. Generally, one studies the western the better to understand the role of the landscape in the formation of American culture. So, one thinks about America's past. One tries to analyse how the epic or tragic genres were manipulated and utilised to construct a mythical rather than a historical past. One looks upon the heroes of the western as an Odysseus and an Aeneas: the western heroes' wanderings and incidents along the way seemed aimed at weaving a geography, thereby constructing a topology of these new spaces, just as the wanderings and the adventures of both Odysseus and Aeneas had designed the map of the Mediterranean. In this context, the desert is just one of the possible landscapes, a fact confirmed by the presence, in both literature and film, of many other scenarios, such as prairies, mountains, lagoons and rivers. On the other hand, one cannot deny the automatic parallel drawn between the American desert and the western from the director John Ford onward. There is good reason for this. The desert in the western is a bare, wild, inexorable and fierce place, where one meets only Indians and criminals; literally, beings living outside civilisation and law. The perfect scene for representation of the epic imposition of order. The anthropomorphised

137

Alessandra Ponte
The house of light and entropy:
inhabiting the American desert

9.1 P. Reyner Banham in the desert

landscape represents another enemy that the hero must defeat. Ford speaks of the desert as the main protagonist of his films.[3] Again, in this logic, architecture and modernity had no place.

But what kind of modern architecture is being discussed? Tompkins maintains that it is a *monumental* and *monolithic* architecture. This is interesting; in fact, it is understandable in historical terms: the idea of a natural monument has a long tradition in the culture of the Western world. Nevertheless, the monument and the monolith are, to say the least, problematic figures for the modern. Thus, it might be useful to read what P. Reyner Banham, historian and critic of modern architecture, has to say of the American desert:

> … The desert measurably offers immeasurable space. It is therefore an environment in which 'Modern Man' ought to feel at home — his modern painting, as in the works of [Piet] Mondrian, implies a space that extends beyond the confines of the canvas; his modern architecture, as in the works of [Ludwig] Mies van der Rohe, is a rectangular partition of a regular but infinite space; its ideal inhabitants, the sculptures of [Alberto] Giacometti stalking metaphysically through that space as far as it infinitely extends. And modern man's last frontier of exploration, in case you'd forgotten, is space itself — which is how we came to be stumbling about lunar landscapes that are uncomfortably like the desert of the earth.[4]

Banham confirms some terms of the equation (the desert as a space of modernity) and adds new ones: the domestic and the future. The desert is the place where modern man should feel at home. (Note, however, that Banham's 'modern man' is not the average man: he cites Mondrian, Giacometti, Mies van der Rohe.) The desert resembles both the alien surroundings discovered by space exploration and those described by science fiction, whose themes Banham often revisits.

Monument/house: the architecture of the modern struggles with these two irreconcilable terms. Could one hypothesise that the American desert is the place where this opposition is resolved or sublimated? Could it be that to inhabit the modern means to inhabit this desert that is also, and simultaneously, the stage on which the drama of the past unfolds and future events are projected? The American desert seems the place where past and future collapse into the present; it is also the place where the primitive and the futurist inhabit monumentality.

Two paintings by Mark Tansey: *Robbe-Grillet Cleansing Every Object in Sight* (1981) and *Purity Test* (1982). In the first of the two monochromatic canvases, the French writer and filmmaker Alain Robbe-Grillet, equipped with bucket and brush, kneels in the middle of the desert and scrubs the stones strewn across the ground. Looking more closely, one realises that what look like stones are not stones at all, but miniature monuments (Stonehenge, the Sphinx, the monoliths of Monument Valley, and so on), elementary forms and icons of various types. Judi Freedman, in a commentary on Tansey's works, writes: 'Through his determined scrubbing, Robbe-Grillet attempts to strip these stones of their content, no doubt a reference to his wish to remove hidden meanings from every object.'[5] In *Purity Test*, a group of Indians on horseback looks at Robert Smithson's *Spiral Jetty* (1970) from a rocky promontory. About this canvas Freedman writes: 'Smithson had sought to create a pure image. The Indians, unaware of the spiral's function as a work of art, attempt to decipher it as a symbol instead. These Indians and *Spiral Jetty* clearly did not coexist; instead they come together as two of Tansey's trajectories, not precisely oppositions but irreconcilable forces that meet on a plane.'[6] Smithson probably did not exactly intend to create a pure image, but this will be addressed below. What is interesting in Tansey's paintings is how the American desert becomes the 'plane' on which irreconcilable forces meet: domesticity and monumentality, past and future, primitive and civilised, art and nature.

Even if Tansey appears to confirm these hypotheses, he does not help in explaining them. Thus, one starts all over.

The house of light

> But the work I do is with light itself and perception. It is not about those issues; it
> deals with them directly in a non vicarious manner so that it is about your seeing,
> about your perceiving. It is about light being present in a situation where you are,
> rather than a record of light or an experience of seeing from another situation.
> (James Turrell, 1985)[7]

In 1898, John Charles van Dyke, Professor of Art History at Rutgers University, sick with asthma, ventured into the great American deserts seeking relief in their dry climate. He wandered for three years, alone, suffering more and more, and plagued by bouts of fever, to come out of the desert in 1901 with a manuscript for *The Desert*, the first celebration of the American desert and a future cult book.[8]

One can accept the reasons that cause van Dyke to wander through the desert. 'I was just ill enough', he writes in his autobiography, 'not to care about perils and morbid enough to prefer dying in the sand, alone, to passing out in a hotel with a room maid weeping at the foot of the bed.'[9] It is more difficult to understand why he stays in the desert, since his health worsens instead of improving and the solitude torments him. Van Dyke presents it as an inescapable fate: '… I began to long for the sight of familiar faces, and the sounds of friendly voices. Still I kept on alone. There seemed no alternative.'[10] The same things that van Dyke himself describes as the horrors of the desert transform it into the only place where it is possible for him to survive — or is it perhaps the only place where it is possible for him to *live*? 'The weird solitude', he explains in *The Desert*, 'the great silence, the grim desolation, are the very things with which every desert wanderer eventually falls in love. You think that very strange perhaps? Well, the beauty of the ugly was sometime a paradox, but to-day people admit its truth; and the grandeur of the desolate is just as paradoxical, yet the desert gives it proof.'[11]

This is clearly the writing of an art critic. From the seventeenth century on one of the major preoccupations of aesthetic theory has been to explain the 'beauty of the ugly'. The elaboration of the definitions of the Picturesque and the Sublime identified sources for the pleasure derived from the contemplation of the terrible scenes offered by an implacable nature (inaccessible peaks, stormy seas, immeasurable chasms, and so on) and of the signs caused by the painful passing of time, or by poverty (wrinkled faces, corroded rocks, ruins, twisted trunks, beggars, rags, and so on). Thus, van Dyke speaks as a connoisseur but proposes something more interesting than the gratifying description of a 'difficult' landscape. He introduces other conditions necessary for enjoyment. First, the present, the now, the particular historical moment; then himself as historical subject. Others before him could not have appreciated that desert; comparing his own capabilities of perception with those of the farmers and the Indians who lived on the fringes of the arid and desolate areas of the great American desert, van Dyke comments: 'A sensitive feeling for sound, or form, or color, an impressionable nervous organization, do not belong to the man with the hoe, much less to the man with the bow. It is to be feared that they are indicative of some physical degeneration, some decline in bone and muscle, some abnormal development of emotional nature. They travel side by side with high civilisation and are the premonitory symptoms of racial decay.'[12]

He is forced into the desert by two ailments, the first physical (his respiratory difficulty), the second more subtle and insidious: discontentment with society. Certainly the dates correspond. Only a few years before, in 1893, the historian Frederick Jackson Turner, in his famous speech given to the American Historical Association during the World's Columbian Exposition in Chicago, had declared the frontier closed and the conquest of the 'greatest gift' ever offered to civilised man — the wild territory of the West from the Alleghenies to the Pacific — completed. The destiny of America was sealed. Certainly the great expositions celebrated not only the taming of the 'Wild West', but also the rapid industrialisation of the country, the growth in urbanisation, the incredible changes in the standard of living brought about by mechanisation. On the other hand, nationalism and the corresponding faith in industry, in the governmental system, and in the arts called upon to celebrate and represent them were challenged by the harsh realities that were a result of those same changes.[13] There were also pernicious dangers — dangerous uncertainties undermining that same American individuality. As Turner himself had explained, was it not the frontier that had formed the character of the ideal American citizen? Now that the glory of victory and the strenuous battle to conquer the land were over, what would forge men's spirits as strongly and purely? Would not this 'high civilisation', these new and immense riches provoke nausea, weariness and waste, weakening the fibre of the race? This is what van Dyke believed. In *The Money God* (1908), a work in which he sharply criticises contemporary American society from a socio-economic and moral standpoint, van Dyke dedicates an entire chapter (appropriately titled 'Discontent') to a list of the evils that afflict the newly rich: boredom, vacuity, neurasthenia and suicidal tendencies.[14]

Van Dyke is the American who moves with ease in the exclusive salons of the East and yet simultaneously declares that only in the desert does he truly feel at home. In *The Open Spaces: Incidents of Nights and Days Under the Blue Sky* (1922) he writes: 'What a strange feeling, sleeping under the wide sky, that you belong only to the

Alessandra Ponte
The house of light and entropy:
inhabiting the American desert

142

Cirrus, cumulus, and r

9.2 'Cirrus, Cumulus and Nimbus over Desert Mountains' in van Dykes *The Desert*

over desert mountains.

143

Alessandra Ponte
The house of light and entropy:
inhabiting the American desert

universe. You are back to your habitat, to your original environment, to your native heritage. With that feeling you snuggle down in your blankets content to let ambitions slip and the glory of the world pass by you. . . . At last you are free. You are at home in the infinite, and your possessions, your government, your people dwindle away into needle-points of insignificance.'[15] It would be unjust, however, to reduce van Dyke's living in the desert to an escape from civilisation or a 'nostalgic' return to the roots of the American experience. In this case the desert would simply be revalued as the last 'wild' space left in America, whereas his encounter with this area has more of the character of an aesthetic revelation. *The Desert* belongs in the wider context of the conception of the work of art previously elaborated by van Dyke.

The Desert originally had a subtitle that has strangely disappeared in the most recent reprints. The complete title of the 1901 edition is *The Desert: Further Studies in Natural Appearances*. The 'further' refers to a previous work by van Dyke, namely *Nature for Its Own Sake: First Studies in Natural Appearances* (1898), which in turn represented the continuation of a discussion begun some years earlier in *Art for Art's Sake: Seven University Lectures on the Technical Beauties of Paintings* (1893). In the Introduction to this last, van Dyke asserts his intention of writing on the subject of painting from the artist's point of view, ignoring the opinions of the metaphysicians and the public. He proceeds by clarifying the greatest misunderstanding between the artist and the public. The average person, van Dyke explains, asks for the expression of 'ideas' or 'stories' in painting without appreciating the '. . . pictorial beauty which of itself is the primary aim of all painting'.[16] The painter is neither writer, scientist, philosopher, historian nor preacher; he does not possess the same qualities and background, nor does he strive for the same goals. 'As a Painter', writes van Dyke, 'he has one sense and one faculty, both of which, by the necessities of his calling, are perhaps abnormally developed. The sense is that of sight, and the training of it has enabled him to see more beauties and deeper meanings than the great majority of mankind. The faculty lies in his ability to make known, to reveal to mankind, these discovered beauties and imports of nature by the means of form, color, and their modifications.'[17] The artist does not reason; he observes. The artist does not recount what he thinks abstractly but presents what he sees concretely. According to this logic, landscape painting, a pure play of forms and colors, light and shadow in which even the title is superfluous to complete 'pictorial' enjoyment, is celebrated as the highest practicable genre while that of history is degraded as 'illustration'. Van Dyke admits that the idea exists in painting but he specifies that the 'pictorial idea' is understandable only through the sense of sight to the exclusion of all the other senses and functions as a stimulant to our emotions more than to our intellect.

If the artists of Greece had been forced to represent the ideal and those of the Renaissance to become educators and decorators, modern art has become the 'means of sympathetic and emotional expression given to the individual man'.[18] In van Dyke's discussion such a change justifies 'that essentially modern product, the landscape',[19] one that differs from the classical or romantic landscape in which the painter gleaned his subject matter from the historian, from the poet, from the novelist. In the past, for example, 'The desert existed not so much for its white light, rising heat, and waving atmosphere, as for the home of the roaming lion, or the treacherous highway of the winding Bedouin caravan.'[20] The contemporary painter has rejected such associations to concentrate solely on the beauty of form and color in a nature considered independently of human actions.

It is tempting to trace a parallel between van Dyke's oeuvre and biography and those of his more famous contemporary Bernard Berenson. Both are Americans. Both write and travel a great deal. Both can be considered 'connoisseurs' rather than art historians. It is known how Berenson combined a literary criticism modelled after that of Walter Pater with the scientific methods of Morelli to fashion innovative attributions. Van Dyke, with equal fastidiousness, presented to the American public (in twelve slim volumes published in 1914 with the title *New Guides to Old Masters*) the most important collections of paintings conserved in European museums. In 1923, with *Rembrandt and His School*, he scandalised both critics and collectors by reducing the nearly eighty paintings traditionally attributed to Rembrandt to fifty, basing his findings on the minute observation of microscopic technical and stylistic discrepancies. Ernst H. Gombrich, Roberto Salvini and many others have demonstrated that Berenson's oeuvre must be placed within the milieu of the theories of visual perception developed in the aesthetics of Konrad Fiedler, Adolf von Hildebrand, Alois Riegl and Heinrich Wolfflin.[21] The sources of the 'pure visibility' of van Dyke (*Sichtbarkeit* in the terms of the Viennese school) are not as clear.[22] As a means of maintaining the independence of his own impressions about the work of art, van Dyke intentionally refused to read contemporary literature. Nevertheless, he continually cited John Ruskin and seemed to consider him much more than just a simple point of reference.

The obsession with sight, the almost hallucinatory concentration of the gaze had already been one of the central and more modern elements of Ruskin's thought. Ruskin has already been spoken of as a 'visibilist' before the letter, and Rosalind Krauss recently made Ruskin's childhood the point of departure for a study on modernism and the modernist vocation of looking.[23] For Ruskin the child, 'playing' meant the fascinated and fixed observation of the decorative motifs of the drapes and the carpets at home. The total polarisation of the essence of being in sight, which he theorised and practised throughout his career, is an open window on abstraction. The world of tangibles and meanings dissolves into pure form and color. Ruskin invoked *the innocent eye*: 'The perception of solid Form is entirely a matter of experience. We see nothing but flat colours; and it is only by a series of experiments that we find out that a stain of black or grey indicates the dark side of solid substance, or that a faint hue indicates that the object in which it appears is far away. The whole technical power of painting depends on our recovery of what may be called the *innocence of the eye*; that is to say, of a sort of childish perception of these flat stains of colour, merely as such, without consciousness of what they signify, — as a blind man would see them if suddenly gifted with sight.'[24]

He does not seek this visual innocence only in painting. In the end, for Ruskin, the act of seeing was more important than the process of reproducing. In *The Elements of*

145

Alessandra Ponte
The house of light and entropy:
inhabiting the American desert

Drawing he affirmed: 'I believe that the sight is a more important thing than the drawing; and I would rather teach drawing that my pupils learn to love Nature, than teach the looking at Nature that they may learn to draw.'[25] Observing nature is an act closer to reading than to drawing; a way of reading, however, in which the characters take on the appearance of decorative, symbolic and hieroglyphic motifs. So, for Ruskin, writing and travelling are the actions that correspond to seeing. To travel means to see, to see implies to describe, 'as plainly as possible', exactly that which one sees.[26] This is Ruskin's mission. This is the lesson mastered by van Dyke.

There remains, however, a fundamental difference between Ruskin and van Dyke. Even though he preaches the abstraction of the gaze, its concentration on pure form and pure color, Ruskin does not relinquish theorising a superior level of 'vision' and interpretation in which nature, beings and things become invested with symbolic significance. Ruskin cannot ignore the moral question, nor can he forget his own religious conception of nature. The pleasure obtained from his burning visual passion is justified by the fact that observing nature for Ruskin means observing God and all His works. Seeing is also an act of adoration. It is known how much Ruskin was perturbed by the scientific thought of the time that distanced itself more and more from the biblical version of creation. In spite of his love for geology, he asked that the geologists leave him in peace. He claimed to hear the clinking of their hammers at the end of every line of the Bible.

Van Dyke looks at nature for nature, with no sentimentality. In the Introduction to *Nature for Its Own Sake*, he explains:

> The word 'Nature,' as it is used in these pages, does not comprehend animal life in any form whatever. It is applied only to lights, skies, clouds, waters, lands, foliage.... Nature is neither classic nor romantic; it is simply — nature. Nor is it, as some would have us to think, a sympathetic friend of mankind endowed with semi-human emotions. Mountains do not 'frown,' trees do not 'weep,' nor do skies 'smile;' they are quite incapable of doing so. Indeed, so far as any sympathy with humanity is concerned, 'the last of thy brothers might vanish from the face of the earth, and not a needle of the pine branches would tremble.'[27]

146

Nature for Its Own Sake is not meant for painters. The question of representation has been completely surpassed in that everything is already there, present: a scene whose elements, colors, and lights need not be selected or rearranged. After having dispensed with the question of meaning — nature, like art, needs no interpretation because it has no hidden thoughts and teaches nothing — van Dyke eliminates the mediating figure of the painter. What remains is the observer or, better yet, the eye of the observer. In these books in which van Dyke systematically explores nature, the narrator has neither a body nor any sense other than that of sight. Heat, cold, thirst, hunger, encounters, dialogues, desires: everything is suppressed to give room to the 'plain description' of what is seen. Numerous scientific observations are utilised to clarify the mechanisms of perception: digressions on the theme of refraction, reflections on the effects of humidity in the air, considerations of the processes of erosion that have brought to light materials of a certain tonality, analyses of the changing of colors brought on by the shifting angles of the light rays with the rising and the setting of the sun. Van Dyke describes what *appears*. He knows the current thesis on the mechanism of perception: he cites Charles Blanc, Eugène Chevreul, and the experiments of the French Impressionists.

The American desert is the house of light and color. This is the great aesthetic revelation that van Dyke experienced. Everything in the desert is coloured, even the air. Van Dyke speaks of yellow, saffron-coloured, rose-coloured, azure, steel blue, ruby-red, topaz, lilac, and violet air. The colours are saturated, so intense as to appear distinct from any substance. The absence of humidity and the presence of dust particles suspended in the air create dense fields of color completely independent of the form and real position of things. The desert is also the house of illusions. A whole chapter of *The Desert* is dedicated to them, and it is exactly the improbability and the abstraction of these illusions that enchants van Dyke: 'And there we have come back again to that beauty in landscape which lies not in the lines of mountain, valley and plain, but in the almost formless masses of color and light.'[28] Living in the desert means inhabiting a space defined by light, imbued with color. The desert is the house of pure visibility; this is why van Dyke feels at home there. Total triumph of the visible. Complete evacuation of meaning. Art/Nature: no longer in opposition, but a simultaneous happening. On the 'plain' of the desert the mediating figure of the painter becomes unnecessary: there is no need for imitation or representation. The 'innocent gaze' of modern man recognises and inhabits this space as a space of pure perception, an artistic space and no longer a natural one. The nature of the desert is in fact denatured by a gaze that no longer 'reads' form and its meaning but strives to perceive only the abstraction of light and color.

It has been said that van Dyke's entering the desert and losing himself in fascination corresponds to entering and losing oneself in the infinite galleries of the greatest of all museums. I believe instead that van Dyke stepped into a space that could be entered only in that particular historical moment: the impossible space of representation. His eye does not see but 'inhabits' light and color. It seems that this is what impelled the first generation of American modernist artists to go to the desert. For Georgia O'Keeffe it was the only possible home. In the 1920s she wrote from Taos, New Mexico: 'I am West again and it is as fine as I remembered it — maybe finer — There is nothing to say about it except the fact that for me it is the only place.'[29] The desert, she continued is *'painting country*. Out here, half your work is done for you.'[30] A reaction confirmed in the negative by Stuart Davis: 'I spent three or four months there [New Mexico] in 1923 — until late fall — but did not do much work because the place itself is so interesting. I don't think you could do much work there except in a literal way, because the place is always there in such a dominating way. You always have to look at it.'[31]

147

First possible conclusion

Q. What do you mean by an architecture of space?
A. I am interested in the weights, pressures, and feeling of the light inhabiting space itself and in seeing this atmosphere rather than the walls.

Alessandra Ponte
The house of light and entropy:
inhabiting the American desert

Q. Are you talking about volume?

A. Atmosphere is volume, but it is within volume. Seeing volume as a whole is one thing, but there are densities and structuring within a space that have to do with a penetration of vision and a way of seeing into it.

Q. Seeing, as opposed to being inside it?

A. You can inhabit a space with consciousness without physically entering it, as in a dream. You can be in it physically and see it in that manner also. But whether you're in a space and looking at it or outside and looking into it, it still has qualities of atmosphere, density, and grain so that your vision will penetrate differently in some areas than others. Some areas will be more translucent or more opaque, and other areas will be free to the penetration of vision.

...

Q. Are there references for the use of color or density of light or the particular experience you're creating? It is something that you have seen elsewhere or experienced before?

A. A lucid dream or a flight through deep, clear blue skies of winter in northern Arizona — experiences like these I use as source.... Spaces within space, not necessarily delineated by cloud formations or storms or things like that, but by light qualities, by seeing, and by the nature of the air in certain areas.
(interview with James Turrell, 1985)[32]

It is possible to align minimalist criticism of the museum and architecture with the choice of the American desert as the site for works of art that, as James Turrell explains, are not 'objects that go up an elevator into an eastside apartment'.[33] The work of art is no longer subordinated to or contained by an architecture, be it that of the museum or of the house, but creates in and of itself an atmospheric architecture intended to be inhabited by light and by sight. Turrell has been at work for years on the construction (reconstruction?) of Roden Crater in the Painted Desert of Arizona. He utilises a natural formation, the cone of an extinct volcano to create a 'powerful place'. A series of spaces — 'bunkers' excavated in the crater — will be filled with light. Roden Crater is not just an invitation for one to redefine one's notions about art, architecture and living through the mere use and manipulation of light and space. It will be an architecture suspended between geological time and astronomical time. Situated in a desert that 'uncovers an enormous quantity of time', the crater will become a celestial observatory.[34] Balanced between a remote past and an infinite future Roden Crater poses questions about its essence: is Turrell restoring the ruins of an ancient natural monument or is he creating an impossible monument to the future? One cannot help but recall the 'New Monuments' of Smithson.

The house of entropy

I have a ranch on the north end of the range overlooking the Rio Grande called Ayala de Chinati. This has two small houses which I've thought a lot about, but done little about, since I hate to damage the land around them. Here, everywhere, the destruction of new land is a brutality. Nearby a man bought a nearly untouched ranch 3 or 4 years ago, bulldozed roads everywhere so he could shoot deer without walking and last fall died. (Donald Judd)[35]

It seems that in the desert it is difficult to concentrate on architecture in the present and independent of its surroundings. The same can be said about the landscape. One looks at the ground and at the boulders and thinks of their past and their future: this is perhaps because the desert seems to be a lesson in geology. There are no trees, bushes, grasses or mirrors of water to dress the skeleton of the earth. There is no sign of youth or laughter, nothing of the reassuring or the picturesque. There are only bare bones on which it is easy to read the processes of erosion and calcification. And the time spans are vast; they are counted a thousand years at a time. How long did it take to dig this canyon? How long did it take to pulverise the less resistant rock surrounding the monoliths of Monument Valley? How long did it take to dry up what was once a whole sea on whose banks rose cities and villages?

One of the most beautiful chapters of *The Desert* describes in extraordinarily poetic and agonising terms the process of the evaporation of an ancient sea (known today as the Salton Sea) that left behind it a chain of beaches upon which can be seen the traces of settlements created and then abandoned in the search for water. Van Dyke speaks of the incredible beauty of the light and colours perceived from the bottom of its dried basin. This is one of the landscapes that most fascinates Banham, an aficionado of van Dyke. The strange thing is that Banham, like everyone else, cannot verify the truth of van Dyke's statements. Owing to accidents during drainage and irrigation projects, the waters of the Colorado River flooded the ancient sea from 1905 to 1907 – that is to say, shortly after the publication of *The Desert*. Van Dyke had foreseen the vulnerability of that precarious beauty. Banham is ambivalent about the event. He complains vaguely about this casual destructive action, but he cannot quite condemn it: 'Salton Sea, calm as death under its veil of mist, reflecting the stranded trivia of human construction in its mirror-smooth surface. This accidental sea may indeed be – Hell, no. It *is*! – as beautiful as the back shores of the Venetian Lagoons. But it is not the same beauty. It will be forever shot through with the irony that this beauty is the product of a careless human ambition to produce something entirely different.'[36]

From 1963 to 1964, J. G. Ballard wrote *The Drought* (1965), the account of an ecological cataclysm, one easily imaginable in the near future. In the story the accumulation of pollution had caused the formation of a film on the surface of the seas and oceans of the earth, which impeded the evaporation of water and thus also the formation of clouds and rain. The catastrophic drought that resulted was experienced by the reader through the eyes of the protagonist, Dr Charles Ramson, who witnessed the drying up of the large river next to which rose the city in which he lived. The area was evacuated and Ramson was among the last to leave. At first he hoped to isolate himself in the new sterile lands, 'putting an end to time and its erosions'.[37] He lived in a

Alessandra Ponte
The house of light and entropy:
inhabiting the American desert

houseboat, marooned on the sand, in which he collected mementoes. The most important of these was a paperweight of limestone that as a child he had cut out from the gypsum of a hill, the shell fossil imprisoned in the surface of which carries a 'quantum of jurassic time, like a jewel'. In the end he is forced to depart, leaving the city prey to fires and partially submerged in the sand. Fish, birds and human beings have perished by the thousands. His departure is the beginning of a long voyage toward the 'bitter sea', in search of water but without possibility of salvation. At the end of the story, Ramson returns and ponders the meaning of his return journey. Initially he believes he is returning to the past to take up the thread of his previous life. He then realises that the dry river bed is carrying him in the opposite direction: 'in the opposite direction, forward into zones of time future where the unresolved residues of the past would appear smoothed and rounded, muffled by the detritus of time, like images in a clouded mirror. Perhaps these residues were the sole elements contained in the future, and would have the bizarre and fragmented quality of the debris through which he was now walking. None the less they would all be merged and resolved in the soft dust of the drained bed.'[38] The novel ends with Ramson entering a state of living death, and he never realises that it has begun to rain again.

Ballard has never really visited America. In an autobiographical fragment he explains that, all things considered, he preferred not having seen it; in this way he succeeded in avoiding all the clichés of the American landscape in his stories: 'I had to invent my own landscape, and I invented something which was much truer to myself and also much closer to the Surrealists (who were my main inspiration). In fact, I had to invent my own America.'[39] It is unsettling to realise just how much this imagined America is immediately recognisable and believable; the coincidence between the description of the progression of the drought in van Dyke and in Ballard is perturbing up to the last 'surreal' detail: the basin of the Salton Sea becomes accidentally inundated and Ramson does not realise that it has begun to rain again. Both accounts are pervaded by a sense of ineluctability and inanity. The landscape that van Dyke sees and the one that Ballard imagines seem suspended, like Turrell's crater, between the past and the future, between geology and astronomy. This is not to say that they are in the present; rather, they create a present in which the past and the future collapse on the plain (so to speak) of the desert.

The Surrealists are not Ballard's only inspiration. In 1956 when he is still just beginning his career as a writer of science fiction, the famous Independent Group exhibition, *This Is Tomorrow*, opened in London. Science fiction, with other images of popular culture after the Second World War, was a central part of the exhibition and had from the beginning fascinated the members of the Independent Group: Eduardo Paolozzi, Richard Hamilton, John Voelcker, John McHale, Peter and Alison Smithson, and Reyner Banham.[40] Ballard already knew the group; like them, he was interested in looking at consumer goods, advertising images, popular cinema and 'the media landscape' with a new eye. It seemed to him that the research of the Group had something in common with that of the new science fiction. This was what impelled him to visit *This Is Tomorrow*. Years later, he still remembered very clearly the impact of the show: 'Richard Hamilton had on show his famous little painting.... And there were a lot of other Pop artifacts there, which impressed me a great deal. It struck me that these were the sorts of concerns that the SF writer should be interested in. Science Fiction should be concerned with the here and now, not with alien planets but with what was going on in the world in the mid-'50s.'[41] Through the exhibit Ballard became friendly with Paolozzi, Hamilton and Banham.

Even though Ballard is interested in the experiments of the Group, he disdained the science fiction sources utilised by it. He does not like the robots, the spaceships, the futuristic weapons and technology, or the genre of space fantasy. He focussed on the processes of deterioration and transformation of the environment and on how they affected their inhabitants, as in *The Drought*, or in *Terminal Beach* (in which the protagonist, the anti-hero Traven, goes to and stays in the deserted place where a nuclear bomb has exploded), or again in *The Cage of Sand* (set in a Florida, which has become a desert). Ballard's gaze is an entropic one. The desert that fascinates him is that of *Mad Max II: The Road Warrior*, by George Miller (1981) and not that of *Star Wars*, by George Lucas (1977). It is the desert after a catastrophe, in which can be seen the signs, traces and monuments of a banal, everyday, domestic past (the paperweight with the imprisoned fossil, a jewel of time). It is the desert of de-evolution. Ballard's desert is populated; strange figures roam it, archaeologists of the future. They unearth residues of the present — of their present and of ours: cars, machines, houses. They are uncertain; like Ramson, they do not know whether they are contemplating their past or their future.

Smithson, in America in the 1960s, like the Independent Group in England in the 1950s, used science fiction, including Ballard's, to formulate a new aesthetic. It is known that Smithson opened his famous paper 'Entropy and the new monuments' with a quote from a science fiction novel by John Taine, *The Time Stream*: 'On rising to my feet, and peering across the green glow on the desert, I perceived that the monument against which I had slept, was but one of thousands. Before me stretched long parallel avenues, clear to the far horizon, of similar broad, low pillars.'[42] For Smithson, the images evoked by Taine were not science fiction; instead, they suggested a new kind of monumentality that had much in common with the works of Donald Judd, Robert Morris, Sol LeWitt and Dan Flavin. The new monuments celebrated an 'inactive history', the future as the 'obsolete in reverse', the universe transformed into an 'all-encompassing sameness'. What in physics is called entropy. (LeWitt prefers the term 'sub-monumental', especially when referring to his proposal to insert a fragment of goldwork by Benvenuto Cellini in a block of cement; is this Ballard's fossil?).

Less well known is the beginning section of 'The artist as site-seer or a dintorphic essay', a work of Smithson's that long remained unpublished. Here, Smithson quotes Ballard's *Terminal Beach*: 'The system of megaliths now provided a complete substitute for those functions of his mind which gave to it its sense of the sustained rational order of time and space....'[43] Smithson is interested in the recurring appearance of monoliths in Ballard's desert, in particular those described in another story, *The Waiting Ground*. There, inscriptions are chiselled into great rectangles of stone. They are, Smithson explains by quoting Ballard, 'strings of meaningless ciphers ... intricate cuneiform glyphics … minute carved symbols … odd cross-hatched symbols that seemed to be numerals'.[44] He asks himself if there is a language at the root of these monuments, just as mathematics lies at the root of geometry. The characters are enigmatic. Do they allude to a lost language of the past or one readable in the future? Of what is the monumental monolith a memory? Smithson explains that it is a monolith to whose aesthetic we have been accustomed by 'The much denigrated architecture of Park Avenue known as "cold glass boxes," along with the Manneristic modernity of Philip Johnson, [which] have helped to foster the entropic mood.'[45] What is *Spiral Jetty*'s perfect geometry a memory of, with its complex crystalline formation destined to disappear in a post-apocalyptic landscape? A future scenario that dissolves in a prehistoric, deserted past? Smithson's spiral is enigmatic, like the monolith of Stanley Kubrik's *2001: A Space Odyssey* (1968) that appears for the first time in the desert, at the dawn of civilisation, and then again in space in the age of spaceships.

It is strange that even though Banham knows and esteems Ballard, he does not relate Ballard's stories to the American desert or to the chain of entropic associations that Smithson, Judd, Michael Heizer and Walter DeMaria bring to bear on that scenario. Instead, Banham looks to Frank Herbert's *Dune* or Ray Bradbury's Martians. Strange, but not coincidental: Banham is not much interested in Land Art or Minimalism. He defines Smithson's sculptures in the desert as 'pure creative will exercised on a defenceless landscape'.[46] For Banham, the most spectacular artefact in the American desert is the solar telescope at Kitt Peak: 'it looks, so hugely and imperturbably elegant sitting there at the junction of earth and sky, humming busily to itself as all large enigmatic machines should. Its forms are as clean-cut as those of an abstract concept…. And it leaves an image of absolute clarity on the retina of memory, a monumental sign of human presence inscribed on a background of empty air, above a brown desert of unfathomable beauty.'[47] Compared with this: 'the desert earth works of sculptors like Robert Smithson, or John Heizer [*sic*] are trifles, as is the minimalist sculpture of an artist like Robert Morris. I happen to know that Morris is an admirer of Stonehenge, so that he might also see the point of all this as a henge of technology, shaped and textured very like one of his own sculptures, but multiplied not only by the sheer factor of size, but also by the factor of purpose whose absence cripples so much modern art.'[48] It seems that Banham's modernist moralism keeps him from grasping the extent to which these *earth works* obey the logic of the American desert.[49]

Yet Banham intuits the entropic fascination of the American desert. He roams the desert preoccupied with the aesthetics of its ruins, with the state of preservation of its monuments and the future of its buildings. He is fascinated by the meticulous perfection with which the train station of Kelso has been preserved, a perfection that renders it not so much an oasis in the desert as something preserved in a bubble beyond time. He compares it with the ungainly ruins of Marl Spring or of Government Hole, which he defines 'a sick joke'. He looks at Las Vegas, which had already fascinated Robert Venturi, Denise Scott Brown and Steven Izenour, as the symbol of the impermanence of man in the desert. It appears to him as an image from science fiction, a human encampment on a hostile planet, doomed to perish from the very beginning: 'it is already beginning to fade', writes Banham, 'as energy becomes more expensive and the architecture less inventive. It won't blow away in the night, but you begin to wish it might, because it will never make noble ruins, and it will never discover how to fade away gracefully.'[50] Banham offers many other examples, but two are particularly significant: those that refer to the architectures of Frank Lloyd Wright and of Paolo Soleri. This is how Banham concludes the chapter dedicated to them: 'In the end, it seems to me, neither Wright nor Soleri has produced structures that are, in any normal sense, sympathetic or proper to the desert. Both brought an inherently alien vision with them and imposed it on the desert scene, and the results are, in their way, as foreign as the mad townscape of Las Vegas.'[51] Perhaps, Banham is once again blinded by his functionalist interpretation of modernism.

Banham maintains that Wright had built dwellings too light for a climate that demanded thick walls to temper the extreme changes in temperature. This objection is perfectly consistent on the part of Banham, the author of *The Architecture of the Well-Tempered Environment* (1969), among other books. However, if one considers Wright's houses as entropic monuments, their 'lightness' takes on a completely different meaning. The first house built by Wright in the desert was Ocotillo Camp, an encampment built in 1927 with the help of his 'apprentices', so that he could closely monitor the progress of a project — never realised — for the San Marcos Hotel. The camp was in a commanding position on a vast rocky summit. The design followed the 'character' of the Arizona desert landscape. Here Wright transformed his preferred straight line into a broken line to achieve harmony with the dominant lines of the 'astounding' scenario of the desert. He drew inspiration from the desert: 'The great nature-masonry we see rising from the great mesa floor is all the noble architecture Arizona has to show at present and that is not architecture at all. But it is inspiration.'[52] Wright explained in his autobiography that the encampment was the most suitable kind of home: 'a camp we shall call it. A human inhabitant of unmitigated wilderness of quotidian change — unchangeably changing Change. For our purpose we need fifteen cabins in all. Since all will be temporary we will call them ephemera. And you will soon see them like a group of gigantic butterflies with scarlet wing spots, conforming gracefully to the crown of outcropping of black splintered rock gently uprising from the desert floor.'[53]

153

The shacks, of simple lumber, had entrances and ceilings covered with canvas cloth hung from a frame and were connected to a low fence painted dusty rose. The isosceles triangles of canvas at the ends of the roofs were scarlet like the flower of the ocotillo, a desert plant. Even though everything was short-lived, it had been built and planned with great care. And everything disappeared within a year. Banham related that only fragments and traces remained on the rocky promontory. The encampment had been specifically planned for this result, a disquieting site of the archaeology of the modern. Wright was proud that the image and the idea of his camp were preserved by something essentially modern and mechanical — photographs published in German and Dutch magazines a couple of months after it was completed.

A similar strategy was subsequently used for the construction of Taliesin West,

Alessandra Ponte
The house of light and entropy:
inhabiting the American desert

154

9.3 Taliesin West, by Frank Lloyd Wright. (Photograph by the author)

Alessandra Ponte
The house of light and entropy:
inhabiting the American desert

Wright's winter residence in the desert, built years later on more solid foundations. But once again, Wright insisted on lightness and on the idea of encampment. Even if the walls and fireplaces were made of solid local stones, held together by cement, the coverings were of impractical cloth through which the rain entered freely. The theme is again that of impermanence. Wright's house was ready to become a ruin, an enigmatic monument. One of his apprentices pointed to a mysterious recurrence of a geometric motif. Large rocks found in the general area had been brought to the camp and set up as sculptures. On those rocks one could see pictograms traced by 'prehistoric campers'[54] One in particular represented two interwoven spirals at right angles. This interlacement, combined with a red square, became the mark of the Fellowship created by Wright. The enigmatic symbol appeared on the Fellowship's letterhead and the road signs that led the way to the camp. It indicated the entrance. It can be seen in other forms in the construction of the camp itself.[55] Even if one does not want to stretch the interpretation, it is impossible not to draw certain parallels. Wright does not mention entropy explicitly, but what other message could one glean from his architecture? These are houses and at the same time monuments, designed and constructed with an eye to the past and to the future. Inspired by the ancient architecture of geological formations and the works of its prehistoric inhabitants, they prefigure the remains that they will leave behind: fragments in the case of Ocotillo; heavy walls of stone covered and marked with mysterious hieroglyphs in the case of Taliesin West.

Soleri was one of Wright's apprentices. He enjoyed a certain degree of popularity during the 1970s and early 1980s thanks to the gospel he preached together with his architecture. For a long time Soleri succeeded in convincing young architectural students to work for free on the construction of his fantastic and impossible project, Arcosanti, near Phoenix in Arizona. The idea was to create a hi-tech, high-density community – gigantic, but compact and ecologically correct. Arcosanti is only one of the 'arcologies' that Soleri dreamed up and designed. His arcologies are an answer to entropy and are in uninhabitable locations. Novanoah I, for example, is intended for continental platforms or the open sea, while Babelnoah is destined for a flat coastal region. Arcoforte rises from reefs, Logology on hills, Arckibuz in the desert (probably that of North Africa), Veladiga on top of a dam … there is even one in space: Asteromo. The only arcology that was ever started is, in fact, Arcosanti, a city for 25 000 people built on a rocky terrain similar to the landscape in which the Indians built their pueblos. Clearly, the ancient indigenous people are one of Soleri's reference points. Another is undoubtedly G. B. Piranesi, dark poet of the ruins of ancient Rome: compare the plan of Arcosanti to that of 'Un Ampio e Magnifico Collegio'. (Banham compares living at Arcosanti to camping amid the great ruins of the Baths of Caracalla in Rome.) Piranesi, an impossible architect, is an appropriate source. Arcosanti will never be completed but will always remain in a state of ruin, an entropic monument, a ruin of the future like those described by Smithson. Perhaps it is not coincidental that *arcology*, the neologism used by Soleri to designate the monumental habitations of the future, sounds so much like *archaeology*.

Notes

1   Jean Baudrillard, *America*, trans. Chris Turner (London: Verso, 1988), p. 63; originally *Amerique* (Paris: Grasset, 1986).

2   Jane Tompkins, *West of Everything: The Inner Life of Westerns* (York: Oxford University Press, 1992), p. 76.

3   For example, in an interview given in 1964, Ford says, 'Actually, the thing most accurately portrayed in the Western is the land. I think you can say that the real star of my Westerns has always been the land', repr. in Robert Lyons (ed.), *My Darling Clementine: John Ford, Director* (New Brunswick: Rutgers University Press, 1984), p. 139.

4   P. Reyner Banham, *Scenes in America Deserta* (Cambridge, MA: MIT Press, 1982), pp. 61–62.

5   Judi Freedman, 'Metaphor and inquiry in Mark Tansey's "Chain of Solutions"', in *Mark Tansey*, ed. J. Freedman (San Francisco: Los Angeles County Museum of Art and Chronicle Books, 1993), p. 37.

6   *Ibid.*, pp. 46–51.

7   Julia Brown, 'Interview with James Turrell', in *Occluded Front: James Turrell*, ed. J. Brown (Los Angeles: Lapis and The Museum of Contemporary Art, 1986), p. 23.

8   Although he became famous thanks to his book on the desert, van Dyke has never been the subject of a true monographic analysis and has been overlooked in the history of art criticism. The author is only aware of Peter Wild, 'A Western sun sets in the East: the five "Appearances" surrounding John C. van Dyke's *The Desert*', *Western American Literature*, 25/3 (1990), pp. 217–231.

9   Van Dyke's autobiography is still not published, and the manuscript has not been available for inspection. The quote is from Richard Shelton, 'Introduction', in John C. van Dyke, *The Desert* [1901] (Peregrine Smith, 1980), pp. xiv–xv.

10 *Ibid.*, p. xxvi.

11 Van Dyke, *The Desert*, p. 19.

12 *Ibid.*, p. 13.

13 The classic thesis on this historical period is Alan Trachtenberg, *The Incorporation of American Culture and Society in the Gilded Age* (New York: Hill & Wang, 1982). Also *The American Renaissance: 1876–1917*, exh. cat. (New York: Brooklyn Museum and Pantheon, 1979).

14 On the neurasthenia and other 'illnesses of civilisation' in America, see Anson Rabinbach, *The Human Motor: Energy, Fatigue, and the Origin of Modernity* (New York: Basic, 1990).

15 John C. van Dyke, *The Open Spaces: Incidents of Nights and Days Under the Blue Sky* [1922] (Salt Lake City: University of Utah Press, 1991), pp. 20–21.

16 John C. van Dyke, *Art for Art's Sake: Seven University Lectures on the Technical Beauties of Painting* (New York: Charles Scribner's Sons, 1893), p. 6.

17 *Ibid.*, p. 8.

18 *Ibid.*, p. 25.

19 *Ibid.*

20 *Ibid.*, p. 26.

157

Alessandra Ponte
The house of light and entropy:
inhabiting the American desert

21 Ernst H. Gombrich, *Art and Illusion: A Study in the Psychology of Pictorial Representation* (London: Phaidon, 1977 [1959]); Roberto Salvini, *La critica d'arte della pura visibilità e del formalismo* (Milan: Garzanti, 1977); and Philippe Junod, *Transparence et Opacité: Essai sur les fondementes théoriques de l'Art Moderne* (Montreux: l'Age d'Homme, 1976).

22 As already mentioned, the history of art criticism has overlooked van Dyke. However, see Craig Hugh Smyth and Peter M. Lukehart, *The Early Years of Art History in the United States* (Princeton: Department of Art and Archaeology, Princeton University, 1993) on art history in America during these years.

23 Rosalind E. Krauss, *The Optical Unconscious* (Cambridge, MA: MIT Press, 1993).

24 Quotation in Christopher Newall, 'Ruskin and the art of drawing', in *John Ruskin and the Victorian Eye*, exh. cat. (New York: Harry N. Abrams in association with the Phoenix Art Museum, 1993), pp. 81–115, 94.

25 *Ibid.*, p. 81.

26 For these themes, see also Lindsay Smith, *Victorian Photography, Painting and Poetry: The Enigma of Visibility in Ruskin, Morris and the Pre-Raphaelites* (Cambridge: Cambridge University Press, 1995).

27 John C. van Dyke, *Nature for Its Own Sake: First Studies in Natural Appearances* (New York: Charles Scribner's Sons, 1989), pp. ix–x. To this first study on 'natural appearances', van Dyke adds (in addition to *The Desert*): *The Opal Sea: Continued Studies in Impressions and Appearances* (1906); *The Mountain: Renewed Studies in Impressions and Appearances* (1916); *The Grand Canyon of the Colorado: Recurrent Studies in Impressions and Appearances* (1920); and *The Meadows: Familiar Studies in the Commonplace* (1926).

28 Van Dyke, *The Desert*, p. 127.

29 Quotation in Roxana Robinson, *Georgia O'Keeffe* (New York: Harper Perennial, 1990), p. 36.

30 *Ibid.* On O'Keeffe in New Mexico, see Christine Taylor Patten and Myron Wood, *O'Keeffe at Abiquiu* (New York: Harry N. Abrams, 1995).

31 Quotation in Katherine Plake Hough and Michael Zakian, *Transforming the Western Image in 20th Century American Art* (Palm Springs: Palm Springs Desert Museum, 1992), p. 26.

32 Julia Brown, 'Interview with James Turrell', in Brown, *Occluded Front*, pp. 14–19.

33 *Ibid.*, p. 13.

34 On Roden Crater, see *Mapping Spaces: A Topological Survey of the Work of James Turrell* [published on the occasion of an exhibit at Kunsthalle Basel] (New York: Peter Blum, 1987).

35 Donald Judd, 'Ayala de Chinati', in *Donald Judd Architektur* (Cantz, 1992), pp. 55–63 (p. 60).

36 P. Reyner Banham, 'The man-mauled desert', in *Desert Cantos: Photographs by Richard Misrach*, exh. cat. (Albuquerque: University of New Mexico Press, 1987), pp. 1–6 (pp. 3–4).

37 J. G. Ballard, *The Drought* [1965] (London: Triad Panther, 1985), p. 81.

38 *Ibid.*, p. 152.

39 J. G. Ballard, 'From Shanghai to Shepperton', *Re/Search*, 8/9 (1984), pp. 112–124 (on p. 118).

40 On the relationships between Ballard, the Independent Group and Smithson, see Eugene Tsai, 'The sci-fi connection: the Independent Group, J. G. Ballard, and Robert Smithson', in *Modern Dreams: The Rise and Fall and Rise of Pop* (Cambridge, MA: MIT Press, 1988), pp. 70–75. On the subject of the Independent Group, see Dick Hebdige, *Hiding in the Light: On Images and Things* (London: Routledge, 1988); and Anne Massey, *The Independent Group. Modernism and Mass Culture in Britain, 1945–1959* (Manchester: Manchester University Press, 1995).

41 Quotation in Tsai, 'Sci-fi connection', p. 73.

42 Robert Smithson, 'Entropy and the new monuments', *Art Forum* (1966); repr. Nancy Holt (ed.), *The Writing of Robert Smithson: Essays with Illustrations* (New York: New York University Press, 1979), pp. 9–18 (on p. 9).

43 Robert Smithson, 'The artist as site-seer; or, a dintorphic essay', in *Robert Smithson Unearthed: Drawings, Collages, Writings*, ed. Eugene Tsai (New York: Columbia University Press, 1991), pp. 74–80 (on p. 74).

44 *Ibid.*, p. 75.

45 Smithson, 'Entropy and the new monuments', p. 11.

46 Banham, *Scenes in America Deserta*, p. 86.

47 *Ibid.*, pp. 188–189.

48 *Ibid.*, p. 188.

49 For Banham's cultural and educational background, see Nigel Whiteley, 'Banham and "Otherness". Reyner Banham (1922–1988) and his quest for an *architecture autre*', *Architectural History*, 33 (1990), pp. 188–221; and Alan Colquhon, 'Reyner Banham. A reading for the 1980's, *Domus* (1988), pp. 18–24.

50 Banham, *Scenes in America Deserta*, p. 43.

51 *Ibid.*, pp. 86–7.

52 Frank Lloyd Wright, *An Autobiography* (New York: Duell, Sloan & Pearce, 1943), p. 309.

53 *Ibid.*, p. 310.

54 Curtis Besinger, *Working with Mr. Wright: What it was Like* (Cambridge: Cambridge University Press, 1995), p. 47.

55 Donald Leslie Johnson talks extensively on Ocotillo Camp and Taliesin West in *Frank Lloyd Wright Versus America: The 1930s* (Cambridge, MA: MIT Press, 1990).

Section Four
Observing, recording

Rhona Richman Kenneally

10 Landscape to inscape: topography as ecclesiological vision

'Travellers are very pleasant people', noted Nathaniel Parker Willis in 1840. 'They tell you what picture was produced in their brain by the things they saw; but if they forestalled novelty by that, I would as soon read them as beseech a thief to steal my dinner. *How it looks to one pair of eyes* would be a good reminder pencilled on the margin of many a volume.'[1]

This admonishment directly addresses a central aspect of the problematic of vision. In the course of engaging with a particular landscape and its architecture, 'one pair of eyes' inevitably transposes versions of a perceived environment. How can the interstices between the actual landscape, the picture it produces in an individual's brain, and the articulation of that visual experience be profitably evaluated? Does prior knowledge of a building as it is being explored — its cultural significance, its iconography, its position within (or outside of) the architectural canon — affect what is viewed? Does exposure to a description or analysis of a particular building or landscape before actually seeing it — a guidebook, an architectural paradigm, even a map — indeed not 'forestall novelty' at least to some extent by creating a hegemonic lens through which the subject is to be understood, even on first encounter?

Given recent research in the history of travel and tourism, these questions have particular resonance when they address the absorption of visual images outside of the context of familiar, everyday reality. What has been called the 'tourist gaze' by John Urry and others presupposes a differentiation of vision as it pertains to visited or tourist sites, as opposed to familiar or immediate ones: it is the nature of sightseeing, of experiencing new vistas, that the traveller gaze upon special target sights in a distinctive way, namely with particular 'interest and curiosity' resulting from the fact that those sights elicit distinct pleasures 'which involve different senses or are on a different scale from those typically encountered in everyday life'.[2] 'Socially organized and systematized', this gaze is at once influenced by the personal experience of the viewer, and authorised through such cultural discourses as education or 'enlightenment',[3] by a variety of professionals such as photographers, travel writers, and tour operators.[4] Dean MacCannell simplifies this issue into a relationship between 'a tourist, a sight, and a

163

Rhona Richman Kenneally
Landscape to inscape: topography
as ecclesiological vision

marker'. He defines a marker as being an indicator of information about a sight; it derives from guidebooks, plaques or other informational notices, slide shows, souvenirs, etc. and serves as the lens which focuses broader perceptions and interpretations about that object for the viewer's consumption, by framing the cultural matrix in which that object resides.[5] Jonathan Culler goes so far as to argue that the markers demarcate the very authenticity of a tourist sight.[6] The records of such a tourist gaze, then, become useful tools in trying to reconstruct the act of visualising and internalising a newly perceived landscape, and to evaluate various aspects of the processing, through vision, of space as place.

One particularly revealing collection of documents that records manifestations of this tourist gaze consists of several hundred multi-page forms called church schemes, dating from the late 1830s to the 1850s, which have never before been studied collectively. Their importance lies in their dual nature: on the one hand, they are records of several hundred visits or 'excursions' to medieval parish churches made by two key figures in the history of Gothic Revival architecture, Benjamin Webb and John Mason Neale, two clergymen who founded the Cambridge Camden Society in 1839. These schemes, then, record the act of vision and do so fairly immediately; that is, the information contained has probably not been subject to subsequent rewriting or reformulating. On the other hand, these church schemes themselves subsequently become influential markers to the sites they depict, capable, then, of motivating and to some extent predetermining the visual reactions of others who later visited these churches.

The purpose of this chapter is to posit a close analysis and interpretation of church schemes both as residues of visual experience, and as subsequent bridges that propose and justify these sites as worthy subjects to subsequent tourists. In a pivotal collection of essays entitled *Topographies*, literary critic J. Hillis Miller offers a methodological point of departure. Assembled due to their overlapping attention to the writing about place, these articles consider the works of such diverse writers as Thomas Hardy, Gerard Manley Hopkins and Wallace Stevens.[7] Miller, too, is concerned with the act of encapsulating a landscape as manifested in literature and philosophical texts, as both a unique gesture, and one which might have future implications on subsequent considerations of that landscape. To him, the creation of a discreet geographical entity, in essence its transformation from undifferentiated space to encultured place, comes significantly from the act of topography (defined as place-writing), which embodies or captures the actual landscape by substituting words used to name or identify it.[8] Miller draws attention to the dynamic, non-linear interrelationship between text and landscape, each legitimizing and qualifying each other in an ongoing process.[9]

I would like to argue that as topographical texts in their own right church schemes encrypt the nexus between the actual and the articulated landscape of the churches they describe. The very format of the schemes, the direct as well as tacit instructions which accompanied them, and the method of recording data on them can all be scrutinised in an effort to see how they reflect, both intentionally and unintentionally, the appropriation of the act of vision by an architectural paradigm whose impact would become widespread and pervasive. In Miller's terms, church schemes can be explored as texts with performative implications: their existence precipitates subsequent activities that in turn coincide with the actions and ideas of a much wider constituency. In an England newly accessible thanks to an expanding railway system, where tourism is promoted as never before in a multitude of guidebooks and by advocates of empirical exploration, and is undertaken by a more diversified cultural group than hitherto, church schemes have their own role to play. They become their own impetus for educational travel and for determining which sites are worthy of perusal. Moreover, they contribute in their own right to the dissemination of Neo-Gothicism, both geographically, in the sense of demarcating destinations so sanctioned, and demographically, by striving to attract audiences interested in medieval churches by facilitating the means by which information about them was to be learned and gathered.

In terms of the ideas derived from travel theory encapsulated above, Miller's assertion in *Topographies* is that words are particularly powerful tools in the creation of markers, through which distinctly configured 'place' is designated and delimited in the landscape. Words or other signs, for example a song or poem, can serve as a *locum tenens*, a place holder or place maker which puts definite boundaries and measurements around previously undemarcated environments.[10] Here place names have a special role to play: 'The power of the conventions of mapping and of the projection of place names on the place are so great that we see the landscape as though it were already a map, complete with place names and the names of geographical features.... Place names make a site already the product of a virtual writing....'[11] Further, he argues that even when literary texts appropriate a particular geographic setting which already exists, the writing and the reading of the resulting fiction are to be understood as a continuation of the very activities which collectively identified the site to begin with; hence, 'novels themselves aid in making the landscapes that they apparently presuppose as already made and finished'.[12] In short, a landscape as place does not in itself pre-exist: it becomes landscape by the 'living that takes place within it', transformed, indeed, made 'human' in an 'activity of inhabitation' — being mapped or by the making of a picture, the placing of a story or a novel in that setting — that the writing of a novel 'repeats or prolongs'.[13]

The defining power of topography is so strong that Miller interprets the actual landscape and the text of the novel that refers to it as having not a linear relationship — original conditions become setting pure and simple — but, rather, as affecting each other in series. According to this rather deconstructivist point of view, the actual geographic space in question exists not only 'in itself', but on the basis of previous transpositions, for example as photos or maps. These maps are subsequently reconfigured in the novel which alludes to them, by being shot through with the characters and activities which carry the novel's plot. Thus, novels can be seen as 'figurative mapping', which traces the movements and emerging relationships that converge to form an imaginary environment, one which is ultimately a synthesis of the original actual landscape and the overlaid subjective meaning imposed by the manipulations of the novel.[14] From this perspective, Mississippi is ultimately 'what it is' in

Rhona Richman Kenneally
Landscape to inscape: topography
as ecclesiological vision

part because of William Faulkner's Yoknapatawpha novels, Dorset's identity acknowledges Thomas Hardy's Wessex, as Paris is recast through Balzac and Marcel Proust, for example.[15]

Church schemes were not the first or the only written texts that serve as markers to highlight and legitimate medieval churches as tourist destinations in the nineteenth century, but they do have a distinct and unique role to play. From about the mid-eighteenth century, streams of architectural writing and design advocating a renewed understanding of and respect for the Gothic were already evident in England, and the Neo-Gothic fiction of the day — from Sir Walter Scott to the torrid exploits in the penny journals — attracted further attention to the field. By the early nineteenth century there were repeated didactic gestures by the Cambridge Camden and other similar societies, by guidebooks to individual buildings and later by more comprehensive guidebooks, or individuals familiar with the Gothic paradigm, to encourage as many people as could be made interested, to study and appreciate medieval buildings.[16]

Increasingly driving these groups was the impetus to teach about Gothic architecture by direct, hands-on scrutiny of medieval churches. As mentioned above, the Cambridge Camden Society, later called the Ecclesiological Society, was established in 1839 with the purpose of studying medieval architecture and religion and with a mandate to instigate a reawakening to Anglican worship both in England and in the colonies.[17] Shortly thereafter, a number of groups with overlapping raisons-d'être, for example, the Oxford Architectural Society and the Exeter Diocesan Architectural Society, followed suit. Many of these groups advocated and organised 'excursions' or short visits to Gothic churches in England (and some also went abroad to study European Gothic churches).[18] For example, the Oxford Architectural Society Report of General Meetings dated 16 June 1852 laments that only one excursion was made by its members during the previous term, during which three churches were visited. Members were reminded that

> much more real architectural information is derived from the ocular inspection of a few good examples, than from the perusal of books however correctly and beautifully illustrated and in this lies the chief benefit to be derived from architectural excursions, such as these. It is to be hoped that some arrangements may be made by which these excursions may be placed on a more permanent footing and become a source of further advantage. Our Sister Society the Ecclesiological Society, while still appertaining to that University derived much advantage from these expeditions.[19]

The goal of these excursions was to satisfy the perceived need to gain familiarity with medieval church architecture through direct empirical analysis, and for this, the blank forms the Cambridge Camden Society called church schemes were devised and disseminated. Indeed, the use and value of such questionnaires were recognised beyond the field of medieval church architecture: *Archaeologia Cambrensis, A Record of the Antiquities of Wales ... and the Journal of the Cambrian Archaeological*

Association offered its members a similar set of 'instructions, questionnaires, or formularies, by which the antiquary will be greatly aided in his operations, from knowing *what* and *how* to observe'. The precedent in this case was said to be similar documents from the 'French Government Commissions' as well as those of other societies. The goal: 'Antiquarian research may thus be carried on ... on something like an uniform plan; discoveries may be more easily compared, illustrated, and classified; difficulties may be more readily solved; and communication of knowledge more rapidly sustained.'[20] Blank forms were also used by the Dorset and Wiltshire Archaeological and Natural History Societies, and by the Somersetshire Archaeological and Natural History Society.[21] From the late 1830s to perhaps 1850, mass-produced forms were made available by many of the ecclesiological societies to facilitate the process by which their members could locate, identify and study each individual component of the church. Schemes from the Cambridge Camden Society appeared in multiple editions, on which were preprinted headings such as window, pier, roof and font (Fig. 10.1). Information was to be written in a specially encoded language that encouraged uniformity to enable effective comparative analysis. Members were to bring blank schemes to the churches they visited, complete the schemes on site as part of the learning process, then return a copy to the societies to create a database of information. A prototype for a form called Notes on Churches was designed by Sir Henry Dryden in 1841, presumably to be issued to members of the Oxford Architectural Society. The format differed to some extent in that the preprinted portion of the Oxford form was primarily a checklist that charted the presence and absence of particular architectural elements − clerestory, dripstones, rood screen, and so on. The main descriptive component was meant to be summarised on blank pages appended to the preprinted sheets.[22]

Whereas other textual markers collectively authenticate the medieval churches and other destinations that were their subject, the church scheme and the other variations cited above do so in an immediate way, right on-site, simultaneous to initial visual contact with the subject, that is, in direct conjunction with the 'tourist gaze' activated by the excursion. In Miller's terms, they are so interesting because they are records of the overlay of subjective meaning upon the previously relatively undifferentiated actual landscape. The Cambridge Camden Society schemes, then, can be studied as the superposition of theories concerning medieval architecture − framed and textualised as the pedagogical writings of the Cambridge Camden Society and other related sources − directly applied to the church building itself. Moreover, the schemes may also be viewed as concrete manifestations of figurative mapping, the trait Miller ascribes to novels − the literary legitimators of the landscapes they encompass − mapping which 'disarranges' the actual landscape to serve the needs of the text.[23] In other words, they record the act of envisioning the churches through the influential lens imposed by the topography of ecclesiology.

Even a blank church scheme (Fig. 10.1) shows itself to be integrally about topography, about place writing and place naming. The premise of the scheme is the perception of a church as a composite of place names such as altar, nave and transept.[24] And the visualisation of the building in these terms is meant to be

Cambridge Camden Society.

The Society trusts that its Members, while pursuing their Antiquarian researches, will never forget the respect due to the sacred character of the edifices which they visit.

Date.   Name of Visitor.

Dedication.   **Diocese.**
Parish.   **Archdeaconry.**
County.   **Deanery.**

I. Ground Plan.

    1. Length } of Chancel {   { Nave {   { Aisles {   }
    2. Breadth }   {   {   }

                Transepts {   { Tower {   { Chapel {   }

    3. Orientation.

II. Interior.

    I. *Chancel.*
        1. East Window.
        2. Window Arch.
        3. Altar.
            α. Altar Stone, fixed or removed.
            β. Reredos.
            γ. Piscina.
                (1) Orifice.
                (2) Shelf.
            δ. Sedilia.
            ε. Aumbrye.
            ζ. Niches.
            η. Brackets.
            θ. Easter Sepulchre.
            ι. Altar Candlesticks.
            κ. Altar Rails.
            λ. Table.
            μ. Steps—number and arrangement.
        4. Apse.
        5. Windows, N.
                     S.
        6. Window Arches, N.
                           S.
        7. Piers, N.
                  S.
        8. Pier Arches, N.
                        S.
        9. Chancel Arch.
        10. Stalls and Misereres.
        11. Chancel Seats, exterior or interior.
        12. Elevation of Chancel.
        13. Corbels.
        14. Roof and Groining.
    II. *North Chancel Aisle.*
        1. Windows, E.
                      N.
                      W.
        2. Roof and Groining.
    III. *South Chancel Aisle.*
        1. Windows, E.
                      S.
                      W.
        2. Roof and Groining.
    IV. *North Transept.*
        1. Windows, E.
                      N.
                      W.
        2. Transept Arch.
        3. Roof and Groining.
    V. *South Transept.*
        1. Windows, E.
                      S.
                      W.
        2. Transept Arch.
        3. Roof and Groining.
    VI. *Lantern.*
        1. Windows.
        2. Groining.
    VII. *Nave.*
        1. Nave Arch.
        2. Panelling above Nave Arch.
        3. Rood Screen.
        4. Rood Staircase.
        5. Rood Doors.
        6. Rood Loft.
        7. Piers, N.
                  S.
        8. Pier Arches, N.
                        S.
        9. Triforia, N. 1st. Tier.

10.1 Portion of a Church Scheme, 7th edn, by the Cambridge Camden Society. Collection, Canadian Centre for Architecture/Centre Canadien d'Architecture, Montréal.

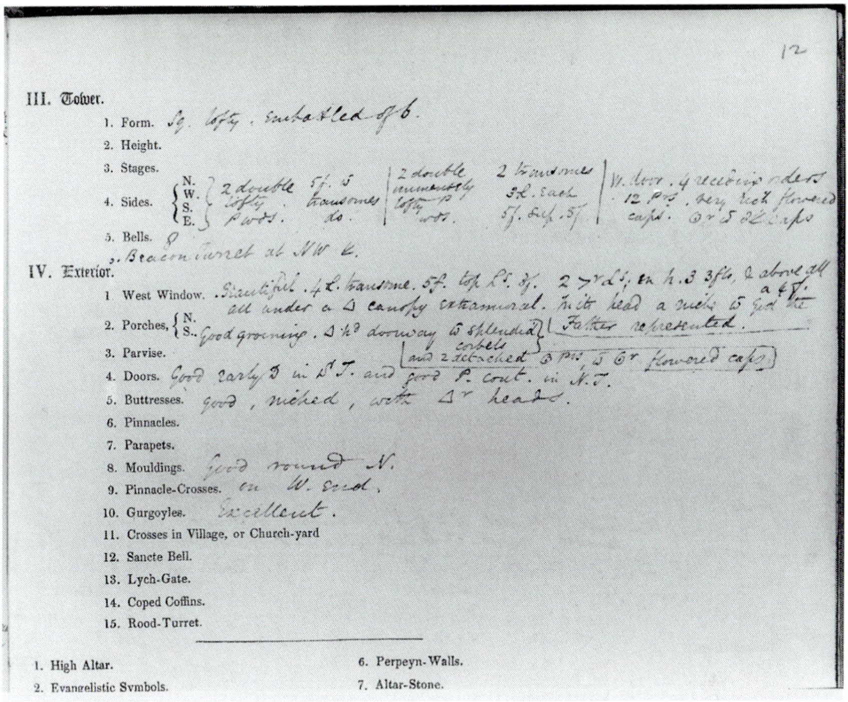
III. Tower.
1. Form.
2. Height.
3. Stages.
4. Sides. N. W. S. E.
5. Bells.
IV. Exterior.
1. West Window.
2. Porches, N. S.
3. Parvise.
4. Doors.
5. Buttresses.
6. Pinnacles.
7. Parapets.
8. Mouldings.
9. Pinnacle-Crosses.
10. Gurgoyles. Excellent.
11. Crosses in Village, or Church-yard
12. Sancte Bell.
13. Lych-Gate.
14. Coped Coffins.
15. Rood-Turret.
1. High Altar.
2. Evangelistic Symbols.
6. Perpeyn-Walls.
7. Altar-Stone.

10.2 Church Scheme for Howden Collegiate Church, Yorkshire, 3 July 1840, by Benjamin Webb, Cambridge Camden Society. British Architectural Library, Royal Institute of British Architects

transposed immediately into text. Schemes seem to be designed to be filled primarily by using text or words, rather than sketches or drawings. Fig. 10.2 shows a portion of a scheme depicting Howden Collegiate Church, Yorkshire, completed by Benjamin Webb on 3 July 1840. Both the blank and the completed versions reveal that there are no large spaces dedicated specifically for sketching, just long narrow blocks or linear spaces next to the printed words. Two explanations might be suggested: that the user of the scheme would possibly be more adept at textual rather than visual description, and that the form was meant to be filled in rather quickly, a requirement more readily satisfied by text than by drawing.

These hypotheses are confirmed when supplemental documents on ecclesiology are examined. Schemes are indeed intended to be text based. The main handbook on ecclesiology and the church scheme, a Cambridge Camden Society pamphlet entitled *A Few Hints on the Practical Study of Ecclesiastical Antiquities*, includes a prototype filled-in scheme that has no illustrations at all.[25] The justification given for text-only is to facilitate a speedy recording of salient architectural details:

> It is plain, that the only safe way to arrive at any general principles of Ecclesiology, is to observe and describe the details and arrangements of

Rhona Richman Kenneally
Landscape to inscape: topography
as ecclesiological vision

unmutilated churches, or parts of churches; and from a large collection of such observations, if carefully recorded, much advantage may accrue to the science. But it is equally plain, that if all these are to be sketched, a visit to the poorest church would scarcely be comprised in the longest day; and a degree of trouble, attended with no results of proportionate value, would ensue. For this reason the Cambridge Camden Society, on its first formation, issued those Church Schemes which have now reached a ninth edition, and the value of which has been amply proved by the experience of three years. They are by no means intended to supersede sketching, but simply to assist and corroborate it, and to supply its place in the less valuable details of the churches examined.[26]

This is a potentially paradoxical argument: notwithstanding the fact that schemes are not intended to supersede sketching, they are offered as a replacement for sketching to alleviate 'a degree of trouble' that drawing would cause, trouble 'attended with no results of proportionate value'. It is true that the Society hoped that church visitors would bring along materials for drawing and rubbing brasses, a measuring tape, a pocket telescope and a compass.[27] But there is no evidence in the approximately five hundred church schemes located by this researcher or in the books into which they were eventually bound of any of these instruments being used on a regular basis. Only a portion of the schemes report building dimensions; and the category of compass direction is virtually ignored, even in the sample scheme given in the promotional pamphlet. And only a few of the several hundred filled-in schemes have drawings or sketches, located either on an appended page or next to printed textual categories which did not elicit a written response. (It is of course possible that schemes that did have substantial illustrations were separated from the others and do not survive.) Images that appear on collected schemes consist of isolated small sketches of details. One example is a simple line drawing of a pinnacle cross and an hourglass frame on a scheme for St Mary Church, Lacombe, Hertfordshire.[28] And whereas members are implored to make accurate measurements of mouldings using a leaden tape, 'and the

170

rough sketch reduced to any required size by the Pentegraph [*sic*]', extant sketches of mouldings were drawn free-hand, apparently rather quickly.[29]

What seems significant here is the willingness to let text take a major role in describing the churches which were visited, a role substantial enough to warrant the accumulation of probably thousands of schemes by the Cambridge Camden Society and the distribution of these documents to other sympathetic societies. In February 1841, the Cambridge Camden Society reportedly sent hundreds of filled-in schemes to the Oxford Architectural Society as an information-sharing gesture; the Exeter Society also shared schemes with these two organisations, and by 1847 had itself advocated the collection of schemes as a research tool for interested members.[30] It seems, then, that this sort of topography reconfigured the churches within a framework compatible with the tenets of ecclesiology. As markers, then, the schemes not only authenticated the churches as architectural 'places', but also imposed a way of seeing them which replaced image with word.

As mentioned above, the schemes may be read as the figurative mapping of the church as part of the realm of the text. Such a map reflects the transformation of the real landscape as affected by the writing of the paradigmatic text. Each completed scheme is a figurative map in this way. It traces out the story of the person as s/he explores the church at that particular time on that particular day. Each scheme thus becomes in its own right an analysable encryption of the narrative.

What does understanding the scheme in this way reveal? It confirms the degree to which the processing of the visual experience, and, apparently, the act of vision as well, were so thoroughly permeated by ecclesiological dogma. What is consistent among the prototypical scheme in *A Few Hints*, in the Cambridge Camden Society schemes and in the proposed 'Notes on Churches' of the Oxford Architectural Society, is the specially encoded language instituted and utilised for the purposes of documentation. It is beyond the scope of this essay to dwell on the taxonomy of medieval church architecture espoused by ecclesiology, beyond noting that it was based on a style/chronology index of all the isolated elements of the structure and ornamentation.[31] Returning to the schemes themselves, it is obvious that observations had to be recorded succinctly, and, in the interest of comparison when sent to the Society database, consistently. As a result, *A Few Hints* supplies the necessary abbreviations and urges its members to use them.[32] The nave piers in the prototype scheme, for example, consist of 'six fine D. i-v 4 clustered, each cluster of 3 semi-cir. shafts with vertical bead: finely moulded cir. caps. and bases. vi.3 semi-cir. shafts, with similar caps. Base to vi. S. of very wide spread, and EE character, on sq. plinth'.[33] The schemes of Neale and Webb show an even more encrypted version of this abbreviation system. For example, the west window of Howden Church, Yorkshire, is described as follows (Fig. 10.2): '4L.transome.5f.top L^s.3f. 2>rL^s; ea h.3 3fls, & above a 4f'.[34] The window thus consists of four cinqfoiled lights, above which is a transom, above which are aligned four trefoiled lights. Above those in turn are two lights described as angular, each of which has a head containing three trefoils; above them is a quatrefoil. Fig. 3 is a visual equivalent to this description by Edmund Sharpe in his *Architectural Parallels* dated 1848.[35] Through the description in the scheme, it is possible to imagine the basic shapes that comprise the window, although such information as size, location of the window (how high or low it is situated in the wall) and, in this case, what architectural chronologic/stylistic period it belongs to are not available. Nevertheless, the 'inscape' — the original church-landscape overwritten by ecclesiology — is effectively captured.[36]

What can one say about this topographical system? For one thing, it is a gesture to make ecclesiology accessible to the amateur, perhaps someone who is more proficient in writing about than drawing landscape. The expectation seems to be that it is relatively simple to learn the nomenclature, which is quite clearly spelled out in *A Few Words* and may indeed have been easy enough to learn by someone dedicated to the cause and willing to consult with those who were more cognisant. Indeed, neophytes are particularly welcomed and encouraged to participate in excursions and apply the established principles:

Rhona Richman Kenneally
Landscape to inscape: topography
as ecclesiological vision

10.3 West façade of Howden Church, Yorkshire, from Edmund Sharpe, *Architectural Parallels, or The Progress of Ecclesiastical Architecture in England Through the Twelfth and Thirteenth Centuries* (London: John van Vorst, 1848), n.p. Department of Rare Books and Special Collections, McGill University

If you are anything of an equestrian, do not fail to accompany the members of your Society on 'Field-Days.' In these cases a route will be marked out with the special object of comprising as many and as interesting churches as can be seen within the limit of a day, and you will then have the benefit of the advice and suggestions of more experienced persons than yourself. You need not feel any reluctance in obtruding yourself on a strange party, for Camdenians are all friends and brothers, and will feel pleasure in assisting you.[37]

Schemes, then, fulfil a dual purpose. They are the handy receivers of visual data, interactive in the sense that they also prompt the viewer on what to see. But they also establish, by their very presence, an already-defined context.

There is another key issue that permeates Miller's topographical reflections, which considers the performative capacity of literature and language. A performative, by his definition, 'is a contingent act in the human and social world that makes something happen … though it can never be known for sure beforehand exactly what that something will be'.[38] All true performatives 'make something happen that was not predictable from the elements that were there to start with. … They exceed the intentions of the builders or singers'.[39] As has already been indicated above, Miller is convinced that 'the topography [in this sense configurations] of a place is not something there already, waiting to be described, constatively. It is made, performatively, by words or other signs, for example, by a song or a poem'.[40] He adds that 'the naming of places is one of the most important performatives'.[41] Designating a place with a name, for example New York, is a performative act that subsequently attracts events to take place *there* – say the building of Frank Lloyd Wright's Guggenheim Museum – which could not be anticipated when the city received its name.

Can a church scheme be seen as a performative and, if so, what implications do schemes have on nineteenth-century architecture? If textualising a space to make it a place is a performative act, then schemes are performatives in bestowing appellations on the various portions of the church which becomes each scheme's subject. The words 'piscina' and 'sedilia', for example, have the power to bring the scheme's user to seek out those parts of the church and also imply that the visitors understand the functions of these isolated elements and their role in religious worship.[42] The word 'font', singled out because of the significance of baptism and the ecclesiological stipulation that it be ideally located near the church's entrance, encourages the visitor to note and study it, and at the same time provokes an evaluation of whether the font's position is right or wrong vis-à-vis the imposed rules. Theoretically, such a designation might even result in the font being moved as the result of an excursion, reiterating the unpredictability that characterises a true performative.[43]

Indeed, the very sequence of the categories of the church scheme has performative consequences, and turns the process of experiencing the church into a narrative whose chapters – altar, nave, transepts – are meant to be viewed in a predefined order. The number of headings that comprise the scheme increased in succeeding editions, but the sequence did not essentially change. After allocating space for identifying the location of the church, the scheme has space for a 'ground plan', which, rather than requiring an architectural drawing, asks to note whether the church has aisles, chapels, transepts, and so on. Dimensions are requested in later schemes, but, as indicated above, are not usually supplied. The church interior is addressed first, starting with the chancel. The nave, the 'ornaments' such as shrines and niches, and the font follow this. Characteristics of the tower, inside and out, are then proceeded by categories related to the exterior.

To follow the sequence of the scheme and view the church according to the order of the headings was to reiterate the priorities of the ecclesiologists. The east window is the first category, given primacy because it is closest to the altar, and the style of window tracery was considered a highly effective means of dating – read classifying – a church. The altar is considered right away and is parsed into small details (and this is a section that becomes increasingly more precise with successive editions) because it is the strongest repository of the spirit of God. Next are the transepts, traditionally off limits to the congregation and still the domain of the clergy. The headings then progress back toward the nave and aisles, moving outward toward the tower, but not before stopping at the font, which, as has already been mentioned, ought to have been near the door. The tower, the church's exterior and the crypt are next on the list, followed by a checklist of relatively minor objects such as the alms chest, and tangential buildings such as a library or a well connected to the church.[44] In this way, the building and the paradigm are inextricably linked.[45]

Rhona Richman Kenneally
Landscape to inscape: topography
as ecclesiological vision

Church schemes had wider-reaching performative dimensions. On the one hand, the paradigm of ecclesiology was itself reinforced by its own successful applicability as a means of church topography, by the fact that its rules and logic were so useful in cataloguing and representing the church. On the other hand, the churches themselves were legitimised by the process as well. Whereas a wider-based (that is, beyond the paradigm of ecclesiology) resurgence in interest in medieval architecture in England was already over half a century old by this time, the focal points of interest had generally been in more monumental or picturesque architecture, for example cathedrals and ruined abbeys or particularly special parish churches. It was the ecclesiological societies that brought the relatively modest Gothic parish churches under consistent scrutiny and it was these buildings which comprised the vast majority of architecture documented by the church schemes.[46] In some ways, then, the excuse of filling out a scheme was the incentive for an excursion to visit an obscure parish church, not the other way round.

More widespread proscriptive implications are harder to prove, but do suggest themselves. First, ecclesiologists were very much of their age in inscribing English sights for tourist consumption. Widespread laying of railway track throughout the country, a vested interest on the part of the railway companies to increase passenger use of the trains, and, apparently, an increasingly accommodating audience substantially accelerated the proliferation of travel guidebooks and articles on travel available to the British public as well as visitors from abroad.[47] More importantly, however, there seems to be a strong projection of the ecclesiological paradigm beyond the intended scope of the initiators. Records of associations such as the Cambridge Camden Society reveal the members to be predominantly clergy, but, as has frequently been recorded, architects were also members, notably those who were major practitioners of Gothic — George Gilbert Scott, George Edmund Street, and William Butterfield. What is revealed in the research on church schemes as well as other non-traditional primary sources such as travel guidebooks and penny journals, is that exposure to the language of Gothic architecture was made available by and for a considerably broader constituency of potential tourist gazers and ultimate admirers of Gothic architecture, ones who had neither a religious nor a professional agenda in learning about these buildings. Even in texts that did not show partiality to Gothic architecture over other styles, its taxonomy and terminology were utilised. One such example is the *Railway Travelling Charts* composed by Sir Henry Cole under the pseudonym of Felix Summerly.[48] This unique blend of a map and a guide annotated interesting landmarks between the departure and destination points of a particular train excursion. The London-to-Brighton chart, for example, contains details on Merstham Church in Surrey, including drawings of its double *piscina*, font, west door and chancel arch (Fig. 4), presented for the edification of any potential excursionists to this destination. Cole asserts right in the text that the church 'will interest ecclesiologists', but has not presented the charts with only them in mind. *Sharpe's London Magazine*, a journal of popular culture, ran a series in 1845 entitled 'Rural Sketches; with Hints for Pedestrians' that describe a visit to an unnamed village church and briefly refer to the different periods of medieval architecture.[49] A

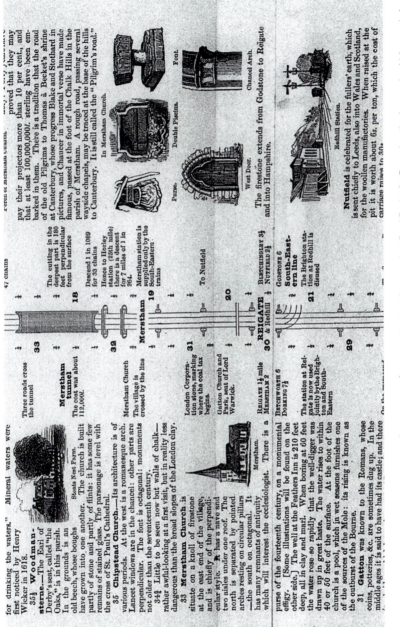

for drinking the waters," Mineral waters were first noticed by Henry Wicker in 1618.

35½ **Woodmansterne.**—The Earl of Derby's seat, called "the Oaks," is in this parish. In the grounds is an old beech, whose boughs have grown into one another. The church is built partly of stone and partly of flints: it has some few remains of stained glass. The parsonage is level with the cross of St. Paul's Cathedral.

35 **Chipstead Church.**—Its architecture is of various periods. At the west is a romanesque arch. Lancet windows are in the chancel: other parts are perpendicular. The font is octagonal: monuments not older than the seventeenth century.

34¾ Little is to be seen now but walls of chalk—rather awful-looking at a first visit, but in reality less dangerous than the broad slopes of the London clay.

33 **Merstham Church** is situate on a knoll of firestone at the east end of the village; and is chiefly of the perpendicular style. It has a nave and two aisles under one roof. The north is separated by pointed arches resting on circular pillars —the south on octagonal. It has many remnants of antiquity which will interest the ecclesiologist. There is a

purse of the fourteenth century, on a monumental effigy. [Some illustrations will be found on the other side.] The well at the Feathers Inn is 210 feet deep, all in clay and marl. When boring at 60 feet the water rose so rapidly that the well-digger was drawn up in great haste. The water rises to within 40 or 50 feet of the surface. At the foot of the church is a pool, which in wet seasons furnishes one of the sources of the Mole: its rising is known as the outburst of the Bourne.

31 **Gatton** was known to the Romans, whose coins, potteries, &c. are sometimes dug up. In the middle ages it is said to have had its castle; and there

Stoats Nest Farm.

Merstham.

Three roads cross the tunnel — 33

Merstham tunnel The cost was about 112,000l. — 32

Merstham Church The village is crossed by the line

London Corporation stone, marking where the coal tax begins. — 31

Gatton Church and Park, seat of Lord Warwick.

REIGATE & Redhill — 30

REIGATE 1¾ mile MARSTHAM 2 — 31

BETCHWORTH 6 DORKING 7½

The station at Reigate is now used jointly by the Brighton and South-Eastern

BLETCHINGLY 2½ NUTFIELD 2½

Godstone 6 **South-Eastern line**

The station at Redhill is disused — 21

29

---

47 chains

The cutting in the deepest part is 180 feet perpendicular from the surface. — 18

Descend 1 in 1089 for 33 chains

Hence to Horley station (25¾ mile) there is a descent for 7 miles of 1 in 264. — 19

Merstham station is supplied only by the South-Eastern trains. — **Merstham**

To Nutfield — 20

... proved that they may pay their projectors more than 10 per cent, and that at least 100,000,000l. sterling have been embarked in them. There is a tradition that the road of the old Pilgrims to Thomas à Becket's shrine at Canterbury, whose progress Blake and Stothard in pictures, and Chaucer in immortal verse have made famous, passed at the foot of the Chalk Hills in the parish of Merstham. A rough road, passing several wayside chapels, may be traced at the base of the hills to Canterbury. It is still called the "Pilgrim's road."

In Merstham Church.

Font.

Double Piscina.

Piscina.

Chancel Arch.

West Door.

The firestone extends from Godstone to Reigate and into Hampshire,

Nutfield is celebrated for the fullers' earth, which is sent chiefly to Leeds, also into Wales and Scotland, for the woollen manufactories. When raised at the pit it is worth about 6s. per ton, which the cost of carriage raises to 30s.

Redhill Station.

10.4 Merstham Church, Surrey, from Felix Summerly [Sir Henry Cole], *Railway Travelling Charts; or Iron Road Books, for Perusal on the Journey: in which are noted The towns, villages, churches, mansions, parks, stations, bridges, viaducts, tunnels, cuttings, gradients, &c.* (London: Railway Chronicle Office, [1845–71]), London to Brighton portion, n.p. V&A Picture Library

Rhona Richman Kenneally
Landscape to inscape: topography
as ecclesiological vision

more specific two-part essay devoted to 'Remarks on the Church Architecture of England' is distinctly pedagogical: 'We all know how very much difference is to be seen between churches of a different date, and so it seems desirable that, as the difference exists, we should have proper words to express it in, and thus be able to say in one word what the particular date or *style* of this or that building may be.'[50] Not only is the terminology presented and explained, but also numerous diagrams and illustrations are provided to clarify it.[51] Churches both monumental (Salisbury Cathedral) and humble (Tysoe, Warwickshire) are then discussed in these terms.[52]

There is no question that Gothic Revival architecture, especially Gothic Revival church architecture, is by the 1840s well on its way to achieving its predominant position in Britain; one of the assertions of this chapter is that the establishment of identifying markers on Gothic buildings by ecclesiologists and the other more general guides entrenches the connection between Victorian culture writ large and the medieval-style building. Indeed, the image of the Gothic church may arguably derive its status at this stage, as a fundamentally iconic representation of middle-class English life, depicted, for example, on countless Christmas cards.[53] The pervasiveness of Neo-Gothic architecture (of varying degrees of fidelity to the original forms) in the nineteenth century and indeed today — witness the continued use of Gothic and Tudor elements in suburban domestic architecture, for example — may be related to the performative aspects of medieval-architectural topography in general, including that emanating from ecclesiology. That is, Gothic architectural topography encouraged public interface with and appropriation of Gothic architecture, encouraged every interested individual — from those with vested interests to the merely curious — to participate in the activation of Gothic spaces as the stage sets that would accommodate his or her own life as well. Although rooted even earlier in the ideas of the picturesque, this renewed attention to Gothic architecture was formalised and its identifying characteristics made accessible to an Anglican evangelical audience, and later to a more diversified one, thanks in no small measure to ecclesiology. Church schemes, in their capacity both to reveal and to create, in participating in the metamorphosis from landscape to inscape, were an effective and integral part of the strategy.

Acknowledgements

This chapter contains research and analysis undertaken for my doctoral dissertation in architecture at McGill University, for which I gratefully received a fellowship from the Social Sciences and Humanities Research Council of Canada. I am also indebted to Annmarie Adams and Ricardo Castro for comments and suggestions.

Notes

1   Nathaniel P. Willis, *Letters from Under a Bridge* [1840], cited in Christopher Mulvey, *Transatlantic Manners: Social Patterns in Nineteenth-Century Anglo-American Literature* (Cambridge: Cambridge University Press, 1990), p. 3.

2   John Urry, *The Tourist Gaze: Leisure and Travel in Contemporary Societies* (London: Sage, 1990), pp. 1, 11–12.

3   *Ibid.*, p. 135.

4   Carol Crawshaw and John Urry, 'Tourism and the photographic eye', in *Touring Cultures: Transformations of Travel and Theory*, eds Chris Rojek and John Urry (London: Routledge, 1997), p. 176.

5   Dean MacCannell, *The Tourist: A New Theory of the Leisure Class* (New York: Schocken, 1976), p. 41.

6   Jonathan Culler, *Framing the Sign: Criticism and Its Institutions* (Oxford: Basil Blackwell, 1988), p. 160.

7   J. Hillis Miller, *Topographies* (Stanford: Stanford University Press, 1995). Indeed, the articles addressing these three authors were, along with the Introduction, the most useful in developing this paper: 'Philosophy, literature, topography: Heidegger and Hardy' (pp. 9–56); 'Naming, doing, placing: Hopkins' (pp. 150–168); and 'The ethics of topography: Stevens' (pp. 255–290).

8   Miller constantly tempers and reconsiders the definition of topography in the articles, from the graphic delineation of a physical space or the 'configuration' of its surfaces, to one more closely derived from the literal meaning of topos or place merged with graphein, to write (*Topographies*, p. 3). I will focus on the third of these meanings, which Miller explores in the sense that 'topography substitutes the names of things for the things themselves' (p. 280).

9   The transformation of space to place has been the subject of a number of studies. For example, Yi-Fu Tuan, *Space and Place: The Perspective of Experience* (Minneapolis: University of Minnesota Press, 1977); and Kent C. Ryden, *Mapping the Invisible Landscape: Folklore, Writing, and the Sense of Place* (Iowa City: University of Iowa Press, 1993). Essentially, space is geometrical, undifferentiated, with 'no fixed pattern of established human meaning; it is like a blank sheet on which meaning may be imposed'; Yi-Fu Tuan, *Space and Place*, p. 54. Place 'is necessarily anchored to a specific location that can be identified by a particular set of cartographic coordinates, but it takes in as well the landscape found at that location and the meanings that people assign to that landscape through the process of living in it'; Ryden, *Mapping the Invisible Landscape*, p. 38.

10 *Ibid.*, pp. 276–277. It is important to note here that Miller's terminology has shifted slightly *vis-à-vis* distinctions between undifferentiated *space* and defined *place*. Here, the distinction is articulated as between 'mere place' and 'a world' to coincide with the use of these words in Stevens' poem *The Idea of Order at Key West*. The contrast between the two is still to be understood in the same terms.

11 Miller, *Topographies*, p. 4.

12 *Ibid.*, p. 16.

13 *Ibid.*, p. 21.

14 *Ibid.*, p. 19.

15 *Ibid.*, p. 16.

16 The list is enormous. The search for the picturesque, as motivated by Edmund Burke in his *A Philosophical Enquiry into the Origin of Our Ideas of the Sublime and Beautiful* (1757) and explored by such advocates as William Gilpin from the 1780s, attracted travellers to

medieval ruins among other destinations, as did Romantic poets such as William Wordsworth. Antiquarian pursuits that developed in seventeenth-century Britain placed a premium on exploring the relics of Britain's past, and were advocated by the work of such figures as William Stukeley (1687–1765). For example, John Towner, *An Historical Geography of Recreation and Tourism in the Western World 1540–1940* (Chichester: John Wiley, 1996). As early as the 1750s, Horace Walpole began the design and construction of Strawberry Hill in Surrey and he merged text and architecture by using this setting for his novel *The Castle of Otranto (1764)*, and William Halfpenny published his *Rural Architecture in the Gothick Taste (1752)*, which serves as a pattern book for *Temples, Garden-seats, Summer-houses, Lodges. . . . With Instructions to Workmen, and Hints Where with Most Advantage to be Erected* (London: R. Sayer, 1852). John Britton's series on the history and antiquities of the cathedral churches of England of 1814–35 was influential. Writers on the taxonomy and language of medieval architecture include Thomas Rickman, Matthew Holbeche Bloxam, J. L. Petit, John Henry Parker, Robert Willis, John Milner and, of course, Augustus W. N. Pugin, whose ideas on the subject were absorbed to a large extent into the paradigm of the Cambridge Camden Society.

17 Key secondary sources that address ecclesiology and the Gothic Revival include Megan Aldrich, *Gothic Revival* (London: Phaidon, 1994); Chris Brooks, *The Gothic Revival* (London: Phaidon, 1999); Chris Brooks and Andrew Saint (eds), *The Victorian Church: Architecture and Society* (Manchester: Manchester University Press, 1995); Basil F. L. Clarke, *Church Builders of the Nineteenth Century: A Study in Gothic Revival in England* (London: SPCK, 1938); Kenneth Clark, *The Gothic Revival: An Essay in the History of Taste* (London: Constable, 1928); Peter Collins, *Changing Ideals in Modern Architecture 1750–1950* (Montreal: McGill-Queens University Press, 1965); Charles L. Eastlake, *A History of the Gothic Revival* [1872], ed. with an Introduction by J. Mordaunt Crook (Leicester: Leicester University Press, 1970); George L. Hersey, *High Victorian Gothic: A Study in Associationism* (Baltimore: Johns Hopkins University Press, 1972); Henry-Russell Hitchcock, *Architecture: Nineteenth and Twentieth Centuries*, 4th edn. Pelican History of Art (Harmondsworth: Penguin, 1977); *idem, Early Victorian Architecture in Britain*, 2 vols (New Haven and London: Yale University Press, 1954); James Macaulay, *The Gothic Revival 1745–1845* (Glasgow: Blackie 1975); Christopher Miele, 'The Gothic Revival and Gothic architecture: the restoration of medieval churches in Victorian Britain', PhD thesis, New York University, 1992; Phoebe Stanton, *Pugin* (London: Thames & Hudson, 1971); *idem, The Gothic Revival in American Church Architecture: An Episode in Taste* (Baltimore: Johns Hopkins University Press, 1968); and J. F. White, *The Cambridge Movement: The Ecclesiologists and the Gothic Revival* (Cambridge: Cambridge University Press, 1962).

18 For example, 'travelling Committees which have been formed from time to time for the purpose of visiting more distant Churches, and collecting information upon their architectural beauties or peculiarities'; Quarterly Report read on 24 July 1845, *Transactions of the Exeter Diocesan Architectural Society*, 2 (1847), p. 105. A 'Report of Visiting Committee' read at a Quarterly Meeting of the Exeter Diocesan Architectural Society, 13 November 1845, describes the churches visited during that period; *ibid.*, pp. 119–132.

19 Oxford Architectural Society Report of General Meetings dated June 16 1852; *ibid.*, pp. 206r, 217r.

20 'On the study and preservation of national antiquities', *Archaeologia Cambrensis*, I (1846), pp. 3–16.

21 'Queries relating to the archaeology of Somersetshire, Somersetshire Archaeological and Natural History Society', completed for the parish of Stogumber, 18 December 1849; Somerset Studies Library. Miele notes that in 1851 the Somerset Archaeological and Natural History Society used the Cambridge Camden Society scheme as a model for its own questionnaire: perhaps the 1849 version is a precursor; Miele, 'The Gothic Revival and Gothic architecture', p. 500.

22 'Notes on Churches', proposed and presented by Sir Henry Dryden to the Oxford Architectural Society, completed for Great Easton Church, Leicester, 12 August 1841; Bodleian Library, Oxford. A reason for advocating a combination of printed form and blank sheets for the Oxford Note has to do with the redundance of the Cambridge long and detailed format for recording a small church. Dryden admits to some potential confusion with

his system: when 'Door arches are marked X it is uncertain in what division of the church it it [*sic*] is, or whether in all.' Nevertheless, 'To have a perfect note paper you must have *nearly the whole* of the columns Interior and Exterior repeated 23 times ie under each Division besides having some things repeated 4 times in each for N, S, E [and] W. Such a paper would be absurd for a little barn church with no aisles or tower' (emphasis in original). The description on the blank pages of the Oxford Note uses terminology in keeping with that of the Cambridge schemes: the tower of the church used for the prototype, Great Easton in Leicester, is 'EE all up [and] of 3 stages. In 3d stage 1 double 2L EE wd on each face with clustered shafts. S of W wds have tooth ornament. N plain [and] E nail ornament.' The Note is dated 12 August 1841 and is part of the holdings of the Oxford Architectural Society at the Bodleian Library.

23 Miller, *Topographies*, p. 20.

24 This focus on place names reinforces the absence from consideration of issues not related to description and analysis on the basis of place-naming and -identifying. Questions such as the size of the congregation of a particular church, and whether it was High- or Low-Church in orientation (a point that might be expected to have concerned ecclesiologists bent on reinforcing religiosity) are not accounted for on the schemes.

25 Cambridge Camden Society, *A Few Hints on the Practical Study of Ecclesiastical Antiquities, for the Use of the Cambridge Camden Society* (Cambridge: Cambridge Camden Society, 3rd edn, 1842), pp. 37–45.

26 *Ibid.*, p. 16.

27 *Ibid.*, p. 17.

28 Church Scheme of St Mary, Lacombe, Hertfordshire, 17 March 1840 [Benjamin Webb], Cambridge Camden Society, vol. II, no. 56; The Royal Institute of British Architects, British Architectural Library. In contrast to the Cambridge schemes, however, the Oxford prototype 'Notes on Churches' has three small but quite intricately rendered drawings of the church on the blank sheets used for the description.

29 Cambridge Camden Society, *A Few Hints* (1842 edn), pp. 15–16.

30 Miele, 'The Gothic Revival and Gothic architecture', pp. 79–80.

31 Architectural elements were classified as belonging to a particular medieval subgenre, each of which was temporally demarcated: the Decorated style, for example, was said by the Cambridge Camden Society to coincide with the reign of the Edwards in the late thirteenth and most of the fourteenth centuries (Edward I was excluded from this list in the 2nd 1840 edition of *A Few Hints* of 1840 but was admitted by the 1842 third edition). Identifying characteristics included equilateral arches; much-enlarged mullioned windows, the heads filled with geometrical tracery or with 'wavy or flowing lines'; groined vaults divided 'into numerous compartments by intricate ramifications', and so on; *ibid.*, 1842 edn, pp. 8–9. Experts debated about the details, for example, with regard to terminology: Rickman uses the more secular 'water-drain' for what the Cambridge Camden Society called a *piscina*, and in the 1842 edition of *A Few Hints*, Perpendicular is divided into Plantagenet and Tudor. However, the basic terms – Norman, Early English, Decorated, Perpendicular – are generally consistent and continue to be in use well into the twentieth century. Residues of this system may be viewed, for example, in the *Buildings of England* series edited by Nikolaus Pevsner (Harmondsworth: Penguin, from 1951 and various edns).

32 Cambridge Camden Society, *A Few Hints* (1842 edn), p. 15.

33 *Ibid.*, p. 39.

34 Church Scheme of Howden Collegiate Church, Yorkshire, 3 July 1840 [Benjamin Webb], Cambridge Camden Society, I, no. 77; The Royal Institute of British Architects, British Architectural Library.

35 West façade, Howden Church, Yorkshire. Edmund Sharpe, *Architectural Parallels, Or, The Progress of Ecclesiastical Architecture in England Through the Twelfth and Thirteenth Centuries* (London: John van Vorst, 1848), n.p.

36 Miller borrows 'inscape' from the journals of poet Gerard Manley Hopkins, and as explanation refers back to Hopkins, who describes verse, for example, as 'inscape of spoken sound'; G. M. Hopkins, *The Journals and Papers of Gerard Manley Hopkins*, eds Humphry House and Graham Storey (London: Oxford University Press, 1959), p. 289, cited in Miller, *Topographies*, p. 168. Hopkins seems to ascribe to the word an imagined or formulated potentiality that successively overwrites a landscape out there. For example, the end of March and the beginning of April 'is the time to study inscape in the spraying of trees, for the swelling buds carry them to a pitch which the eye could not else gather – for out of much much more, out of little not much, out of nothing nothing: in these sprays at all events there is a new world of inscape'; *Journal* (17 March 1871), p. 205. In September 1872, Hopkins notes catching 'an inscape as flowing and well marked almost as the frosting on glass and slabs; but I could not reproduce it afterwards with the pencil'; *ibid.* (17 September 1872), p. 227. Later, in a longer quote worth citing here, the quality of an inscape as composed out of the random of landscape – with which Miller's topographical analysis clearly echoes – is clearly articulated: 'In the snow flat-topped hillocks and shoulders outlined with wavy edges, ridge below ridge, very like the grain of wood in line and in projection like relief maps. These the wind makes I think and of course drifts, which are in fact snow waves. The sharp nape of a drift is sometimes broken by slant flutes or channels. I think this must be when the wind after shaping the drift first has changed and cast waves in the body of the wave itself. All the world is full of inscape and chance left free to act falls into an order as well as purpose: heaps of snow made by the cast of a broom. The same of the path trenched by footsteps in ankledeep [*sic*] snow across the fields leading to Hodder wood through which we went to see the river'; *ibid.* (24 February 1873), p. 230.

37 'How to attain some knowledge of church architecture', *The Ecclesiologist* (April 1842), p. 89.

38 Miller, *Topographies*, p. 157.

39 *Ibid.*, p. 279.

40 *Ibid.*, p. 276.

41 *Ibid.*, p. 150.

42 A *piscina* is a basin recessed into a wall of the chancel and is used to receive the water with which the clergyman rinsed the chalice after use and where he washes his hands. *Sedilia* are seats also built into the wall, usually south of the altar, used by priests at the administration of the Eucharist.

43 Perhaps this performative quality can be taken a step farther: countless medieval churches were renovated by Neo-Gothic architects during the Victorian period, partly to compensate for years – centuries – of neglect, and partly to purge the churches of modifications made to them in the past that were inconsistent with the architectural style of their origin. In other words, a predominantly Decorated church with a Perpendicular window could well have been 'restored' by removing the anomalous portion and replacing it with a new window in the Decorated style. This became a contentious issue in the 1850s and 1860s and by the last quarter of the nineteenth century preservation came to be the accepted strategy where the building fabric was to be stabilised, but nothing – medieval, Georgian or Regency – altered. Central to this transformation was the establishment of the Society for the Protection of Ancient Buildings in 1877 by William Morris. For varying points of view with regard to these interventions, see Miele, 'The Gothic Revival and Gothic architecture', pp. 532–550; Martin S. Briggs, *Goths and Vandals: A Study of the Destruction, Neglect and Preservation of Historical Buildings in England* (London: Constable, 1952); and J. Mordaunt Crook, *The Dilemma of Style* (London: John Murray, 1987). As Miele points out, 'The scientific historiography of Rickman and his followers in effect led to a belief that one could have a perfect and absolute knowledge of medieval architecture, and armed with this knowledge architects set out to restore buildings, rebuild them, add new features in period style, or reconstruct others from archaeological evidence without compromising an artifact's integrity as such' (p. 532). Is this a consequence, at least to some extent, of the performative quality of church schemes and the perception of churches they reflect and reinforce?

44 The relatively lesser significance of the tower is confirmed in another Cambridge Camden Society pamphlet, *A Few Words to Church Builders* (1841), that offers advice on

determining which are the most important parts of a church and how they ought to be designed. Whereas a chancel was 'absolutely essential', a tower 'though a highly ornamental, is not at all an essential part of a church, and should not for a moment be thought of [in designing a new church], till [*sic*] Chancel, Nave, and Aisles ARE COMPLETELY FINISHED' (original emphasis). Indeed, the text goes on to ask, 'Does not the contrary assertion in the number of the Dublin Review seem to symbolize one of the errors of Romanism, — the excessive love of show?'; *A Few Words* (Cambridge: Cambridge University Press, 1841), pp. 5, 8.

45 Actually, by 1842, the scheme was printed in two formats: one on a long strip of folio paper and the other on a quarto sheet on which the rough draft was to be transcribed and sent to the Society. The advantage of the long strip format was said to be that it was easily torn apart, and individual pieces distributed among a large group visiting a church together: each would then study a portion of the building and the group would thus be more easily disbursed; Cambridge Camden Society, *A Few Hints* (1842 edn), p. 16. Extant schemes are in the quarto format, and the number of visitors usually ranged from about two to four or five, perhaps groups small enough not to have to split up. Moreover, by comparing schemes compiled by John Mason Neale and Benjamin Webb, it can be observed that when they went together to visit a church, each man filled out his own scheme. It seems likely that a scheme would be followed sequentially: *A Few Hints* (1840 edn), p. 13, explains that 'the arrangement adopted has been founded on the principle of allowing the describer to remain in one spot of the Church till that is finished, and to spare him the trouble of running backwards and forwards, as he proceeds onward with his paper', repeated with the word 'work' substituted for 'paper' in the 1842 edn, p. 16.

46 The desire to bring obscure churches to light is declared in *A Few Hints*: 'It is the Society's wish to procure a complete and accurate description in detail of as many Churches as possible; but especially of such as either, from their antiquity or any other causes, may contain objects particularly worthy of record, or, from their remote situation, may have hitherto escaped the researches of Ecclesiologists'; *A Few Hints* (1840 edn), p. 12.

47 Wolfgang Schivelbusch, *The Railway Journey: The Industrialization of Time and Space in the Nineteenth Century* (Leamington Spa: BERG, 1977), p. 7; Jack Simmons, *The Victorian Railway* (London: Thames & Hudson, 1991), p. 272; Esther Moir, *The Discovery of Britain: The English Tourists 1540–1840* (London: Routledge & Kegan Paul, 1964), p. xv; W. Fraser Rae, *The Business of Travel: A Fifty Years' Record of Progress* (London: Thos. Cook & Son, 1981), p. 16.

48 Felix Summerly [Sir Henry Cole], *Railway Travelling Charts; Or, Iron Road Books, for Perusal on the Journey: in which are noted The towns, villages, churches, mansions, parks, stations, bridges, viaducts, tunnels, cuttings, gradients, &c.* (London: Railway Chronicle Office, [1845–47]), 'Merstham Church, London to Brighton', n.p.

49 'Rural Sketches, with Hints for Pedestrians', *Sharpe's London Magazine*, 1/1 (1 November 1845), pp. 5–7; 1/2 (8 November 1845), pp. 22–3; 1/3 (15 November 1845), pp. 38–9.

50 *Ibid.*, 1/12 (17 January 1846), p. 186.

51 *Ibid.*, 1/18 (28 February 1846), p. 276.

52 *Ibid.*, p. 278.

53 Chris Brooks, 'Introduction', in Brooks and Saint, *Victorian Church*, p. 8.

Katherine Wentworth Rinne

11 Fluid precision: Giacomo della Porta and the Acqua Vergine fountains of Rome

The fountain networks of baroque Rome are in principle no different from those in other pre-industrial cities. Here as elsewhere the need for a reliable and pure public water supply was a complicated interplay of public policy, patronage and real estate development. However, the underlying determinants in the development of an urban water distribution system were the limitations of gravity-flow technology and the specific topography of the areas to be served. Rather than simply directing water where it was wanted, urban development was optimised in areas where water could be delivered. Time and again elaborate political alliances were forged or strengthened depending on the potential for water delivery to a particular site.

Water and geography also impose their own very strict rules on the design process. Unlike mechanical systems that force water into unnatural contortions, a gravity system nurtures, exploits and enhances water's natural abilities as it flows through its watershed. Allowing for seasonal variation in volume each Baroque fountain was designed around the potential of the water at a specific location. Whether the water shot in a lofty jet, fell in a rushing cascade, bubbled from a low nozzle or slipped slowly over a stone lip, it did so because the symbiosis between gravity and topography had been exploited by the design. Hence, each fountain told a topographic story that linked it simultaneously backward and forward to the other fountains in its network, to its aqueduct and to its source outside the city.

Three gravity-flow aqueduct networks each with its own clearly bounded 'watershed' area, outside of which the water can not flow, still operate in Rome: the Acqua Vergine (1453 and 1570), a low-pressure network serving the densely populated Campo Marzio; the high-pressure Acqua Felice (1585–87) serving the Velabrum, and the Esquiline, Quirinal and Capitoline hills; and the high-pressure Acqua Paola (1605–12) serving the Vatican, Trastevere and the entire left bank of the city. This chapter will specifically address a series of public fountains designed by Giacomo della Porta from 1570 to 1591 for the Acqua Vergine network. I will investigate how his understanding of the relationship between topography and gravity evolved through the course of this work until it began to precede and influence other design considerations.

Katherine Wentworth Rinne
Fluid precision: Giacomo della Porta and
the Acqua Vergine fountains of Rome

Della Porta translated this growing mastery of technical and topographical data into formal solutions that established a distinct identity for the fountains within the Vergine watershed.

Hydraulics

Roman fountains until the twentieth century were fed by a vast, yet simple aqueduct system that exploited the natural law of gravity. Water flowed continuously, and its distribution to fountains depended upon the altitude of the springs at their source and their distance from the city, the grade of flow, the altitude of holding tanks along the route, the elevation of the various service areas, the material and construction of the conduits and pipes, as well as the amount of water flowing through them. Each aqueduct delivered water to a holding tank, called a *castellum*, often located just inside the city wall. Here, the water was held at a high elevation, divided into smaller quantities, and sent to smaller secondary *castelli*, to be delivered to public and private fountains in various neighbourhoods. From the spring to the *castellum*, the water flowed in large channels, at an average drop of only 50 centimetres per kilometre, with room for air circulation within the channel. From the *castellum* to the fountains, the water flowed under the streets in pipes that constricted its flow and created pressure. The more pressure in the pipes, and the greater the difference in elevation between the level of the *castellum* and the level of the fountain, the higher the water could shoot when finally released. The elevation at which water left the *castellum* determined the theoretical, maximum height it could attain in another location. The higher the pipe was placed in the *castellum* wall, the greater the elevation that the water could reach at the next *castellum* or fountain. The lower the pipe was placed, the greater the available pressure for water displays such as jets and sprays. At various points along the distribution route the water might flow into another, lower *castellum*, to be divided again, after which the water could never regain its original elevation.

The first *castellum* within the city was often embellished with a major fountain known as a *mostra*. The Fontana di Trevi served as the *mostra* for the Acqua Vergine, while the Fontanone on the Janiculum hill, and the Fontana del Mose on the Quirinal hill, served as *mostre* for the Acqua Paola and Acqua Felice networks respectively. These *mostre* announced and celebrated the arrival of water into the city, literally flaunting their waters in front of the bedazzled and thirsty citizens. From the *castellum* at the back of the *mostra* the water flowed in underground pipes to all the other fountains in its network. The elevation of the *castellum* in relation to subsequent fountain sites determined to a large part how the water was displayed. Typically, with less water, fountains diminished both in size and in the flamboyance of the water display, as distance from the source increased.

The task of designing an entire gravity-flow water network (as opposed to designing a single fountain) was fraught with considerable difficulty. It is important to note that the formula to accurately calculate water flow was not generally known and accepted until the eighteenth century. This meant that the elements of the water distribution system of ancient Rome, which during the Constantinian period included

184

eleven aqueducts and 1212 public fountains, as well as numerous private fountains, imperial baths and other water features, were all designed and constructed without accurate hydraulic formulas.[1] In spite of the writings of Leon Battista Alberti and experiments by Leonardo da Vinci and others in the fifteenth century, and the survival of ancient hydraulic texts by authors such as Vitruvius, Frontinus and Hero of Alexander,[2] most hydraulic planning was the result of empirical, rather than precise scientific knowledge. This is not to say that Giacomo della Porta was without procedural and design guidelines. Like many renaissance architects he was also a knowledgeable engineer and had previous experience with fountain design.[3] The problem for della Porta in 1570, as for the ancient Romans, was to deliver an unknown and seasonally variable quantity of water, from a specific location and elevation, to a series of fountains each located at different distances, and different elevations from the source. Additionally, it was essential that the water be delivered in quantities sufficient to provide for the needs of each service area (whether for laundry, bathing, drinking or industry, and so forth), and in a manner appropriate for those needs.

Della Porta's fountains for the Acqua Vergine

The antique Aqua Virgo originally arrived near the Pantheon, but as the structure deteriorated during the medieval period its terminus receded eastwards.[4] It was restored several times during the medieval and renaissance periods. By the time a major restoration was completed under the sponsorship of Nicholas V in 1453 the aqueduct terminated in the Piazza di Trevi. Nicholas renamed it the Acqua Vergine, and commissioned Alberti to replace an existing fountain with a new Fontana di Trevi, which survived until 1643.[5] The elevation of the water as it fell from the aqueduct into the fountain was 20 metres above sea level.[6] The Acqua Vergine was restored again in 1570 and a new *castellum* (with a *limnaria*, or settling tank) known as the San Sebastianello *bottino*, was built near the Piazza di Spagna. Nearly 750 metres further north the water achieved a level of 20.7 metres above sea level.[7] This added a crucial 70 centimetres of head to the network, and the more northerly location served portions of the low-lying Campo Marzio, such as the Porta di Ripetta and the Piazza del Popolo, that could not be reached from the Trevi. This small advantage was of considerable consequence as there was only about an 8-metre fall in elevation over the entire 2 square-kilometre distribution area.

185

As technical advisor to the *Congregatione cardinalitia sopra le fonti* Della Porta, 'architetto del popolo Romano', was called upon in 1570 to design and supervise the distribution of Vergine water to a group of eighteen new public fountains, in the first major water distribution program in Rome in at least 1200 years.[8] Of the eighteen, he singled out nine for immediate construction. These included one in the Piazza del Popolo at the northern gateway into the city, one each in the Piazza Colonna, Piazza della Rotonda, and Piazza San Marco (now Piazza Venezia) and two in the Piazza Navona all in the heart of Campo Marzio. Three fountains were designated for the south-west area of the Campo Marzio with one fountain each in the Campo dei Fiori, the Piazza Giudea and the Piazza Montanara.[9] The first seven fountains were built as planned, but a single

Katherine Wentworth Rinne
Fluid precision: Giacomo della Porta and
the Acqua Vergine fountains of Rome

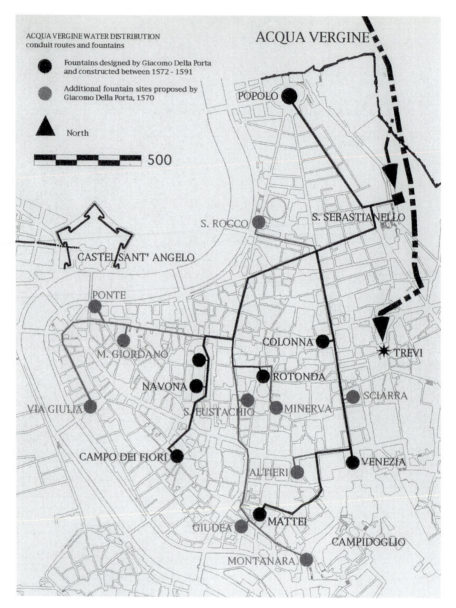

ACQUA VERGINE WATER DISTRIBUTION
conduit routes and fountains

ACQUA VERGINE

● Fountains designed by Giacomo Della Porta
  and constructed between 1572 - 1591

● Additional fountain sites proposed by
  Giacomo Della Porta, 1570

▲ North

500

POPOLO

S. ROCCO

S. SEBASTIANELLO

CASTEL SANT' ANGELO

PONTE

COLONNA

M. GIORDANO

TREVI

ROTONDA

NAVONA

SCIARRA

VIA GIULIA

S. EUSTACHIO

MINERVA

CAMPO DEI FIORI

VENEZIA

ALTIERI

GIUDEA

MATTEI

CAMPIDOGLIO

MONTANARA

186

11.1 The 1570 proposal for Acqua Vergine water distribution by Giacomo della Porta, shown in relation to the present day street plan. Computer Map by K.W. Rinne. © K.W. Rinne

fountain, built in the Piazza Mattei, was substituted for those in the Giudea and Montanara. These fountains were built later and supplied with water from the Acqua Felice.[10] A conduit was laid from San Sebastianello north to the Piazza del Popolo, and another was directed west to the Piazza Caetani (now Piazza Goldoni), where a branch line turned south along the Via del Corso for distribution to the Colonna and San Marco fountains. The main conduit line continued west to the Via della Scrofa where it turned

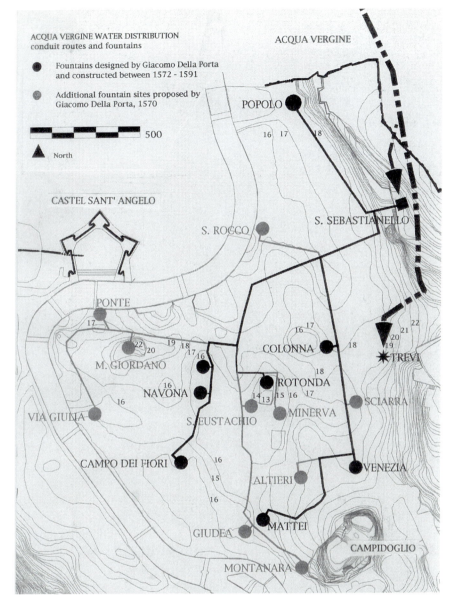

The map contains the following labels:

ACQUA VERGINE WATER DISTRIBUTION
conduit routes and fountains

ACQUA VERGINE

● Fountains designed by Giacomo Della Porta
and constructed between 1572 - 1591

◉ Additional fountain sites proposed by
Giacomo Della Porta, 1570

500

▲ North

POPOLO

16 17 18

CASTEL SANT' ANGELO

S. SEBASTIANELLO

S. ROCCO

PONTE

17

22 20 19 18 17

M. GIORDANO

16

NAVONA

16

VIA GIULIA

S. EUSTACHIO

CAMPO DEI FIORI 16

15

16

COLONNA

16 17

18

19 20 21 22

TREVI

ROTONDA

18

14 13 15 16 17

MINERVA

SCIARRA

ALTIERI

VENEZIA

GIUDEA

MATTEI

CAMPIDOGLIO

MONTANARA

187

11.2 The 1570 proposal for Acqua Vergine water distribution by Giacomo della Porta, shown in relation to the present day topography which is drawn at one-meter intervals. Computer Map by K.W. Rinne. © K.W. Rinne

south to serve the Navona, Rotonda and Campo dei Fiori fountains. This line was also originally intended to serve the Giudea and Montanara fountains (Figs 10.1 and 10.2).

I would like to consider how della Porta might have proceeded with the daunting task of organising an entirely new public water distribution program. In Rome itself there were no practical examples to which he could refer, and although there were several models outside Rome none was particularly relevant for the Campo Marzio. Only two

Katherine Wentworth Rinne
Fluid precision: Giacomo della Porta and
the Acqua Vergine fountains of Rome

possible models will be cited here, both close at hand and probably well known to him.[11] First were the surviving medieval aqueducts and their fountains in other Italian cities. Siena, Naples, Perugia and Viterbo,[12] for example, all had operating fountain networks to which he might have looked for inspiration. However, in general, their topographies allowed for a far greater range of design options than those suitable for the relatively flat Campo Marzio. Second, the luxuriant new gardens recently built outside Rome, such as the Villa Lante at Bagnaia and the Villa d'Este at Tivoli, offered examples of water distribution networks designed and implemented more or less at a single stroke. However, these too were inappropriate not only because of their dramatic topographies, but also because much of the water flowed directly from one fountain to the next, losing pressure along the way. The extremely shallow topography of the Campo Marzio meant that none of the ornamental fountains could act as a *castellum* for any other ornamental fountain — each needed its own dedicated water line.[13]

In addition to distribution networks, there were individual, free-standing urban fountains that della Porta could look to for inspiration. Rome in 1570 however, was served by only a handful of functioning, fresh-water, public fountains.[14] In addition to Alberti's Trevi fountain, there were three others near San Pietro and another near San Giorgio in Velabro. Two other fountains, one at Santa Maria in Trastevere, the other at Santa Maria Maddelena near the Pantheon, were both functioning in the fifteenth century but may have been dry in the late sixteenth century.[15] There were medieval fountains such as the Fonte Gaia in Siena, the Fontana Maggiore in Perugia and several others in nearby Viterbo, all orthogonal and richly carved. This style was superseded in the Renaissance by new sculptural fountains such as the 'Neptune' fountains in Messina by Giovanni Angelo Montorsoli (1554–57) and in Florence by Bartolomeo Ammannati (1560–75). A third type combined the orthogonal basin with a tall central chalice as seen in the fountain located in the Piazza di Santa Maria in Trastevere.[16] In all three of these fountain types the water itself, the real subject as it were of the work, typically played a very minor role to the sculptural program. Often in these fountains the water merely spurted from a jet before it trickled or dripped into the basin, or else it fell in a thin stream from a spigot for drinking or filling jugs. This was principally due to extremely limited water resources, but perhaps it also represented a particular lack of appreciation for the design potential of water within an urban setting.

Della Porta chose the 'chalice' type fountain as his first model. It is difficult to document whether the *Congregatione* encouraged him to imitate existing chalice fountains, or if it was his choice from the beginning. Regardless, the first two fountains that he designed for the Acqua Vergine network both derive from this type. I would like to suggest, however, that as he became more familiar with the topography of the Acqua Vergine watershed and developed a more intimate understanding of water and hydraulic engineering, that he radically altered his approach to create a series of fountains that specifically responded to the Campo Marzio.

Della Porta's remaining six ornamental Vergine fountains were lower and broader than the other fountain types. Their basins were often more like pools and several were placed below ground level. In his first two fountains he had attempted to use gushing jets, but with the later six fountains he turned to the image of a bubbling spring. With only one notable exception sculpture was never the dominant element of the design. It was the water itself and the basin in which it was contained, both undulating, fluid and approachable, which were the dominant features. However, he did not develop this formula overnight. Rather, he was engaged in a process of empirical and probably embarrassing experimentation, as he struggled to translate the demands that Campo Marzio topography placed on Acqua Vergine water, into a series of site-specific public fountains.

Della Porta's first fountain was for the Piazza del Popolo,[17] designed in 1572 and essentially complete but perhaps not yet functioning by 1575 (Fig. 11.3). However, in autumn 1577 the upper chalice was removed and a new one substituted 'in order to lower the fountain'.[18] Several authors have mentioned this modification but none has asked why it was necessary. A little simple arithmetic makes it clear that topography and gravity supply convincing answers. The San Sebastianello *bottino*, which supplied water to the fountain was about 750 metres away and, as previously mentioned, the level of the water was 20.7 metres above sea level. After the 1577 modification, the fountain stood approximately 4 metres high, measured from the original steps to the top of the upper nozzle.[19] Because the fountain was moved to make way for Valadier's redesign of the Piazza del Popolo (1805–23), it is difficult to know the precise level of the piazza in the 1570s, but if it were any higher than about 15 metres above sea level there would not have been enough room for any significant water display. Had the elevation of the piazza been lower there might not have been any reason to lower the upper chalice.[20]

189

11.3 Piazza del Popolo fountain, now in Piazza Nicosia. Giacomo della Porta was required to substitute a new upper chalice in 1577 'in order to lower the fountain'

Katherine Wentworth Rinne
Fluid precision: Giacomo della Porta and
the Acqua Vergine fountains of Rome

There are several reasons that help to explain why the 1577 design modification may have been necessary. This was della Porta's first commission for a free-standing urban fountain fed by its own conduit. Previously he had restored the 1453 Trevi and he had designed a public laundry fountain at the site of a natural spring in Piazza di San Giorgio in Velabro. Neither design, however, involved the use of underground distribution conduits. Second, the conduit leading from the *castellum* to the fountain was made of terracotta, rather than travertine or lead, both of which can withstand greater pressure.[21] Made by hand the terracotta pipes also had rough inner surfaces that created friction, thus slowing water flow. Third, the water supply was seriously reduced due to persistent illegal tapping by private users for both domestic and industrial uses such as laundries.[22] Finally, because water flow is subject to seasonal variation, depending upon rainfall, it is entirely possible that a dry winter in 1577 could have significantly lowered the distribution and display potential of the Vergine during the following summer.[23]

Conditions such as these would directly impact the amount of water that could be delivered to any fountain and hence would necessarily become part of the design equation. However, while technological solutions could produce more sophisticated conduits and more accurate calculations, and while laws and fines could help stabilise the water supply for public use, rainfall could not be controlled. Therefore, it was absolutely necessary for della Porta to insure that the design of the Piazza del Popolo fountain (as well as all others to be built in the network) specifically address the topography of the site, and not to rely on regulations and technology alone.

On 25 September 1574 construction was authorised for the next four Vergine fountains, one each for the Piazza della Rotonda and the Piazza Colonna, and two for the Piazza Navona.[24] In 1575, apparently before the design problems with the Piazza del Popolo fountain became evident, della Porta had already proposed a second chalice type fountain, even though, according to Cesare D'Onofrio, a site had not yet been chosen for it by the *Congregatione*.[25] In any case, authorisation to begin construction of a terracotta conduit from the corner of S. Agostino to the Piazza della Rotonda, and another to the Piazza Giudea, was given on 20 March 1576. The Piazza della Rotonda, where the chalice fountain was eventually placed, was the only proposed site in the Campo Marzio where it could have functioned properly considering the interplay between the elevation of the site (probably about 14 metres above sea level at the time), distance from San Sebastianello (about 1.35 kilometres), the level of water in the *bottino*, the height of the fountain as originally designed (probably about 3.5 to 4 metres high) and the use of a terracotta conduit. The theoretical head at this site was about 19 metres above sea level. As shown in a fabulously exaggerated 1675 print by Gianbattista Falda, there was originally a central chalice with a jet of water instead of the current obelisk which replaced it in 1711. Although Falda would have us believe there was a 4-metre-high jet, it was probably not much more than 1 metre high, even during the rainiest years (Fig. 11.4).

The *Congregatione* had also considered this fountain design for the Piazza Colonna, which was more than 2 metres higher in elevation than the Piazza Rotonda.

11.4 'Fontana nella Piazza della Rotonda' by Gianbattista Falda, *Le Fontane di Roma* (Rome, 1675). The exaggerated scale of the fountain in relation to the site suggests that it had an enormous geyser of water. However, this is clearly impossible due to the relationship of the piazza to its water source at San Sebastianello (Fiske Kimball Library, University of Virginia)

While della Porta may have been literally 'feeling his way' through the design of the new water distribution system, he was too accomplished an architect to make the mistake of designing a 4-metre-tall fountain for a piazza that was less than 3 metres lower than the water source. It is interesting to speculate how he convinced the *Congregatione* that something altogether different was required at this location since none of the problems associated with the Piazza del Popolo fountain were yet apparent.

Today, the elevation of the Piazza Colonna at the base of its fountain is 17.5 metres above sea level — only about 2.25 metres lower than the theoretical head that Acqua Vergine water could achieve at this location. It seems unlikely that della Porta would not have intuitively understood that a tall chalice fountain would not work in this location. Yet, a dramatic statement was necessary at this important site along the Via del Corso. His innovative response was to fill as much of the piazza as possible with a horizontal plane of water to compensate for the lack of verticality. Nearly 7.5 metres in length and 5.5 metres across,[26] the 1-metre-high basin was raised on two shallow steps and was originally surmounted by a slightly larger and more elaborate chalice than the one seen today. Nonetheless, in this expansive fountain with its undulating and inviting basin, for the first time water, not sculpture, was the focal point of the design.[27] Della Porta dispensed with strong vertical elements to create a new type of public fountain that responded to the specifics of Vergine topography. By creating what is essentially an over-scaled garden pool, similar to those which 'were regularly used to adorn the garden beds' of mid-sixteenth century Roman villas,[28] he respected the essential nature of water, which is to flow, not shoot up into the air. He created an urban oasis with

Katherine Wentworth Rinne
Fluid precision: Giacomo della Porta and
the Acqua Vergine fountains of Rome

11.5 The low undulating basin of the Piazza Colonna fountain breaks with the Renaissance tradition of vertical, sculptural fountains

allusions to nature and to the surrounding villa gardens. From this point on his Vergine fountains nestled closer to the ground until they were finally submerged by the topography itself into fountains that connote spring-fed grottoes. In turn, della Porta's fluid, billowing pools may in fact have become models for later garden *peschiera*, or similar broad and low, free-standing pools. As MacDougall points out 'water itself becomes more important in the seventeenth century; in sheets or pools or falls it comes to dominate the architectural framework' of early seventeenth-century suburban villa gardens (Fig. 11.5).[29]

His fountains for the north and south ends of the Piazza Navona (at 16 and 15.5 metres above sea level respectively) were even broader than the Colonna fountain — nearly 10 by 12 metres each. Both fountains have been modified extensively and burdened with large sculptural additions which, while handsome in their own right, tend to de-emphasise the simple, graceful lines of the basins. As illustrated in both the 1593 Tempesta plan and in a 1625 view by Jacopo Crulli, the basins appear to have been placed on two shallow steps like the Colonna fountain. Rather than a central chalice each was originally fitted with a simple, upright, broken column fragment, placed in the middle of the basin that emitted a low jet of water from the top. In the south fountain a small sculpture of dolphins and masks was placed in each of the four straight sides of the basins, and a small kneeling figure was placed in each curved lobe. The north fountain lacked figures until the mid-seventeenth century. From the level of the water in the later sculptural additions which gave the fountains their names, 'Il Moro' and 'Il Nettuno', as well as from the level of the water in the later Quattro Fiume fountain by Bernini in the centre of the piazza, it is clear that the total height of the compositions could not have been more than 2.5 metres above the level of the piazza. According to Fioravanti Martinelli, Borromini later proposed that the steps be removed and the surrounding balustrades be replaced with a ground level basin, thus enlarging and accentuating the pool-like quality of the fountains, and increasing their scale relative to the size of the piazza (Fig. 11.6).[30]

192

11.6 Piazza Navona from the south. Gianlorenzo Bernini added the statue known as 'Il Moro'. The other figures are copies of originals designed by Giacomo della Porta. The ground level basin was a later addition proposed by Borromini

Katherine Wentworth Rinne
Fluid precision: Giacomo della Porta and
the Acqua Vergine fountains of Rome

Next topographically was the San Marco fountain (1587–91) formerly located in front of the Palazzo Venezia at the southern terminus of the Via del Corso. Today the site is about 18.7 metres above sea level, and slightly over 1.5 kilometres from San Sebastianello. Simple subtraction indicates that there was simply no water pressure available in this piazza. Furthermore, the level of the piazza at the time was higher than that of the Via del Corso, down which the conduits were laid. Rather than lower the level of the entire piazza, which would have been exorbitantly expensive for an already over budget project, della Porta submerged the fountain below grade to create an urban grotto down to which one stepped to draw water. For a brief time during 1587 the basin was even ornamented with the antique statue of 'Marforio', a reclining river god, which would have further accentuated the grotto-like quality of the fountain.[31] The final design consisted of an ancient 'vasca' placed in a large rectangular pool that had been 'excavated for the good part of the height of the ancient Egyptian vase'[32] to obtain a decent stream of water.

The original 1570 distribution scheme proposed a fountain for the Piazza Giudea. However, in December 1580, just as the conduits were about to be laid, Matteo Mattei, a wealthy and influential citizen, convinced the *Congregatione* to shift the fountain to the Piazza Mattei in front of his palace.[33] In June 1581, Taddeo Landini was hired to make the fountain, now known as the 'Tartarughe', according to the design and measurements of della Porta, and to complete it by April 1582.[34] The contract spelled out the size of each element – a basin of four *palmi*,[35] figures of six *palmi*, and so on, with the proviso that 'all of the above-mentioned measurements are to be observed, more or less, according to the judgment of Jacomo della Porta' (Fig. 11.7)[36]

11.7 'Fontana su la piazza de SS. Mattei' by Gianbattista Falda, *Le Fontane di Roma* (Rome, 1675). The conch shell basins are fed by Acqua Vergine water and the upper basin is fed by Acqua Felice water (Fiske Kimball Library, University of Virginia)

Acqua Vergine water was inadequate for this fountain as it was finally built. The overall height of the fountain from the level of the piazza, which is about 16 metres above sea level, to the mouth of the upper jet is just under 3 metres. However, this is a full 1.5 metres higher than the theoretical head available in this location, which is a full 2 kilometres from San Sebastianello. Clearly Mattei could exert a great deal of influence on the *Congregatione*, and perhaps he thought that a larger fountain befit his stature in the city, even if it clearly contradicted the hydrological possibilities of Acqua Vergine water at this site. Because of a contract that Mattei held with the *Congregatione* to maintain the piazza and the fountain, he seems to have had a proprietary interest and hence may have exerted influence in the design process.[37] He was certainly able to convince the *Congregatione* to lay a separate conduit, made of lead rather than terracotta, directly from San Sebastianello to the Piazza Mattei.[38]

At any rate, the fountain was not completed until 1588. The inadequate grade differential probably led to prolonged construction delays. Pio Pecchiai cites a decree from the *Congregatione* of 13 March 1584 that alludes to lowering the fountain.[39] This seems to have been done because 418 cartloads of earth were cleared from the piazza on 13 March 1586 'in order to bring it down to the same level as the fountain'.[40] Even with a dedicated lead pipe and a lowered site, there was still insufficient head to deliver water to the upper chalice, which remained dry until 1588. In that year the water of another aqueduct, the higher level Acqua Felice (completed in 1587) arrived at the fountain and served the upper basin. It is generally agreed that the decision to restore the Acqua Alessandrina (the future Acqua Felice) was put forward by Gregory XIII in 1583, nearly two years after della Porta designed the fountain. However, Carlo Fea suggests (but offers no explanation) that the decision was made in 1581.[41] In light of Mattei's influence in the city, he may have been privy to secret information about the intent to bring in the higher aqueduct before it was general knowledge.

The last of della Porta's ornamental fountains for the Vergine network, known as 'La Terrine' was in the Campo dei Fiori where it was specifically intended to serve the largest public market in the city. The Campo site tested the limits of Vergine water distribution. About 1.9 kilometres away from San Sebastianello, it was hampered not only by distance, but also by a severely diminished water supply. Constructed between 1590 and 1594, the design benefited greatly from della Porta's experience. He insured that an adequate supply of water could reach this vital site even during the driest summer months by submerging the fountain almost 1 metre below the level of the piazza, or as one contemporary visitor wrote, 'about half the height of a man'.[42] In 1622 the fountain, shaped like a huge soup tureen, was covered with a stone lid to protect the water supply because the low open basin was constantly filled with debris from the market. The fountain was removed in 1889 to make way for a statue of Giordano Bruno, and in 1924 it was relocated to the Piazza della Chiesa Nuova, where it remains today. The much taller fountains now seen in the Campo dei Fiori is served by the Acqua Paola (Fig. 11.8).

Five additional ornamental public fountains were added to the Vergine network during the Baroque period: the Monte Citorio fountain (*c*.1590) by Francesco da

11.8 The subterranean 'La Terrine' formerly in Campo dei Fiori and now in Piazza della Chiesa Nuova

196

Volterra, the Barcaccia (1627–29) designed by Gianlorenzo Bernini for the Piazza di Spagna, the Quattro Fiume (1648–51) also by Bernini for the Piazza Navona, the Fontana degli Navigatori (1704) by Alessandro Specchi for the Porta di Ripetta, and finally the Trevi (1732–62) designed by Nicolo Salvi. Without going into great detail, I would like merely to suggest that for the baroque drama and innovation of these fountains, particularly those of Bernini, that they are all variations on a theme introduced by della Porta. All five fountains compensate for insufficient pressure with a low centre of gravity and a dominant horizontal composition of cascading sprays of water. Even the largely sculptural Trevi and Quattro Fiume fountains have low, expansive, basins into which the water spews in broad horizontal sheets. The Monte Citorio, Barcaccia and Trevi were all placed below ground level (a full 2 metres for the Trevi) to make maximum use of the minimal water pressure available. Like della Porta's Acqua Vergine fountains, there are only a few jets of water (at the Trevi and the Barcaccia) that act only as compositional highlights. All but the Barcaccia feature craggy rocks as part of the design, reinforcing an image of an urban grotto or sacred spring, down to which the thirsty citizen steps to drink. Taken together these designs all reinforce the horizontal, garden pool schema that della Porta developed from 1570 to 1591 for the original Acqua Vergine fountains (Fig. 11.9).

11.9 The enormous subterranean basin of the Trevi Fountain was excavated fully two metres below the level of the street

Conclusion

Without mechanical pumps no designer could have made Vergine water rise to higher levels. However, I would like to emphasise that each of the Vergine fountains could have taken different forms. There is nothing to suggest that another designer might not have interpreted the relationship between Vergine water and Campo Marzio topography differently, might indeed have failed altogether to understand and respond to the nature of the material. Another designer might easily have relied on existing sculptural prototypes that typically overwhelmed the water to compensate for low pressure, as seen in the Neptune fountains in Messina and Florence. The great accomplishment of della Porta was to understand the limitations that topography placed on gravity-flow water distribution, and at the same time to reveal that complex relationship through a series of site-specific designs. Furthermore, he introduced a new vocabulary of urban fountain design that recalled nature through the use of undulating basins and broad expanses of both animated and reflective water, such as might be seen in garden pools or natural lakes.

197

Water flows naturally to the lowest point in the topography and collects in pools and lakes. The Campo Marzio was, and is, one of the lowest places in Rome. By collecting Acqua Vergine waters into low basins that themselves recall the wave-like motion of water, Giacomo della Porta acknowledged the reality of both the material and the site. His fountains reveal how the demands of a basic infrastructure element, a simple physical law, and the specifics of topography, were respected and harmonised in the creation of a series of uniquely Roman, uniquely Vergine fountains.

Katherine Wentworth Rinne
Fluid precision: Giacomo della Porta and the Acqua Vergine fountains of Rome

Acknowledgements

I thank the Dibner Institute for the History of Science and Technology for its support; and Professor Mirka Benes, Professor David Friedman, Dr Elisabeth B. MacDougall and Professor James Moore for their generous suggestions and comments on an earlier draft of this chapter, which was presented at the 1999 Annual Meeting of the Society of Architectural Historians (USA). Additionally, Joseph Aronson, Professor Meredith Clausen, Professor Joseph Connors, Edward Eigen and Professor William MacDonald all have provided insights and useful bibliographic references. I am grateful to Professor Chuck Hendricks of Lawrence Livermore Laboratory for his help in making sense of complex hydraulic equations. Funding from the Fulbright Commission allowed the author to pursue research for this chapter in Rome.

Notes

1 H. Jordan, *Topographie der Stadt Rom im Alterthum* (Berlin: Weidmannsche Buchhandlung, 1871), II, contains both Latin and German versions of the Notitia Regionum, an early fourth-century inventory of Rome.

2 For an overview of the state of hydraulic knowledge in sixteenth-century Europe, see A. K. Biswas, *History of Hydrology* (Amsterdam: North-Holland, 1972).

3 Before this, he had been involved with a 1563 restoration of the Trevi, and had designed a laundry fountain near St Giorgio in Velabro at the site of a natural spring.

4 The antique Aqua Virgo ran almost entirely underground. It emerged from the slope of the Pincian hill near the southern end of today's Via Gregoriana. From there it travelled on arches to the neighbourhood of the Pantheon. The arcade structure not only deteriorated, but also was buried as the ground level rose several metres in the late antique and medieval periods.

5 For a history of the fountain and the piazza until 1643, see John Pinto, *The Trevi Fountain* (New Haven and London: Yale University Press, 1986), pp. 1–63.

6 This refers to the elevation of the bottom of the *specus* (channel) of the aqueduct at the point where it entered the fountain. The amount of available pressure can vary seasonally depending on the depth of the water in the *specus* above that elevation. Any evidence for pipes that may have been in a *castellum* at the back of the fountain was lost when the fountain was demolished for the 1643 Bernini fountain.

7 This is the elevation of the pipes in the *castellum* Aqueduct elevations supplied by the Azienda Communale Energia ed Ambiente of Rome. 'Schema della distribuzione della rete di innaffiamento', August 1984, sheet 30. Contemporary street elevation from I. Novelli, *Atalante di Roma* (Venice: Marsilio, 1991).

8 C. D'Onofrio, *Le Fontane di Roma*, 3rd edn (Rome: Romana Societa, 1986), pp. 79–80. On 4 November 1570, the *Congregatione* met at the palace of its President Cardinal Ricci da Montepulciano (today the Palazzo Sachetti) in Via Giulia to decide on the distribution programme that was largely authored by della Porta. It is likely that no major water distribution plans were implemented after Constantine moved the capital of the Roman Empire to Constantinople in AD 312.

9 For a discussion of this, and an earlier plan, see *ibid.*, pp. 78–82.

10 Some of the other proposed sites, such as Piazza Sciarra and Piazza Minerva, never received fountains. Some, such as San Rocco, received a smaller mural drinking fountain, and others, such as the Giudea and Montanara, were too far away to receive Acqua Vergine water.

199

11 This is not to suggest that della Porta was unaware of developments outside Italy such as the new aqueduct system for Toledo, Spain designed by Juanelo Turriano in 1565. See *The Twenty-one Books of Engineering and Machines of Juanelo Turriano* [*c.*1590–1600], trans. and ed. Alexander Keller (Madrid: Fundacio Juanelo Turriano, 1999).

12 G. Hersey, *Alfonso II and the Artistic Renewal of Naples* (New Haven and London: Yale University Press, 1969); N. Fasola, *La Fontana di Perugia* (Rome: Libreria dello Stato, 1951); F. Bargagli-Petrucci, *Le fonti di Siena e i loro acquedotti* (Siena: Periccioli, 1974).

13 It was not uncommon for the lower basin of an ornamental fountain to act as a *castellum* for a nearby animal trough or laundry fountain. The Piazza del Popolo fountain, for example, served as a *castellum* for a nearby animal trough and also a laundry fountain.

14 From AD 537 when the invading Goths destroyed the Roman aqueduct system until the early seventeenth century, the Tiber was the primary water source in the city. The hills were essentially abandoned and the low-lying Campo Marzio and Trastevere absorbed most of the population.

15 E. Muntz, *Les arts a la cour des papes pendant le XVe et le XVIe siècle: Recueil de documents inédits* (Paris: Bibliothèque des Ecoles françaises d'Athènes et Rome, 1878),

p.157. Muntz cites a document that states Nicholas V paid for 'fattura di una fontana fatta alla Maddalena, dove stanno I poveri lazari'. The fountain may have been within church property, but it was definitely public. It may even have been placed at the exterior corner in the north end of Piazza della Maddalena. The intersecting street, which is now called Via Collegio Capranica, was known as Via della Acqua Santa before the Collegio was built in the late fifteenth century.

16 An image of the fountain appears in the 1471 map of Rome by Pietro del Massaio but without the distinctive baroque shells, which were added by Bernini.

17 For a catalogue of della Porta's works, see V. Tiberia, *Giacomo della Porta un architetto tra manierismo e barocco* (Milan: Bulzoni, 1974).

18 P. Pecchiai, *Acquedotti e fontane di Roma nel Cinquecento* (Roma: Staderini, 1944), p. 79. Pecchiai includes the pertinent documents from the Registri dei 'Mandati a favore degli Offiziali et artisti del Popolo Romano': credenza VI, vol. XXIII, p. 136 (21 September 1577); p. 138 (25 and 26 October 1577); and p. 140 (13 and 20 January 1578).

19 Today, the fountain is in Piazza Nicosia, where it was placed in 1950. Only the octagonal basin and two top steps are original, while the remaining elements are 'exact' copies.

20 This is made even more difficult than usual because the entire *piazza* was raised perhaps as much as 2 metres during the reconstruction. Today, the elevation at the four corners of the new fountain is about 17 metres above sea level. The surface dips toward the centre of each side to access the drains.

21 Because the laying of the conduits was precariously behind schedule and over budget, owing to serious design errors in the conduits made by Giugliemo della Porta (no relation), Giacomo took over operations and on 2 April 1574 he began the process of substituting terracotta pipes for the travertine pipes laid by Giugliemo. They were much cheaper and were easier to manufacture and install. Because of time constraints to lay out the system as quickly as possible, it was probably more efficient to commission a new upper chalice for the fountain than to endure the ultimate delays in substituting travertine or lead pipes at that time. O. Gracchi, *Projetti degli anni 1575–76*, Archivio Capitolino, credenza VI, vol. XXIII, pp. 127ss, 138ss. Pecchiai, *Acquedotti e fontane di Roma nel Cinquecento*, pp. 33–37, has a detailed chronology.

22 C. Fea, *Esame storico–legale–idraulico dei sifoni impiegati nei condotti dell' Acqua Paola* (Rome: Stamperia Camerale, 1830), p. 31. Fea cites a document issued by the Signori Conservatori del Popolo Romano of 26 February 1583 prohibiting the use of downward angled pipes (rather than horizontal ones) and siphons leading from the *castellum* of the Acqua Vergine because they decreased pressure throughout the network; Archivio Capitolino, credenza 4, vol. CIII, p. 24. Additionally, other published 'editti' strictly forbade laundresses to tap Vergine waters for use in subterranean laundries, hidden in cellars, under a penalty of 500 *scudi*, termination of all water services and other penalties at the discretion of the arbitrator. For an example, see D'Onofrio, *Le Fontane di Roma*, p. 93, who cites an Editto from the Camera Apostolica of 14 June 1608.

23 G. P. Gregori, R. Santoleri, M. P. Pavese, M. Colacino, E. Fiorentino and G. de Franceschi, 'The analysis of point-like historical data series', in *Past, Present and Future Trends in Geophysical Research* (Bremen-Roennebeck: International Association of Geomagnetism and Aeronomy, 1988), pp. 146–211. The year 1577 may have been an extremely dry one because it occurred at the midpoint of the typical forty-one-year cycle of rainfall for Rome and the Tiber basin. Floods in Rome have been recorded from as early as fifth-century Republican Rome. The year 1577 occurred during one of the cyclical troughs, halfway between the devastating 1557 and 1598 floods. As I have not yet obtained accurate rainfall data for the late sixteenth century, it is impossible to confirm this hypothesis.

24 D'Onofrio, *Le Fontane di Roma*, p. 99, citing O. Gracchi, *Notai acque e strade*, vol. 42, cc. 362–365, Archivio di Stato.

25 Leonardo Sormani was hired to begin building the fountain on 6 January 1575. Only ten days later, the Congregatione proposed the same fountain for Piazza Colonna. D'Onofrio, *Le Fontane di Roma*, p.108.

26 B. di Gaddo, *Le fontane di Roma* (Genoa: Vitali & Ghianda, 1964), tab. 13, p. 48. This includes measured drawings of several of the most famous fountains.

27 Originally there were four simple water stanchions rather than the two sculptural groups seen today. They were used for drawing water in jugs, while the central chalice was used for ornamental display of a low water jet. Della Porta had also presented an earlier scheme with the fountain placed at the eastern base of the Column of Marcus Aurelius, with the antique statue of 'Marforio' presiding at the edge of the basin. The statue had survived, more or less in his original position in the Roman Forum since antiquity, but in the late sixteenth century Marforio became the subject of several design proposals. This is illustrated in D'Onofrio, *Le Fontane di Roma*, p. 114, who dates the proposal to 1574.

28 E B. MacDougall, 'L'ingegnoso artifizio', in *Fons Sapientia: Renaissance Garden Fountains* (Washington, DC: Dumbarton Oaks, 1978), pp. 98, 101.

29 E. B. MacDougall, 'The Villa Mattei and the development of the Roman garden style', PhD thesis, Fine Arts Department, Harvard University, 1970, p. 71.

30 D'Onofrio, *Le Fontane di Roma*, p. 103.

31 It is difficult to judge the elevation of the site in the 1580s with currently available information. However, the maximum head must have been about 19 metres above sea level. Although della Porta failed to persuade the Congregatione with his proposal to use the Marforio statue in Piazza Colonna, he did convince them to move it to the San Marco fountain in September 1587. Unfortunately, in the following January the statue was moved again, this time to the Capitoline, thus stripping the Campo Marzio of its first resident river god.

32 F. Martinelli, unpublished manuscript from the Biblioteca Casanatense, Rome, 1652? (Catalogue number f.X.29.3.) I would like to thank Prof. Mirka Benès for this reference.

33 Pecchiai, *Acquedotti e fontane di Roma nel Cinquecento*, p. 48.

34 *Ibid.*, p. 49.

35 According to D'Onofrio, *Le Fontane di Roma*, p. 195, a *palmo* equals 22.26 centimetres; according to di Gaddo, *Le Fontane di Roma*, p. 59, a *palmo* equals 22.34 centimetres.

36 Pecchiai, *Acquedotti e fontane di Roma nel Cinquecento*, p. 49. The fountain itself was also reduced in size. See di Gaddo, p. 59.

37 D'Onofrio, *Le Fontane di Roma*, p. 129, makes such a suggestion.

38 Archivio Capitolino, Registri 'Mandati a favore degli Offiziali et artisti del Popolo Romano', 3 January 1583, credenza VI, vol. XXIII, p. 197. Also, Pecchiai, *Acquedotti e fontane di Roma nel Cinquecento*, p. 82, cites this document as well as others dated 13 April, 1 June and 3 July 1581.

39 *Ibid.*, p. 50, citing a decree from the Congregatione that states, 'attenta nova forma eidem fonti constituenda propter illius depressionem faciendam'. I am convinced that it was necessary to lower the fountain even to insure that Vergine water would flow into the lower basins.

40 *Ibid.*, p. 83, citing 'Mandati a favore degli Offiziali et artisti del Popolo Romano'; credenza VI, vol. XXIV, p. 102.

41 C. Fea, *Storia dell' acque correnti* (Rome, 1832), p. 28. Fea suggests that the decision was made in 1581.

42 Cited in L. Callari, *Fontane di Roma* (Rome: Bardi, 1970), p. 289.

Section Five

Aesthetic analysis

12 New projects for the City of Münster: Ilya Kabakov, Herman de Vries and Dan Graham

How and to what effect can nature, under today's circumstances, be turned into art? Some widely varying answers were given at the 1997 exhibition 'sculpture.projects' in the Westphalian city of Münster in Germany, and the present chapter offers a close reading of three of these — namely Ilya Kabakov's, Herman de Vries's and Dan Graham's contributions to the show.[1] More precisely, it investigates what these works might entail for a discussion of personal identity, focussing on whether the three artists' approaches to nature embrace either a traditional notion of the unitary self, or a postmodern concept of the decentred subject.[2]

The exhibition was the third in a pivotal series, started in Münster in 1977 and held every ten years, devoted to art in the public sphere.[3] At least partly, the conspicuous concern with nature that marked the works of many of the seventy-eight artists who participated in 1997 formed an answer to the city's exceptionally 'green' urban landscape. The fortifications around Münster's medieval centre were demolished from 1764 to make room for a circular tree-lined promenade. This, together with the late eighteenth-century bishop's palace (now a university building) to the west of the city centre, was the work of Johann Conrad Schlaun — Westphalia's foremost Baroque architect — and the less prominent neoclassicist Wilhelm Ferdinand Lipper. The palace grounds, originally planned by Schlaun as a formal French garden, then given a stylistically somewhat hybrid shape by Lipper since 1773 and changed into an English-style landscape garden in 1854, survived as a municipal park after substantial damage in the Second World War. The promenade owes its present grandeur largely to work done on it in the early 1890s.[4] From 1926, the River Aa was dammed at some distance south of the palace to form an inner-city lake, and another large park was created along the lake's banks. Artists at the 1997 'sculpture.projects' made extensive use of this park as well as of the palace grounds, the promenade and the directly adjacent areas.[5]

Ilya Kabakov

Ilya Kabakov's 1997 work, entitled 'Looking Up, Reading the Words', has been permanently installed in its original place on the north-west bank of Lake Aa (Fig. 12.1).

12.1 *Looking Up, Reading the Words*, by Ilya Kabakov, 1997, Münster, Aaseewiesen

12.2 Detail of Fig. 12.1

Approaching it, at first one sees a metal construction resembling a radio transmitter. A steel mast, 15 metres high, carries two aluminium pipes, each 14.45 metres long. These support twenty-two horizontal antennas of differing lengths. As one approaches, they look as if a huge spider's net were woven between them — an effect caused by wire letters welded between the antennas (Fig. 12.2). The only way in which one can comfortably read what they say is to stretch out on the ground under them. The text reads: 'Mein Lieber! Du liegst im Gras, den Kopf im Nacken, um Dich herum keine Menschenseele, Du hörst nur den Wind und schaust hinauf in den offenen Himmel — in das Blau dort oben, wo die Wolken ziehen —, das ist vielleicht das Schönste, was Du im Leben getan und gesehen hast.'[6]

Initially, this simply seems to encourage one to enjoy an idyllic moment, save that the steel structure which supports them reminds us that we are not in Arcadia. However, in the right weather conditions the impact of the expanse of sky above is almost overwhelming. The letters stimulate a sense of scale and thus bring the immensity of space beyond into majestic prominence. They also provide a grid that allows viewers to position themselves in relation to the continual flux of changing shapes, colours and heavenly bodies above (Fig. 12.3). This is a scene that dwarfs the beholder, a sight which is sublime in both Edmund Burke's and Immanuel Kant's sense of the term.

Through the wire words the metal structure — which could have been viewed simply as a sculptural object until one has read what they say — becomes an instrument

12.3 Detail of Figs 12.1 and 12.2

which arrests us point-blank in space and time to make us see a little-noticed aspect of nature. It also tells us, albeit less directly, where to read what the sky above can mean for the viewer's identity. To substantiate this statement, I must take a detour via Russian Constructivism. Alexander Rodchenko's 1929 photograph of the Sukov Tower (Fig. 12.4) is a famous example of this artist's fascination with vertical perspective, and Kabakov could well have had it in mind when designing the Münster installation.[7] With Rodchenko as with Kabakov, what directs one's gaze up to the heavens is a feat of engineering that provides some highly dramatic vanishing lines. From Rodchenko's other photographs, it is clear that for him the tower — though an obvious symbol of the technological age he so strongly believed in — was less important as a motif than the expressive possibilities of vertical perspective as such; equally, from his work as a whole it is obvious that he did not understand nature and technology as mutually exclusive.[8] 'Pines' (Fig. 12.5) — one of a series of photographs taken in 1927 near the poet Vladimir Mayakovsky's *dacha* at Pushkino — shows in what way, for Rodchenko, a forest could take the Sukov Tower's place.[9] And via cultural memory, this image of nature blends into Kabakov's installation.

The photograph of the Pushkino pines also hints at what is probably the single most important textual source behind Kabakov's work at Münster: Rodchenko's image could almost be used to illustrate the second letter in Johann Wolfgang von Goethe's *Sorrows of Young Werther* (1774/87).[10] Here, Werther — an amateur artist — describes to his correspondent a violently emotional response to vivid landscape impressions. Lying in the grass near a stream where only a few rays of sunlight penetrate the darkness of a forest, he observes insect life, and is then prompted to feel

the presence of the Almighty, who … in a state of continuous bliss bears and sustains us — then, my friend, when … the world around me and the sky fully rest

12.4 *The Sukov Tower*, by Alexander Rodchenko, Leica photograph from *Radiosliushatel*, 40 (1929). (Courtesy Niedersächsische Staats- und Universitätsbibliothek Göttingen)

12.5 *Pines*, by Alexander Rodchenko, Leica photograph from *Novyi Lef*, 7 (1927). (Courtesy Niedersächsische Staats- und Universitätsbibliothek Göttingen)

within my soul like the figure of a beloved; then I ... often think: oh if only I could express it all on paper, everything that lives so richly and warmly within me, in such a way that it would reflect my soul, just as my soul is the mirror image of the infinite God! — My friend — but it makes me perish, I succumb to the violence of the splendour of these images.[11]

Kabakov's words in the Münster installation virtually force the viewer to assume a physical position very similar to Werther's, giving him/her a chance to imitate this passionate youth and let sky rest within soul. In view of the fact that during a conversation about his work at Münster the artist explicitly acknowledged his interest in Goethe,[12] it is tempting to take Werther as a main reference figure and to conclude that Kabakov's steel mast is pointing to a sky that has a potential of opening up into a transcendent dimension, thus raising the old theme of epiphany through nature. Kabakov's understanding of this as expressed in his installation would thus seem to be coloured by the Storm and Stress concept — formulated by Johann Gottfried Herder, prominent in Goethe's *Werther*, and later taken up in Romanticism — of nature as a great current of sympathy running through all things, including humankind, and that therefore we have access to the deepest cosmic truths through feeling and our inner voice.[13]

However, of course a mere possibility of epiphany does not afford certainty; at this point, everything depends on how each viewer, lying in the grass and contemplating the sky, interprets Kabakov's central phrase 'perhaps this is the most beautiful thing you have done and seen in your life'. Here it is important to recall that in the 1960s and early 1970s, Kabakov developed a sceptical interest in Suprematist metaphysics. In the light of this, what Kazimir Malevich had to say about the sky in 1919 begins to scintillate as one looks at the Münster installation: 'The blue of the sky has been conquered by the suprematist system, has been breached, and has passed into the white beyond as the true, real conception of eternity....'[14] Kabakov's wire words could be understood as a critique of this, as questioning Malevich's metaphysical aspirations; read in this sense, they would seem to intimate that the sky is in fact the most beautiful sight one can ever contemplate. However, alternatively one could take the crucial word 'perhaps' in his text as a reminder that there may be something beyond the blue sky that is even more beautiful. And this is a reading that would find support in what Kabakov has been saying to his biographer Amei Wallach about his and his Moscow friends' own attitude towards metaphysics: '[We] were interested in white as the holy light and as emptiness — not emptiness as in death or nothingness, but as absolutely positive.... White is like a screen on which from an enormous depth shines a very positive beam, a very positive energy. This is the metaphysical space in our world...'.[15]

Thus, in the end, one is back with a potentially epiphanic sky, and therefore back with Werther. As has been shown, young Goethe's Storm and Stress notion of the self as intimately connected with the cosmos is not at all unthreatening to the subject since there is a risk of perishing 'from splendour'. Yet it remains a notion of the unitary self, and by drawing one's attention to it, Kabakov probes how far it is still, or yet again, valid as a stance from which to confront the natural world. To summarize: in Kabakov's work at Münster, the possibility of epiphany through nature is bound up with a memory of the unfragmented Romantic self, even if such a retrieval here does not mean a simple reinstatement. Nothing limits the viewer to one single reading; several layers of meaning coexist, overlap and question each other. Epiphany can be, but does not have to be experienced as a result of viewing the work. If it is, this results from the potency of a cultural tradition combined with the sublimity — and again this term is used in the eighteenth-century sense of the word — of the natural sky and of infinite space.

Herman de Vries

One must now ask whether, in the landscape of contemporary art, Kabakov's concern with epiphany and his gesture towards the unitary self constitute an idiosyncrasy or whether other artists share such interests. Herman de Vries's architectural installation 'sanctuary' (Fig. 12.6), erected at the northern periphery of Münster's palace grounds, consists of a round brick wall, 14 metres in diameter and 3 metres high, with no gates or doorways but with one bull's-eye opening in each of the four directions of the wind, 65 centimetres wide and placed at about eye level. It is only through these that the

12.6 *Sanctuary,* by Herman de Vries, 1997, Münster, northern periphery of the Schlossgarten

12.7 Detail of Fig. 12.6 showing the interior through a bull's-eye opening

viewer can catch a glimpse of the interior, where nature is meant to develop according to its own laws (Fig. 12.7). The artist did not plant or sow anything here, leaving just the bare soil. In June 1997, a population of mainly nettles had begun to fill the space; less than a year later, the vegetation had already grown to the level of the four openings. The small area of uncultivated nature within the wall contrasts with the surrounding park, which de Vries describes as 'suppressed nature'.[16]

De Vries goes on to explain that the four gilded inscriptions in Sanskrit on the sandstone ledge at the top of the wall above each of the oval openings (Fig. 12.8) are quotes from what he wrongly identifies as the Tsá Upanishad (*sic*), and say: 'om. this is perfect. that is perfect. perfect comes from perfect. take perfect from perfect, the remainder is perfect'.[17] De Vries, who worked as a conservationist earlier in life, has written that he wants the wall to function merely as a frame which protects and presents what is happening within. Obviously, this is misleading. The wall does provide considerable semantic depth, and does so in more ways than just through the inscriptions. For one thing, it is circular, and the circle is, of course, familiar as a symbol of perfection, and of God, no matter if one thinks of ancient China, Andrea Palladio's Italy or of a host of other locations.[18] Form in de Vries thus strengthens the spiritual connotations of the work's title and of the Sanskrit quote. In addition, the brick and sandstone structure frankly declares its indebtedness to Westphalian Renaissance and Baroque architecture and is thus firmly anchored in its geographical and historical environment; for example, the *corps-de-logis* of the Münster Palace, begun by Schlaun in 1767, is also built of red brick and yellow sandstone, and the sandstone entablature on its east façade equally bears a gilded inscription. At the same time and in different formal terms, de Vries's 'sanctuary' is loosely related to a work like Robert Smithson's 'Mono Lake Nonsite' (1968), which features — among other elements — a frame around an empty centre.[19]

12.8 Detail of Fig. 12.6 showing the Sanskrit inscription

However, de Vries's preoccupation is not with emptiness but with the fullness of nature, and one must now ask what his work implies for the investigation of personal identity. As the artist himself has pointed out, the title of his piece has a double meaning: 'sanctuary' in the sense of shrine, and in the sense of nature reserve.[20] It has been seen how through the Sanskrit inscriptions and through the circular form of the wall nature is defined as a source of unity and wholeness. In his text for the Münster catalogue, de Vries predictably describes his work as an act of resistance against commercialism and excessive technology. But what exactly does he understand by nature, which he presents as an antidote? It is 'a *revelation*. As a manifestation, it tells us everything that is vitally important … what am i? — what am i a part of? — what is my life — …? these basic questions of philosophy, and their answers, are all embraced in this primary reality that reveals itself to us'.[21]

Elsewhere, de Vries has mentioned his interest in Gerardo Reichel-Dolmatoff's ethnographic work with the Tukanoan Indians of the North-West Amazon and in what Reichel-Dolmatoff says about their understanding of nature as an analogy of man.[22] Again, this is only mentioned in passing. The questions I am trying to answer here make me propose to set de Vries's all-encompassing idea of nature against a different background, namely that of Jean-Jacques Rousseau's concept of a return to nature. To recapitulate briefly, Rousseau believed that it is possible for man to recover his lost contact with nature by following his inner voice — which he understood as the voice of nature and which, according to him, would help man discover the good. This comes close to de Vries, but as far as I can see the artist does not explicitly mention Rousseau anywhere, which makes me suspect that Rousseauesque ideas have reached him in the reductive form in which they circulate in parts of today's green movement. For Rousseau himself, discovery of the good is made possible only through a fusion of nature and reason. And the description of Mme de Wolmar's wild-looking but actually carefully cultivated secret garden (the 'Elysium') in his novel *Julie, ou la nouvelle Héloïse* (1761–64) makes it clear that for him nature did not necessarily suffer from cautious and sensible human intervention.[23] In other words, he was rather more optimistic about humankind than de Vries, postulating that the source of unity and wholeness is to be discovered within the reasonable self, and not in an unkempt miniature paradise which our instrumental reason is threatening to such an extent that one has to be shut out from it.

Yet, although de Vries places us outside good and holy nature, the sanctuary is there to attract anyone who wants to be healed and hopes to regain a sense of wholeness through contemplating this ideal. If an element of unconscious humour lurks behind the idea of squeezing nature into this tiny temple, this is less relevant in our context than the fact that the 'sanctuary' is meant to draw us towards, once again, a notion of the unitary self which is ultimately rooted in Preromanticism and Romanticism. This is in spite of one very un-Romantic aspect of the work, namely de Vries's minimalization of his own role as creator. The sanctuary's Romantic side comes into the picture only if one centres on the artist's utterly confident attitude towards nature (and perhaps also on his multicultural awareness). If, for de Vries, living specimens of flora and fauna radiate numinous energies that he hopes an absorption in nature can make one grasp, a Romantic writer like Friedrich Schelling's understanding of nature as 'visible spirit' is looming large.[24] Thus, de Vries, too, ends with the issue of epiphany bound up with the unitary self — but in marked contrast to Kabakov he does so didactically, prescriptively and thus ultimately one-dimensionally.

Dan Graham

The third work in the series — Dan Graham's *Fun House for Münster* (Fig. 12.9) — takes one to a completely different concept of the human subject's place in nature. Graham's pavilions, of which *Fun House* is a variant, are all constructed of metal frames and two-way mirror glass. Both sides of this are at the same time transparent and reflective; the more light falls on the surface, the more reflective the glass becomes. *Fun House* is 5 metres long, 2.3 metres high and 2 metres wide. Three of its glass walls are straight and arranged as in a thin parallelogram, the fourth is convex on the outside and concave on the inside. The structure can be entered through an opening in one of the two longer sides. The curved side creates anamorphic distortions of all that is reflected in it — for instance, the trees of the north-east stretch of the Münster Promenade and the viewers. The straight sides in turn mirror these distortions — that is, in addition to the undistorted reflections which they also display. The work was placed close to a

12.9 *Fun House for Münster,* by Dan Graham, a temporary installation on Münster Promenade, summer 1997

childrens' playground and was meant to address children and parents in particular.

Graham's pavilions stand at the end of a long and extremely pluralistic genealogical line that reaches from recent corporate buildings to shopping malls, suburban bus shelters, de Stijl exhibition pavilions, nineteenth-century funfair amusements, the Crystal Palace, Renaissance and Rococo as well as Chinese garden pavilions, Baroque cabinets of mirrors, and last but not least back to the elemental rustic hut whose origin Graham erroneously locates in the writings of Marc-Antoine Laugier instead of in Vitruvius.[25] This somewhat vertiginous path into architectural history also takes us back to Rousseau. In Graham's text *The City as Museum*, he draws a connection between Laugier and the philosopher: 'Like Jean-Jacques Rousseau, Laugier set up his model to criticise the degradation of modern society: architecture would be derived from an uncontaminated Nature. The "rustic hut" was supposed to be a reduction to Man's and architecture's original nature....'[26]

The fact that the artist's pavilions simultaneously allude to modernist glass architecture like that of Ludwig Mies van der Rohe is particularly interesting in that Walter Benjamin, an author frequently referred to by Graham, saw such glass structures as partly responsible for twentieth-century cultural amnesia. Rainer Metzger, who has recently drawn attention to this, goes on to show how Graham, with a somewhat mannerist bow to Benjamin, uses glass and some of the formal vocabulary of such modernist buildings to resuscitate what the artist calls 'that period in time made amnesiac by commodity culture'.[27] As we have seen, this involves resuscitating forgotten, or half-forgotten, reactions to nature.

Where it comes to visual effects, the result of Graham's synthesis of arcadia and modernist architecture can be described in terms of the picturesque. The literature on Graham covers this aspect of his pavilions rather broadly, and the same is true of comments on another eighteenth-century (and modernist) theme they call up, namely utopia.[28] Therefore, it may not be necessary to dwell on either subject here, especially since another aspect of *Fun House* is much more directly relevant to our analysis of identity. Graham himself has mentioned that he has found his artistic stance confirmed in the writings of Jacques Lacan, whose seminal essay on the mirror phase (1949) he explicitly mentions,[29] and it seems useful at this point to sum up briefly some key points of Lacan's thought that are particularly relevant with a view to Graham's pavilions.[30] For Lacan the mirror phase — which a child enters at about six months of age — is the moment of the genesis of the ego. It is the moment when the child, confronted with a mirror, recognizes the distinction between self and other, as well as absence (most conspicuously, that of the mother). In its completeness, the specular image clashes with the child's experience of the world and of its own body, an experience which is at this point in life fragmentary and chaotic. As a consequence, the mirror image becomes an ideal for the ego to strive after. The ego's fascination with specular reflections together with its attempts at compensating the absence of the mother will orient it forever in the direction of imaginary identifications of self with other and other with self; it can thus be seen as a sedimentation of internalized and libidinally invested images of others as well as of the body it inhabits.[31] Through the mirror phase the child enters what Lacan came to call the Imaginary Order — which according to him is not only a stage in the human being's development, but also a lasting level of the psyche.[32]

Obviously, the mirror phase gives rise to social relations with those with whom the human being identifies;[33] however, the Imaginary Order does not bear the stamp of words, but is a domain of unconscious images that shapes the ego's attitude towards others. Language comes later than the onset of the mirror phase, and in Lacan's system it comes at a different level: the human subject (which is not to be confused with the ego) is fully constituted only through what he calls the Symbolic Order, and it is to this latter that language belongs. Lacan's human subject, thus caught between the Imaginary and the Symbolic, is anything but unified and stable; and if one keeps searching for wholeness and unity, in his view one does so very much in vain. While the ego may well give one a feeling of stability, according to Lacan this feeling is nothing more than an illusion, with the ego acting as an alienating armour which masks the subject's underlying 'lack of being'.[34]

It would obviously be inadequate to interpret the fragmentary and irritatingly superimposed flurry of distorted and undistorted reflections of self and other which the viewer sees on all sides of *Fun House* as a straightforward illustration of the many and varied processes of identification, projection and idealization which in Lacan's view constitute the ego — not least because a simple specular image without any anamorphic effects would have been quite sufficient to reflect his views on the mirror phase. Rather, one might say that *Fun House* provides visual impressions that show the average viewer's confidence in what s/he feels to be the basic stability of their own image to be illusory: a slight change of position and of light, and what one thought was an objective mirror image of one's face has turned into a barely recognizable grimace (Fig. 12.10). It is up to the viewers to draw further conclusions and to start wondering if corresponding confidence in their unity and stability as human subjects is as futile as these mirror images are transitory.[35]

In addition, the multiple specular reflections, the changing degree of transparency and above all the anamorphic side of *Fun House* expose one to doubt not only about the truthfulness of one's own image, but also about one's situation in space and in the park environment. The plethora of historical associations which *Fun House* calls up in relation to nature are thus destabilized and questioned along with the unity of the subject, whose face is here literally made to vanish in nature (Fig. 12.10).

Finally, as a focus on the demise or otherwise of the unitary self must inevitably address René Descartes' *cogito* as well as Lacan's *desidero*, one has to face one last paradox. Insofar as one major point of *Fun House* is to foment distrust in visual evidence, paradoxically this work bears witness to nothing less than a Cartesian tradition.[36] While it is common knowledge that Descartes — in his *Discours de la méthode* and in his essay on 'La Dioptrique' (1637) — commented on the deceptiveness of visual impressions,[37] Martin Kemp has more specifically highlighted the relevance of anamorphosis to Descartes in this context and outlined the anamorphic experiments of one of the philosopher's correspondents, the perspective theorist Jean-François Niceron (Fig. 12.11).[38] Obviously, not every detail of this matters with a view to Graham:

12.10 Detail of Fig. 12.9 showing reflections in the concave two-way mirror glass with anamorphically distorted face and hands of the viewer at bottom left

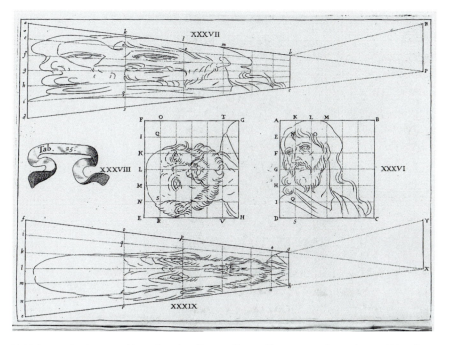

12.11 Anamorphic distortion of faces, from Jean-François Niceron, *Thaumaturgus Opticus* (Paris, 1663 edn), tab. 25. (Courtesy Niedersächsische Staats- und Universitätsbibliothek Göttingen)

the decisive point in relation to *Fun House* must be that if the artist succeeds in bringing an anti-Cartesian concept of the self visually alive, this is thanks to a Cartesian attitude of doubt in visual appearance which he activates in the viewer. And ultimately, his Lacanian alternative to the unitary self is in turn called into question precisely by virtue of such Cartesian doubt in what presents itself to our eyes.[39]

Conclusion

The primary intention in this chapter has been to highlight, through three iconological case studies, some of the most radical differences that exist between contemporary artistic definitions of man's place in nature. It has been shown how each of the artists I have commented on views nature through eyes strongly conditioned by philosophical concepts of personal identity – with results ranging from de Vries's unquestioning acceptance of an ultimately Romantic notion of the unitary self, and Kabakov's vastly more sophisticated approach to this concept, to Graham's Lacanian rejection of any idea of such unity. It has been my particular concern to show that where notions of the unitary self inform the works I have been discussing, these notions are connected with the idea of epiphany through nature – which is either envisaged as a possibility (as in Kabakov) or posited as a firm axiom (as in de Vries).

Going beyond these observations would overstretch the scope of what can be said in a few pages. However, it may be in order to venture a very brief closing remark on the wider philosophical implications of my results. Among the three works, de Vries's offers but limited interest in this respect because of the intellectual simplicity that it betrays, while Graham's pavilion – visually successful and socially stimulating though it certainly is – has been shown to culminate in a conceptual impasse. It is Kabakov who takes us to the cutting edge of contemporary aesthetic thought. Through its carefully qualified evocation of a Romantic concept of the self, his Münster work raises the vital question whether the *Geistesgefühl* of the Sublime – reclaimed for recent philosophy above all by Jean-François Lyotard – is ultimately compatible with any postmodern notion of the decentred subject.[40] In touching this problem, Kabakov's installation also makes one ask whether postmodern aesthetics, for all their merits in stressing the limits of representation, possibly underestimate the subject's capacity to grasp infinity as a force under whose impact any shattered fragments of the self could melt into a unity newly found.

Notes

1 The chapter is based on a paper read at the Association of Art Historians' (UK) annual conference at Exeter on 3 April 1998; see also Ursula Seibold-Bultmann, 'Unangetastete Räume. Natur und Geschichte als Themen neuer Kunst', *Neue Zürcher Zeitung*, 188 (16–17 August 1997), p. 34.

2 Where the term 'nature' is used without further qualification, it is shorthand for the physical facts of flora, fauna and the weather.

3 For the catalogues of the three shows held so far, see K. Bussmann and N. Nobis (eds), *'Skulptur': Ausstellung in Münster 1977* (Münster: Landschaftsverband Westfalen-Lippe & Stadt Münster, 1977); K. Bussmann and K. König (eds), *Skulptur. Projekte in Münster 1987* (Cologne: DuMont, 1987); and K. Bussmann, K. König and F. Matzner (eds), *Skulptur. Projekte in Münster 1997* (Ostfildern-Ruit: Gerd Hatje, 1997); English edn *Sculpture. Projects in Münster* (London: Thames & Hudson, 1997). For the history of exhibitions of sculpture and installations in the public sphere, see C. Büttner, *Art Goes Public: Von der Gruppenausstellung im Freien zum Projekt im nicht-institutionellen Raum* (Munich: Silke Schreiber, 1997).

4 K. Bussmann, F. Matzner and U. Schulze (eds), *Johann Conrad Schlaun 1695–1773: Architektur des Spätbarock in Europa* (Stuttgart: Oktagon, 1995); F. Matzner and U. Schulze, *Johann Conrad Schlaun 1695–1773. Das Gesamtwerk*, 2 vols, ed. K. Bussmann (Stuttgart: Oktagon, 1995), II, pp. 893–895 on Schlaun's plans for the promenade. For Lipper's work there, see K. Bussmann, *Wilhelm Ferdinand Lipper: Ein Beitrag zur Geschichte des Frühklassizismus in Münster* (Münster: Aschendorff, 1972), p. 8. Also B. Haunfelder and U. Oelliges, *Die Promenade in Münster: Vom Festungsring zum Grüngürtel …* (Münster: Aschendorff, 1994), pp. 29, 50–51.

5 For a map with sites, see Bussmann *et al. Skulptur. Projekte in Münster 1997*, pp. 44–45.

6 'My dear friend! You are lying in the grass, with your head thrown back, not a living soul is around, you hear only the wind and look up into the open sky – into the blue, where the clouds float by –, perhaps this is the most beautiful thing you have done and seen in your life' (author's translation); in B. Groys, D. A. Ross and I. Blazwick, *Ilya Kabakov* (London: Phaidon, 1998), p. 87 'das Schönste' ('the most beautiful') is translated as 'the best'.

7 For the 1968 Rodchenko retrospective in Moscow, see A. Wallach, *Ilya Kabakov: The Man Who Never Threw Anything Away* (New York: Harry N. Abrams, 1996), p. 57.

8 For Rodchenko's photographs in general, see S. O. Khan-Magomedov, *Rodchenko: The Complete Work* (Cambridge, MA: MIT Press, 1987), pp. 214–238; H. Gassner, *Rodčenko: Fotografien* (Munich: Schirmer-Mosel, 1982); and A. Lavrent'ev, *Rodchenko: Photography 1924–1954* (Cologne: Könemann, 1995).

9 Rodchenko compared the pines to telegraph poles; P. Galassi, 'Rodchenko and photography's revolution', in *Aleksandr Rodchenko*, eds M. Dabrowski, L. Dickerman and P. Galassi (New York: Museum of Modern Art, 1998), p. 120.

10 I say 'almost' because what is close to Goethe's Werther here is only the visual motif; Rodchenko, as an outspoken exponent of materialism, would have had little sympathy for the spiritual élan expressed in Werther's letter.

11 Johann Wolfgang von Goethe, *Goethes Werke*, ed. E. Trunz, 13th edn (Munich: Beck, 1993), VI: *Die Leiden des Jungen Werther*, p. 9, my translation, with inspiration from Catherine Hutter's in Goethe, *The Sorrows of Young Werther and Selected Writings* (New York: Signet Classic, 1962), p. 25.

12 Information from Dr Ulrike Groos of the exhibition staff, July 1997. After Goethe, the motif of a creative character lying idly in the grass was further developed in German Romantic and Biedermeier literature and art, for example in Joseph von Eichendorff, *Memoirs of a Good-for-Nothing* (1826) [K. Polheim and K. K. Polheim, *Text und Textgeschichte des 'Taugenichts': Eichendorffs Novelle von der Entstehung bis zum Ende der Schutzfrist*

(Tübingen: Max Niemeyer, 1989), I, p. 26] or by the painter Carl Spitzweg [G. Roennefahrt, *Carl Spitzweg: Beschreibendes Verzeichnis seiner Gemälde, Ölstudien und Aquarelle* (Munich: F. Bruckmann, 1960), pp. 294–295, cat. no. 1416].

13 For more on this concept, see C. Taylor, *Sources of the Self: The Making of the Modern Identity* (Cambridge: Cambridge University Press, 1992), pp. 368–374.

14 Statement from the catalogue of the 'Tenth State Exhibition: Nonobjective Creation and Suprematism', Moscow; quoted in J. E. Bowlt (ed.), *Russian Art of the Avant-Garde: Theory and Criticism 1902–1934* (New York: Viking, 1976), p. 144. Wallach, *Ilya Kabakov*, p. 34, erroneously dates Malevich's text to 1916.

15 Wallach, *Ilya Kabakov*, p. 44; also p. 50.

16 De Vries, in Bussmann *et al.*, *Skulptur. Projekte in Münster 1997*, p. 431.

17 *Ibid.*, p. 433; translation by S. P. Swami and W. B. Yeats, *The Ten Principal Upanishads* (London: Faber & Faber, 1937). In fact, the quote is from the *Brihadaranyaka Upanishad* (*ibid.*, p. 159), while the words in the *Eesha Upanishad* (*sic*) are in a different order (*ibid.*, p. 15).

18 M. Lurker, *Der Kreis als Symbol im Denken, Glauben und künstlerischen Gestalten der Menschheit* (Tübingen: Wunderlich, 1981).

19 R. Hobbs, *Robert Smithson: Sculpture* (Ithaca: Cornell University Press, 1981), pp. 112–113.

20 De Vries in Bussmann *et al.*, *Skulptur. Projekte in Münster 1997*, p. 431.

21 *Ibid.*, p. 432. Also A. Meier (ed.), *H. de Vries: To Be: Texte, Textarbeiten, Textbilder* (Ostfildern: Cantz, 1995), pp. 156–157.

22 *Ibid.*, pp. 126, 128; also G. Reichel-Dolmatoff, *Shamanism and Art of the Eastern Tukanoan Indians, Colombian Northwest Amazon* (Leiden: Brill, 1987).

23 Jean-Jacques Rousseau, *Œuvres complètes*, eds B. Gagnebin and M. Raymond, II: *La Nouvelle Héloïse, Théatre-Poésies, Essais littéraires* (Paris: Gallimard, 1964), pp. 470–488.

24 Taylor, *Sources of the Self*, p. 476; E. Brito, *La création selon Schelling* (Leuven: Leuven University Press, 1987), esp. pp. 96–102.

25 D. Graham, *Rock My Religion: Writings and Art Projects 1965–1990*, ed. B. Wallis (Cambridge, MA: MIT Press, 1993), p. 264. Graham's source is Laugier's *Essai sur l'architecture* (Paris, 1755).

220

26 Graham, *Rock My Religion*, p. 258. For a variant statement by Graham, see M. Köttering and R. Nachtigäller (eds), *Two-Way Mirror Pavilions … 1989–1996* (Nordhorn: Städtische Galerie, 1996), p. 87.

27 R. Metzger, *Kunst in der Postmoderne: Dan Graham* (Cologne: Walther König, 1996), p. 168.

28 On Graham and the picturesque, see *ibid.*, pp. 159–161; on utopia, see *ibid.*, pp. 163–166, 170–173.

29 'Le stade du miroir comme formateur de la fonction du Je, telle qu'elle nous est révélée dans l'expérience psychanalytique', in Jacques Lacan, *Ecrits* (Paris: du Seuil, 1966), pp. 93–100. For Graham and Lacan, see B. Pelzer, 'Vision in process', *October*, 10 (1979), pp. 105–119; Metzger, *Kunst in der Postmoderne*, pp. 106–111; and H. D. Huber (ed.), *Dan Graham: Interviews* (Ostfildern: Cantz, 1997), pp. 14–15.

30 For those unfamiliar with Lacan, see E. Roudinesco, *Jacques Lacan: Esquisse d'une vie, histoire d'un système de pensée* (Paris: Librairie Arthème Fayard, 1993); and *idem*, *Jacques Lacan & Co.: A History of Psychoanalysis in France 1925–1985* (London: Free Association Books, 1990).

31 E. A. Grosz, *Jacques Lacan: A Feminist Introduction* (London: Routledge, 1990), pp. 30–49.

32 M. Sarup, *Jacques Lacan* (New York: Harvester Wheatsheaf, 1992), p. 66. For a differing view, see Metzger, *Kunst in der Postmoderne*, pp. 106–107.

33 Grosz, *Jacques Lacan*, p. 43.

34 Sarup, *Jacques Lacan*, pp. 83–87; Jacques Lacan, 'Fonction et champ de la parole et du langage en psychanalyse', in Lacan, *Ecrits*, pp. 237–322.

35 On another level, the anamorphic and fragmentary reflections in and on 'Fun House' could be read as illustrating the human being's disorganized experience of itself at the point of entering the mirror phase, while the undistorted mirror images could be taken to represent the Lacanian ego as engendered by the mirror phase (i.e. a fallacious ideal). Obviously, the social dimension of the mirror phase comes into play when more than one viewer approach Fun House closely enough to be reflected simultaneously.

36 For Lacan's own interest in Descartes, see A. Juranville, *Lacan et la philosophie* (Paris: Presses Universitaires de France, 1984), esp. pp. 140–151, 388–396. I have found no indication that would suggest that Graham consciously takes up this aspect of Lacan's thought.

37 R. Descartes, *Œuvres de Descartes*, eds C. Adam and P. Tannery, VI: *Discours de la méthode & essais* (Paris: Vrin, 1996), pp. 37–39, 141–147.

38 M. Kemp, *The Science of Art: Optical Themes in Western Art from Brunelleschi to Seurat* (New Haven and London: Yale University Press, 1990), pp. 210–211.

39 For Lacan himself and anamorphosis, see Grosz, *Jacques Lacan*, p. 79.

40 For Lyotard's confidence that it is, see, for example, his text on 'Le sublime et l'avant-garde', in Jean-François Lyotard, *L'Inhumain. Causeries sur le temps* (Paris: Galilée, 1988), pp. 101–118 (p. 112, in relation to Burke); and *idem*, 'Beantwortung der Frage: Was ist postmodern?', in W. Welsch (ed.), *Wege aus der Moderne. Schlüsseltexte der Postmoderne-Diskussion*, 2nd edn (Berlin: Akademie Verlag, 1994), pp. 193–203 (p. 199, implicitly, in relation to Kant).

Philippe Nys

13　The Villa d'Este storyboard

First of all, I will set out a theoretical framework, cursory though it may be. Taking as my starting point a generic analysis of the Renaissance by André Chastel, I shall consider the garden of the Villa d'Este at Tivoli as the incarnation of modern beauty embodied in a place, the spatial expression of an understanding created in the midst of a world in crisis.[1] Or, to be more precise, as will be shown, its spatial, aesthetic and conceptual *plan* displays and brings into play, in a manner that is central, a world that is *tilting on its axis*, creating an emotional experience of space in a specific place, which is irreducible to any other aesthetic, poetic, pictorial or musical dimension. All of these media are evoked by the theme of the garden, particularly that of the Villa d'Este. Its garden is, in a profoundly rhetorical sense, a place of memory, an *image agissante*,[2] that takes on the status of a *Pathosformel*[3] by exhuming, literally and fantastically, the figure of Hadrian's Villa in a way that is fundamental and central to the entire future Western imagination.[4] Furthermore, the Villa d'Este encapsulates a vital moment, that of a shift, here firmly controlled by its two creators, Cardinal Ippolito II d'Este and the architect Pirro Ligorio. Among the many emblems scattered around the site as a whole, its most obvious expression is that of the eagle – the Este family coat of arms, prominent everywhere in the villa – able to hold a terrestrial globe in its talons. From a mythical and philosophical point of view, a tension – as much Herculean as Heraclitian – thus emerges between the memory of several different worlds, and of these worlds being swept away by the waters, those of the flood and those of oblivion.[5] With water a main feature of the Villa d'Este gardens, this key theme then becomes a metamorphosis of forms that belongs to a *reversibility* that works *at any point* of its spatial arrangement, as is illustrated at various points with the help of a few examples. For such a truly vertiginous and powerful reversibility to occur *in visu*, *in situ* and *in actu*, in the experience of the space and as a working model in time, there has to be a sort of *cipher*, a secret cipher as much as a manifest secret, here manifested with brilliance, splendour and extravagance. Here the term 'cipher' has a triple meaning: first, in the common sense of 'key to a cryptogram', then in the sense that it is used to indicate how transcendence appears in immanence according to a metaphysical experience that objective thought cannot incorporate,

223

therefore as an *expression* of this transcendence, which leads to the third meaning of the cipher as an 'instrument of philosophical elucidation', in other words, the — non-magical — sense of decrypting, deciphering, referring to an *act* of interpretation and the involvement of an interpreter. The storyboard outlined below invites the reader to participate in the search for and the (re)construction of the place of origin of the phenomenalisation of this cipher. It should be emphasised that this storyboard is very selective, given the abundant polysemy of the many signs embodied in this place. The storyboard, borrowed from the world of film and advertising, can be manipulated like the pieces of a jigsaw puzzle, and consists of a series of sketches or photos showing the sequence of shots or images planned for a film. The storyboard format both creates a montage of images, different in nature and status, and constructs a sequence which one wants to be exemplary, significant in its gaps, leaps and bounds, the whole aiming to produce one or several rhythms specific to the historicity of this place.

Set 1: Gerolamo Muziano's fresco

The fresco was painted on one of the walls of the villa, before the building works were completed. It depicts a profile view of the entire site. At the centre is a tree dedicated to Jupiter, symbolic of the construction of the image which it divides into two separate parts: a flat surface and a steeply slanting plane on the left of the image, presented to the gaze like a kind of writing desk. The base of the tree is at the point where the horizontal plane of the garden rises up into the oblique plane, or, in other words, where the oblique and horizontal planes intersect in unimaginable depths. Reaching to the sky like the axis of a new world, the tree signals that a seminal event is taking place there — a shift. A third part of the image is constituted by the sky — where there are two birds — and a distant horizon. All the elements of the spatial arrangement of the garden are there, as if waiting, waiting for something to happen …

The fresco has been drawn from the inner slope of the hill that supports the plateau of the garden, on an incline, and the building that dominates the whole. It is like a sectional view. Depicting the scene from the other direction, i.e. on arrival by the low road from Rome, would have drawn the eye to the bulk of the hill, rather than to the empty expanse of open sky and landscape. Such a view would have made it impossible to show an aspect of the gardens that is both geographical and symbolic. The choice of this viewpoint effectively directs the eye towards Rome, to the west, thus towards the setting sun, these two horizons melting into the vanishing point of the fresco. The construction of the fresco permits a manipulation, a *jeu de l'esprit*, playing on, and with, directions, certain vistas *in situ* also offering similar spectacular enjoyment. If one is unaware of the orientation of the site or, to put it in more nuanced terms, if one voluntarily suspends geographical objectivity, or going even further, if one abandons oneself to the magic, flowing, ambiguous, dreamlike power exuded by the place, one can imagine that the light striking the obliquely rising hillside is that of a sun rising on the dawn of a new creation, and not that of a sun setting over Rome. The signs then seem to be able to be inverted and to swirl in the evening air, like the promise of a new dawn: it is no longer Rome that dominates the world, it is the cardinal who seems to

13.1 Gerolamo Muziano's fresco in the salon (1565–67)

13.2 Geometric construction of the fresco. (Reconstruction by Martine Bouchier)

13.3 The Hanging Gardens of Babylon. (Engraving by Anathasius Kircher)

13.4 Section of the villa. (Drawing by Christine Dalnoky, 1989)

13.5 La Rometta and the wolf. (Photograph by the author)

dominate Rome, drawing to himself all the conquering strength of the eternal city.

From the moment the gardens of the Villa d'Este were built — and this was an ongoing process — they created an unparalleled *aura*, both in times to come[6] and in the past, thus giving rise to the idea of a continual rewriting of history from the present moment. The combined forces of these narratives and fables gave rise to a continuous summons down through the centuries and thus built the reputation, the renown — the word derives from the French 're-nom' (re-naming) — of the site, through drawings and writings, and later through other media, in a cascade of echoes that appear to speak and reply to each other beyond the barriers of time. Thus, in a fantastical but powerfully heuristic temporal short circuit, the Villa d'Este directly inspired Anathasius Kircher's engraving of the Hanging Gardens of Babylon, a collage in which one can see secondary revision at work in the raw, in this free interpretation of the *Pathosformel* of the Villa d'Este. The well-ordered terracing of the various levels and their supporting vaults are clearly visible, but there is also a remarkable absence, that of the central axis dividing the garden in halves from top to bottom.

An extremely prolific scholar and polymath, Kircher (1602–80) wrote one of the

226

most important treatises on music, which was published in Rome in 1650, making it possible to understand seventeenth-century Italian and German music, as well as a *Phonurgia Nova* (New treatise on phonic energy), published in Kempten in 1673. These writings allow not only a mystical and metaphysical interpretation of the Villa's fountains, in particular those of the water organ in the Fountain of the Flood, also known as the Organ Fountain, but also they give extremely precise technological details of the hydraulic mechanisms and instruments, in particular on the creation and control of the echo. From this point of view, the aura of the villa is therefore not only visual and spatial, but also, and perhaps primarily, resonant.

This section by a contemporary landscape artist, Christine Dalnoky,[7] also shows walls and the supporting vaults, as well as the three or four superimposed plateaux reminiscent of the steps of a large amphitheatre. Unlike Muziano's fresco, Kircher's drawing and, as shall be shown below, Etienne Dupérac's engraving, this is not a bird's-eye view; the section is drawn from a horizontal viewpoint simulating that of the visitor arriving at the site on foot. Suddenly, this view has a twofold effect as it simultaneously conveys the abundance of greenery. Here, the terraces are literally collapsing under the mass of vegetation, demonstrating that these are indeed hanging gardens, artificially created and maintained on the terraces rendered invisible. This lush vegetation enhances the impression of a cascade of sound and visual effects that assails the visitor's senses as his steps take him over the threshold: he forgets, or rather does not realise, that he is walking on a completely artificial 'ground', totally fabricated from nothing. He is floating, but he does not know it … not yet.

Set 2: Verticality, a heavenly attraction
Three elements comprise the direct historical sources of the project, its iconological scheme, an anonymous description dated 1571 describing the salient features of the garden, and Dupérac's engraving of 1573, accompanied by a description of the elements portrayed in the engraving. Contrary to the fresco, which remains connected to the place, and even more contrary to the place itself, Dupérac's engraving is the visual element that has made the greatest contribution to the way the villa has been

227

13.6 Villa d'Este, Tivoli. (Engraving by Etienne Dupérac, 1573)

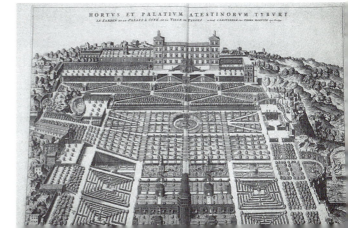

received and perpetuated in Europe as a paradigm for the conception and creation of a garden. Dupérac's engraving constitutes a spatial, global and synthetic model that can be considered as the origin of a long series of typical plans and prototypes in the annals of the European landscaping tradition.[8] Its fundamental power derives from the fact that the engraving is an image that seems immediately accessible and comprehensible whereas the written text needs to be read in conjunction with the image and, more importantly, with the site. The engraving provides access to the place — up to a point — in the absence, physical and circumstantial, of the visitor, an absence that is all the more pronounced when the site itself has disappeared or been obliterated from the landscape,[9] but not from the mental map. The town-planning historian Gaston Bardet pointed out that 'Pérac's sketches transform the fundamental proportions of the Villa d'Este to such an extent that they no longer show the existing gardens but gardens that are *quasi invented* in the manner of [G. B.] Piranesi's famous prisons'.[10] As a 'quasi invention' of the site, the engraving has therefore become more powerful than the site itself, 'superseding' the site on its own terrain. How then can one determine the degree of 'true' observation of the site by the succession of visitors down through the centuries, or the degree of suggestion resulting from representations of it, when people visit the site and experience it for themselves, which is akin to the experience of any garden, and furthermore of any place of pilgrimage. Like a flier or a photographic image, the engraving transports the truth of memory in anticipating, in premonitory fashion, the disappearance of the work, and here, the potential reversion to the amorphousness that was, (in) one day, conquered by the incomparable will and power to transform which was immediately acclaimed by those living at the time. Daniele Barbaro, for instance, wrote:

> Cardinal d'Este has built perfect, magnificent edifices, and done so in different parts of the world, to the great wonder of men … those splendid constructions that he has had built in Rome and Tivoli, where nature, it has to be confessed, has been outdone by art and by his nobility of soul; for, in an instant, gardens

228

13.7 The verticality of the central axis and the marking of the different sections

13.8 The visual cone, and the attraction of the sky. (Reconstruction by Martine Bouchier)

appeared, forests grew up and overnight the trees bore succulent fruits; valleys were transformed into hills, and rocky mountains into river beds; the rock was hewn out to make a channel for the water, to irrigate the arid earth and supply the fountains, streams and rare fishponds.[11]

Even more than a demiurge, the cardinal was thus, in a mythical and rhetorical manner, the very incarnation of the *cosmoplastes*, a manufacturer of worlds.[12] This, in fact, reflects back on the architect, the artists and all the craftsmen who transformed the site into an incomparable wonder.

229

As is clear from a close study of Dupérac's engraving, the layout of the villa's garden is based on a dizzying *proliferation* of axes and interlocking spaces. The garden becomes a labyrinth, made all the more intense and effective by the vegetation that masks the settings and tableaux of the whole, and even obscures some views, for example over the Dragon Fountain or the fountain built by Gianlorenzo Bernini between 1660 and 1661. Constant surprise effects, sudden revelations at a bend in the path, are thus created, but preceded by their sound reverberation. For sound anticipates and tantalises, without disclosing all, reserving the full effect until the last moment, the visual discoveries drowned out by the water. Only the central vertical axis and the various sections the visitor crosses as he follows this axis from top to bottom are depicted here.

There has been much controversy about the location of the actual entrance to the garden: was it from the lower gate that the visitor made his way across the garden to the building, or was it the upper gate that led first of all into an inner courtyard of the building, and only after that into the garden? In the second instance, the visitor discovers the entire garden at a single glance from above, as if standing in the shoes and in the position of the master of the place. This theory is probably the most likely, a testimony to the cardinal's munificence and extravagance in offering an extraordinary total spectacle to his visitors, who were then cast into the waters of oblivion, like a stone carried along the river of time, until finally being swallowed up by the infernal waters of Neptune's Fountain (not built). The lower gate theory is equally plausible; this way the visitor is made to climb the steep slope and to ascend, by degrees, a ladder of being[13] till he reaches a culminating point, one of deliverance and of taking flight. If this path along the axis is followed in a line without deviating, it is an initiation of a Neo-Platonic and magical kind,[14] or an asceticism of a Christian kind.[15] Beyond the choice of gate, here as elsewhere apply the workings of the spatial layout engineered by Ligorio, the mise-en-scène transforming the world into play, with its total reversibility of the overall conception. Any point in the layout is a Janus, Paul Klee's grey point, 'that fateful point between coming into being and dying'.[16]

The manipulation operated here opens up a clear expanse of sky, which makes it possible to encompass the villa and its gardens beneath the visual cone formed by the axes of the engraving. The vanishing point of the construction of the image is located precisely above the vertical axis of the garden. The point of conception of the villa is directly overhead, at the divine viewpoint, inaccessible to humans, other than as transcendence. The construction of the image shows that the terrestrial world, human actions and thoughts, and human destiny are guided, even governed, by a single, superior, transcendent eye. The cardinal remains a Catholic, the *entire* purpose of the villa leading, literally, to heaven.

Set 3

Several important stages mark the visitor's ascent, first of all the entrance via an optical canal designed to be dark and to create a violent contrast not only with the exterior light, but also, even more, with the milky white light of the waters gushing from the many fountains. The second key moment is when the visitor arrives at the Dragon Fountain, which is completely encircled by a double flight of steps – of Spanish inspiration. It is the only time when the gaze and the movement of the body can envelop and dominate a group of statues, which are now badly damaged and rendered unfathomable by the absence of a Hercules slaying the dragons that guard the entrance to the Garden of the Hesperides, a mythological expression of 'Paradise' for ancient and classical Greece.[17] The ascent of the steps invites, or rather almost forces the eye to look back, first of all, towards the path already trodden, which heralds and thus prepares the visitor for the twists and turns to come higher up, climaxing with the viewpoint overhead, the 'absolute' viewpoint from the upper terrace that dominates the entire panorama of the lush Roman countryside stretching out at the foot of the Tivoli hill.

13.9 to 13.16 Following the vertical axis *in situ*, taming the landscape. (Photographs by the author)

13.9

13.10

13.11

13.12

13.14

13.13

13.15

13.16

Set 4: Harnessing the waters

13.17 Plan of the villa's water system. (Drawing by Charles Lamb)

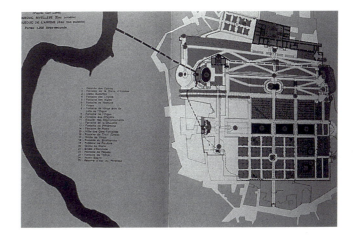

The works began with an inaugural act: the digging of a canal more than six hundred metres long. This made it possible to harness and control the full force of the waters of the Anione River, and permitted numerous metamorphoses and forms through the use of gravitational force alone, reversing falls and cascades in a constant jet. Buried underground, the conduit becomes invisible; it is obliterated, concealing in a hidden art, the 'mechanical' art that metamorphoses the *physis* of the element water, from the drop to the water organ and including the whirlpools, cascades and fountains of all sorts, gentle streams and thundering waterfalls. It is in this application of the treatises of Hero of Alexandria, used in the Roman gardens of Antiquity, and with which Ligorio was perfectly acquainted that this architect, antique dealer, artist and scholar here shows himself to be a master of hydraulic engineering, a creator of automata and of charming aquatic surprises.[18]

13.18 Map of the original site of the city of Rome. (Drawing by Sylvia Pressouye)

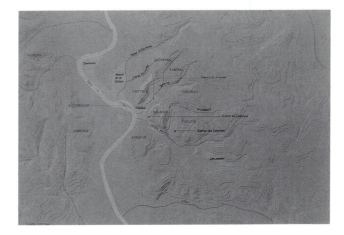

This map of the original site of the city of Rome — of which Ligorio was to draw the *forma urbis* — can be compared with the Villa d'Este site and plans. Like the Tiber, the Anione meanders across the landscape. In the same way as the splendour of Rome and its fountains were to be made possible through the technical and geophysical control of a whole region, similarly, everything is as if the Villa d'Este were a mini-Rome, but in a momentary brilliance, not over the long span of a history.

This contemporary cadastral map of the land around Rome gives a very clear picture of a profound spatial and historic sequence, the transformation of a *chora*:[19] Tibur, ancient Rome and its gardens which developed essentially from the first century BC to the first century AD, Hadrian's Villa and the Villa d'Este, both at Tivoli.[20] Thirty kilometres east of Rome, in a place known since remotest antiquity for the sweetness of

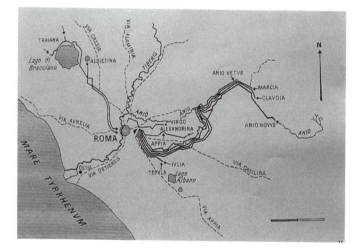
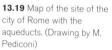

13.19 Map of the site of the city of Rome with the aqueducts. (Drawing by M. Pediconi)

13.20 Avenue of a Hundred Fountains. (Engraving by G. F. Venturini, 1685)

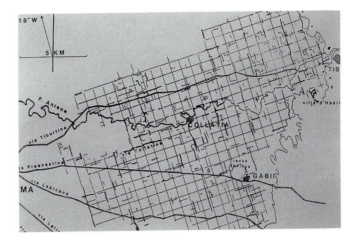

13.21 Cadastral grid and strata of the various sites. (Drawing by Gérard Chouquer *et al.*)

its air and the quality of its waters, Hadrian built his 'villa', which marks a milestone in the history of this typology.[21] Fourteen centuries later, when Cardinal d'Este inherited a convent, once Benedictine, later Franciscan, it was the opportunity for him to compete with the emperor and, through him, with all Rome, both mythical — with Tibur and the Sybilline Oracle at Cumae — and historic, and, probably more to the point, the Catholic Rome of the Counter-Reformation. In transforming this high place, which was relatively wild and remote, into a political and aesthetic manifesto that was singularly attractive for the splendour of its gardens, he pulled off the challenge of turning a bitter failure into a magnificent victory. How was this done?

13.22 The Sybil *in situ.* (Photograph by the author)

Set 5: A doubly historical horizontal axis

13.23 *Forma urbis* of Rome.
(Engraving by G. F. Venturini)

Rejected five times in the election to the pontifical throne, the cardinal was in a way taking his revenge: miniaturising historical Rome, the *frons scaenae* of the Rometta is part of a game, a serious game, on several levels. As demonstrated by Marie-Louise Madonna, an expert on the Villa and on Ligorio,[22] the viewpoint from which this *forma urbis* of Rome *in situ* in miniature has been built (the bulk of which collapsed in the nineteenth century) corresponds to the view of Rome from the hills of Trastevere, beyond the Tiber. Rising up into space, it becomes that of the pope when he gazes down at Rome from the Basilica of Saint Peter's, it substitutes itself for him and takes his place, and even goes beyond. Here, at Este, in a very blatant manner, the path of the horizontal axis extends even further, even deeper in the profundities of time, as it takes the mythical Roma as its starting point, with its Sybilline Oracle, symbolised by three little superimposed channels, to lead to an historic Rome, encapsulated in its silhouette which the master of the place dominates visually and physically. An additional turn of the screw comes with a last manipulation, already alluded to with reference to Muziano's fresco: from the upper terraces of the villa, one can see the very real historic Rome, *in situ*, vanishing each day, set alight by the last rays of the setting sun.[23] Everything is very

236

13.24 La Rometta *in situ*.
(Photograph by the author)

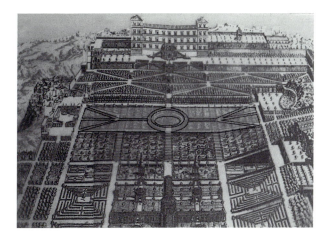

13.25 Dupérac's engraving and the *patte d'oie*'s branching paths. (Reconstruction by Martine Bouchier)

much as if the cardinal were paying homage to Rome while holding it in the grip of the eagle's talons. His viewpoint is effectively superior to any other, for he flies above them.

It is clear that one of the constitutive elements of the functioning of the villa resides in a cumulative and step-by-step burgeoning effect. From a spatial standpoint, other layers of meaning, internal to the layout of the villa's gardens, superimpose themselves on the others. Thus, in addition to the vertical axis, the garden is structured around two horizontal axes, the first leads from the Water Organ to Neptune's fountain, which is clearly visible in the engraving, but which was never built. This axis provides a setting for mythological elements associated with water. The second axis has been highlighted for three reasons: it is higher on the upward path; just below, at its centre, is the Dragon Fountain, located on a vertiginous twist of the vertical path, and, third, that the axis is also a spatial structure that was to have a great future in the art of landscaping. To comprehend what was at stake would need another storyboard to project us into the future of the structural history of the art of garden landscaping as a spatial model. Let us confine ourselves to the key element. This second horizontal axis was indeed to prove, but after the event, to be a fundamental spatial structure in that it *contains* within it what would become known as the *patte d'oie* – the branching path – a point where the vista explodes in the structuring of formal 'French' gardens and, later, of the Haussmann-style city.[24] In this respect, the layout of Vaux-le-Vicomte plays a crucial role in the shift from the formal Italian garden, focused on the interior, to the formal French garden, dominating the surrounding territory.

It is highly significant that a statue of Hercules (the Farnesi Hercules) is placed at the vanishing point of the axis at Vaux on which the visitor sets their sights on arrival. Besides, there is a *patte d'oie* positioned at either end of the axis, on the periphery of the spatial layout and not at its heart. At Vaux, as at Este, everything concurs and converges therefore at one point of density and intensity: the statue of Hercules.

237

Set 6: The figure of Hercules and the Dragon Fountain

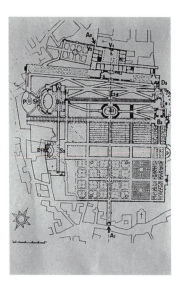

13.26 Iconological scheme of the villa.
(Drawing by Marie-Louise Madonna)

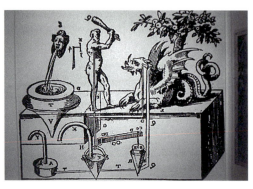

13.27 Hercules slaying the dragon

13.28 Hercules. (Engraving by Hendrick Golzius, 1589)

238

The richness and complexity of the statuary and the associated symbolism, the various names given to certain fountains, the general context of a magic hermeticism and sophisticated alchemy have given rise to fascination and wild interpretations that have resulted in the revival of the mystery, and also in the creation of reservations and reticence.[25] While a philological deciphering of the space and of Ligorrio's writings[26] enables the interpretation of the combination of signs and codes with some degree of accuracy, it also fuels conflicts of interpretation. The theme of Hercules 'at the crossroads'[27] also embodies, very precisely, the manner in which the spatial structure of the garden of the Villa d'Este has been interpreted by many as symbolising the cardinal's split personality. Beyond this identification with an eponymous hero, who was unexceptional at the time and perfectly understandable to the initiated, beyond the moral and Christian interpretation of the paths of the villa — the struggle between good and evil — the theme of a hero who must slay a dragon is also among the most universal legends.

Set 7: The Platonic *khi* and the tilting of the structure of the horizon

13.29 Fountain of the Dragons. (Photograph by the author)

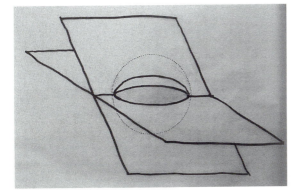

13.30 *Khi.* (Reconstruction by Martine Bouchier)

In several of her studies, Madonna writes of an *anagogic* reading of the gardens of the villa, a reading that she undertakes cautiously based on a series of clues. From a philosophical standpoint, such a position should be directly referred to the history of exegesis and hermeneutics, to the structure of levels of reading, prepared typologically by Origen (?185–?254), permanently instituted by John Cassian (AD 360–430/435) and historicised throughout the Western tradition up to the present day. A sacred text shows a four-level structure that reflects four levels of interpretation: a literal and historic sense that tells us what happened, an allegorical sense that tells us what must be believed, a moral sense that tells us what must be done, and an anagogic sense that supposedly reveals the mysteries of an eschatological nature towards which we are reaching. This is based on a numerical logic, in particular that of the number ten, as evidenced by the Platonic *tetraktys* and the *khi* (x) in the creation of the *cosmos* by the demiurge, in Plato's *Timaeus*: 'This entire compound he divided lengthways into two parts, which he joined to one another at the centre like the letter c, and bent them into a circular form, connecting them with themselves and each other at the point opposite to their original meeting-point'[28] This numerical logic, based on Pythagoras, led to mystical speculations, in particular on the music of spheres and its instrument, for example Robert Fludd's cosmic monochord[29] of which the villa's Water Organ is a representation. Putting it more simply, or more playfully, one could say that the *khi* invokes, in Greek, a phonetic semantics of letters attracting attention to a peculiarity of expression, or an enigma, to be deciphered if not resolved.

This view makes it possible to interpret the garden of the Villa d'Este — and, in my opinion, any place of high culture — as a poetic, spatialising hermeneutics in action, here brought into play by a structure installed at its heart: the Dragon Fountain. This is on one condition: that of playing the game. A game involving an entire world revolving around its axis, like a board game whose story is reversible.

Acknowledgement

The author thanks Ros Schwartz for the English translation.

Notes

1 André Chastel, *Mythe and crise de la Renaissance (1968–1969)* (Geneva: Skira, 1989), p. 68: 'The mythical face of the Renaissance – not its crisis face – permits us to state, as a sort of general law of the period, the connection between intellectual energy and the "spatial". The effort that is required to represent a phenomenon, and therefore to express it in terms of space, is a means of making it tangible and, arguably, visual representation practically becomes a condition of tangibility. In this type of representation, there is not only a coherence that profoundly satisfies the mind, but a manipulation of forms, which gives them a measurable, ordered character, and from which a splendid assurance is born. In pushing the rule of geometry as far as possible, one discovers aesthetic satisfaction, which raises and glorifies the consciousness of the real. The exploration of forms in space and of their properties will be, or can become, over the centuries, almost the condition of "modern beauty."'

2 *Rhétorique à Herennius*, ed. and trans. Guy Achard (Paris: Belles Lettres, 1989), III, 37, p. 122. An *image agissante* is an image–action that is neither mute nor fuzzy. It must be either very beautiful or very ugly, making an impression on the memory that will keep alive the active power – the *force agissante* – of the image. This section comes after a development of the concept of oratory action (*pronuntiatio*) and its two main elements, the quality of the voice (*vocis figuram*) on the one hand, and the movement of the body on the other (*corporis motum*). The conclusion of this section states that 'speaking eloquently has the effect that the words seem to come from the heart'. The art of memory, which is here being developed for the first time, consists of developing that organ of the heart which will permit a discourse of an animated being. All of these elements are fundamental to the Villa d'Este. The body is called on to move and is assailed by the sounds and music created by the abundance of water, the metaphoric and symbolic element of the battle between memory and oblivion.

3 On Aby Warburg and *Pathosformel*, see Philippe-Alain Michaud, *Aby Warburg et l'image en mouvement*, Preface by Georges Didi-Huberman (Paris: Macula, 1998). On the famous atlas of memory images compiled by Warburg, see Italo Spinelli and Roberto Venuti (eds), *Mnemosyne: l'Atlante della memoria di Aby Warburg* (Rome: Artemide, 1998). Also Kurt W. Forster, 'Aby Warburg: his study of ritual and art on two continents', October, 77 (1996), pp. 5–24.

4 Marie-Louise Madonna, 'L'héritage de la Villa d'Hadrien: les villas de Pirro Ligorio', in *Tradition et modernité d'un paysage culturel: La Villa d'Hadrien* [proceedings of a colloquium held in Paris, November 1999] (forthcoming, 2000).

5 For a recent overview of the cultural history of the theme of oblivion in Western culture, see Harald Weinrich, *Léthé: Art et critique de l'oubli* [1997], trans. from the German by Diane Meur (Paris: Fayard, 1999). As regards more specifically the relationship between this question and the art of landscaping and the metaphor of water, which is central in Plato's *Phaedra*, see Philippe Nys, 'La plaine de vérité', in *Le jardin, art et lieu de mémoire*, eds M. Mosser and P. Nys (Paris: Editions de l'Imprimeur, 1995); repr. Philippe Nys, *Le Jardin exploré: Une herméneutique du lieu* (Paris: Editions de l'Imprimeur, 1999), I, ch. 2. As regards the relationship between the fountains and terraces, which is keynote to the aesthetic scheme of the Villa d'Este, see Philippe Nys, 'Terrasses, les mille plateaux du paysage', in *Compar(a)isons* [a journal devoted to landscape, ed. Michael Jakob], nos I–III (forthcoming, 2000).

6 For an initial approach to the history of the villa's reception later on in different milieu (Liszt for music), laudatory writings and speeches (Montaigne), see David R. Coffin, *The Villa d'Este at Tivoli* (Princeton: Princeton University Press, 1960), pp. 125–137. For a recent study of the entire villa, see David Dernie, *The Villa d'Este at Tivoli*, Photographs by Alastair Carew-Cox (London: Academy Editions, 1996), but the author does not intend to explore this aspect here.

7 Christine Dalnoky, *Eléments de jardins: Voyages en Italie 1986–1988* (Rome: Villa Médicis, 1989), p. 37.

8 Lodewijk Baljon, *Designing Parks: An Examination of Contemporary Approaches to Design in Landscape Architecture* (Amsterdam: A. & N. P., 1992), pp. 224–225.

241

9   Two examples will be given here. The first is relatively close to the Villa d'Este, historically, geographically and culturally speaking, since it is the Hortus Palatinus, a garden built in Heidelberg from 1614, most of which was destroyed by the French. This garden makes up the frontispiece of Salomon de Caus's treatise *Le jardin palatin* (1620); repr. with a Postface by Michel Conan (Paris: Editions du Moniteur, 1981), which is an important landmark in the history of this art for the whole of Europe. The second example is a long way removed, historically, geographically and culturally, as it concerns China, but is much closer than might be thought from a theoretical standpoint. In the twelfth century, the gardens of the Emperor were destroyed by his subjects who were furious to see their taxes being constantly raised to pay for the emperor's wild and ruinous pleasure. He was literally 'possessed' by his *furor hortensis*. This episode evokes two elements, the first belongs to a radical and paradoxical logic that is both poetic and moral: the only true garden is the one that does not exist, the Wuyou garden, but which, precisely for that reason, has given rise to speeches of praise and poems celebrating its incomparable beauty that is not of this earth. The second is 'technical' and theoretical. Whereas the 'purely aesthetic' tradition of Chinese gardens is much more ancient than the European tradition, it was not until 1634 that a treatise on the art of landscaping was written: Ji Cheng, *Yuanye* [The Craft of Gardens] (New Haven and London: Yale University Press, 1988); French translation with Introduction, Notes and Critical apparatus by Che Bing Chu (Paris: Editions de l'Imprimeur, 1997). This long wait corresponds to the pre-eminence of the garden-that-does-not-exist over the garden *in situ* conceived as the purpose 'of one' art, an art that uses paradox, deception, setting, irony and affectation.

10 Gaston Bardet, *Naissance et méconnaissance de l'urbanisme* (Paris: Sabri, 1951), p. 91 (emphases added).

11 Daniele Barbaro, dedication to Ippolito II d'Este, in Vitruvius, *De architectura*, 2nd edn (Venice, 1567).

12 From the political and technological viewpoint, the image of the *cosmoplastes* should be compared with a letter from a major landowner, Alvise Cornaro, who both names and masks everything, concealing his economic interests beneath a mythological and religious discourse using the rhetoric-imbued image of God the Creator. For more on Cornaro's role, see Reinhard Bentmann and Michaël Müller, *La villa, architecture de domination*, trans. from the German (Liege: Mardaga, 1975). From a philosophical point of view, Barbaro's dedication should be compared with Pic de la Mirandole's definition of man in *De hominis dignitate* (1486) [*De la dignité de l'homme*, trans. from the Latin and Introduced by Yves Hersant (Paris: Editions de l'Eclat, 1993), p. 5f.], which itself makes direct reference to that of Philon of Alexandria in *De Plantatione* [Introduction, translation and Notes by Jean Pouilloux (Paris: Editions du Cerf, 1963), III, pp. 23–25], where Philon invents the neologism of *cosmoplastes*. For an initial perspective on this figure of the *cosmoplastes*, see Philippe Nys, 'Ethik und Asthetik des Gartens', *Kunstforum International*, 145 (May–June 1999), 'Künstler als Gärtner', pp. 71–85, with microphotographs by Eva-Maria Schön, Innere Gärten-Plankton (1995 and 1997/98).

242

13 Arthur O. Lovejoy, *The Great Chain of Being: A Study of the History of an Idea* (Cambridge, MA: Harvard University Press, 1936, 1964).

14 Joan Petru Couliano, *Eros et magie à la Renaissance. 1484* (Paris: Idées & Recherches/Flammarion, 1984).

15 Christian Heck, *L'échelle céleste dans l'art du moyen âge. Une image de la quête du ciel* (Paris: Idées & Recherches/Flammarion, 1997).

16 Paul Klee, *Théorie l'art moderne* (Paris: Denoël/Gonthier, 1980), p. 56. Gilles Deleuze and Felix Guattari commented on this point in *Mille plateaux* (Paris: Editions de Minuit, 1980), esp. pp. 416f., invoking the figure of the cosmic craftsman, in other words, from our point of view, that of the *cosmoplastes*.

17 For example, Alain Ballabriga, *Le soleil et le tartare. L'image mythique du monde en Grèce archaïque* (Paris: Editions de l'Ecole des Hautes Etudes en Sciences Sociales, 1986).

18 On Hero (third-to-first century BCE according to the exegetes), see Th. Henri-Martin, *Recherches sur la vie and les ouvrages de Hero d'Alexandrie* [papers presented by various

scholars to the Académie des inscriptions] (Paris: Imprimerie Nationale, 1864). *Pneumatica*, in particular, was translated in the sixteenth and seventeenth centuries by Valla who translated fragments from 1501, and Gian-Battista Aleotti, in Ferrara, in 1589. The treatise by Salomon de Caus, *Les raisons des forces mouvantes* (Frankfurt: J. Norton, 1615), is part of this thought trend.

19 'Chora' is a Greek term meaning firstly a land, a region, from a geographic or geoclimatic point of view. Hippocrates uses it in his treatise *Airs, Waters and Places* in opposition to *geo*, the earth, seen as the land, as a geological reality. On this, see Philippe Nys, 'A propos d'un traité d'Hippocrate', in *Le Sens du lieu*, ed. P. Nys, Ch. Younès and M. Mangematin (Brussels: Recueil/Ousia, 1996), pp. 385–434. Things hot up once Plato gets hold of the word to designate, in *Timaeus*, the enigmatic but necessary 'place' of the coupling of two principles, male and female, engendering a third term. *Chora* can therefore be translated as 'receptacle', 'womb/matrix', 'space' or even material (Brisson), which corresponds to the Aristotelian term 'hule', matter, but which is different from *topos*, place, location. Plato adds that the *chora* being an element that is fundamentally hybrid – neither intelligible nor tangible – seizing it, grasping it, comprehending it can only be possible in a dreamlike state. This passage in *Timaeus* has therefore caused to dream, at length and continuously, by giving birth to countless philological studies and metaphysical speculations that should be associated with the subject and challenges of *Timaeus*: the question of the 'place' where the world was begun, of the cosmos. The theme and the term *chora* have been revived both in the field of philosophy and in that of architectural theory (Eisenman and Tschumi) thanks to Jacques Derrida, *Khôra* (Paris: Galilée, 1993), first published in *Poikilia, Etudes offertes à Jean-Pierre Vernant* (Paris: Editions de l'EHESS, 1987), where he distances himself from Luc Brisson's interpretation in *Le même et l'autre dans la structure ontologique du Timée de Platon* (Paris: Klincksieck, 1974), which incidentally gave rise to a new French translation of *Timaeus* in contrast with the old translation by Albert Rivaud, *Les Belles Lettres* (1925). For Eisenman, see *Cinégramme folie: le Parc de La Villette* (Seyssel: Champ Vallon, 1987); for Tschumi, see the journal *Assemblage*, 12 (1991). The question of the *chora* has been the subject of Watsuji Tetsurô's meditations in *Fudo, ningengakuteki kôsatu* (Tokyo: Iwanami Shoten, 1929, revd 1931, completed 1935), and in particular those of Nishida Kitarô, 'The logic of topos and the religious world view', *The Eastern Buddhist*, 19/2 and 20/1 (1945). These speculations have now been taken up by a series of commentators on Nishida. For an update on these debates, see Augustin Berque (ed.), *Logique du lieu and dépassement de la modernité*, 2 vols (Brussels: Ousia, Recueil, 2000). In so far as our own perspective aims to construct a hermeneutics of dwelling, places always singular or made singular by a unique experience, constituting a subject, in so far as it rests on contemporary hermeneutics and its debates, it is appropriate to add the following point. In the seminar on religion organised by Gianni Vattimo and Jacques Derrida, *La religion* (Paris: Editions du Seuil, 1996), Gadamer clearly distances himself from Derrida's perspective on the *chora*: 'mind games', says Gadamer, 'but really nothing more' (p. 232), these games already being those of Plato where the relation of the singular to the universal is always presupposed as taken for granted but not demonstrated or conceptualised as Aristotle did. When I speak of the garden of the Villa d'Este as a structure tilting on its axis, I am thinking very specifically of that oscillation between the image and the concept, which is here constantly maintained in a balance.

243

20 For the cadastral approach, see Gérard Chouquer, Monique Clavel-Lévêque, François Favory and Jean-Pierre Vallat's various works, in particular *Structures agraires en Italie centro-méridionale. Cadastres and paysage ruraux*, Collection de l'Ecole française de Rome – 100, 1987.

21 For a perspective on the structure of the villa in relation to the art of gardens and to the landscape, see James S. Ackerman, *The Villa: Form and Ideology of Country Houses* (Princeton: Princeton University Press, 1990); and Margherita Azzi Visentini, *Histoire de la villa italienne XVe–XVIe siècle*, trans. from the Italian by Laurence Noli and Louis Bonamuli (Paris: Gallimard/Electa, 1996).

22 Maria-Louise Madonna, 'Pirro Ligorio e Villa d'Este: la scena di Roma e il mistero della Sibilla', in *Il Giardino Storico Italiano* (Florence: Leo S. Olschki, 1981). Also *idem*, 'Il *Genius Loci* di Villa d'Este. Miti e misteri nel sistema di Pirro Ligorio', in *Natura e Artificio*, ed. Marcello Fagiolo (Rome: Officina, 1981).

23 It must be added that at Versailles it is the façade of the château itself that is, literally, set alight, especially during the summer solstice, by the last rays of the setting sun which plunge into and are immersed in the waters and the axis of the grand canal, before beginning a new cycle.

24 As far as is known, Bardet, *Naissance et méconnaissance de l'urbanisme*, is the first to have highlighted the impact of this structure.

25 For example, Emanuela Kretzulesco-Quaranta, *Les jardins du Songe: 'Poliphile' et la Mystique de la Renaissance*, Preface by Pierre Lyautey, 2nd corrected and revd edn (Paris: Les Belles Lettres, 1986), esp. pp. 299–312, for the Villa d'Este.

26 On Ligorio's writings, see the works of Ginette Vagenheim, notably 'Les témoignages écrits de Pirro Ligorio sur la Villa d'Hadrien', in *Tradition et modernité d'un paysage culturel: La Villa d'Hadrien*. Proceedings of a colloquium held in Paris, November 1999 (forthcoming, 2000).

27 The seminal work on Hercules is Jean Bayet, *Les origines de l'Hercule romain* (Paris: E. de Boccard, 1926). Also Erwin Panofsky, *Hercule à la croisée des chemins and autres matériaux figuratifs de l'Antiquité dans l'art le plus récent* (1930), translated from the German and Introduced by Danièle Cohn (Paris: Flammarion, 1999).

28 Plato, *Timaeus*, 36b–c, from a previously unpublished translation with Introduction and Notes by Luc Brisson and the collaboration of Michel Patillon on the translation (Paris: GF/Flammarion, 1992), p. 125. 'Alors, tout cette plaque, il [i.e. le démiurge] la découpa en deux morceaux, dans le sens de la longueur ; et les deux bandes ainsi obtenues, il les appliqua l'une sur l'autre en faisant coïncider leur milieu à la façon d'un khi, puis il les courba en cercle pour former un seul arrangement, soudant l'une à l'autre leurs extrémités au point opposé à leur intersection'. (English translation by Benjamin Jowett).

29 Joscelyn Godwin, *Harmonies of Heaven and Earth: Mysticism in Music from Antiquity to the Avant-Garde* (London: Thames & Hudson, 1987 and Paris: Albin Michel, 1994).

244

Caroline van Eck

14 'The splendid effects of architecture, and its power to affect the mind': the workings of Picturesque association

The manipulation of the emotional response of the public to landscape gardens and architecture was one of the central issues in Picturesque theories as they were developed in Britain from the 1740s. 'To move, to melt and elevate the mind' was the aim of landscape gardening according to Richard Payne Knight's poem *The Landscape* of 1795.[1] But given the importance of the impact of art on the memory and emotions of the beholder, Picturesque theories are surprisingly brief on how such direction may be achieved. Most eighteenth-century authors refer briefly to associationist philosophies of perception, memory and aesthetic response, some to the importance of a connoisseur's eye and a memory well stocked with remembrances of works of art from the past. In recent studies of the Picturesque this is not a prominent topic. Yet the associationist view of the workings of the human mind is in an important sense rather meagre, since it only offers an explanation in formal terms of contiguity, likeness, causal or accidental connection. It does not offer a satisfactory explanation why particular works of art excited particular trains of associations and memories in one spectator, but excited entirely different reactions in another. Therefore, this chapter will take a closer look at some eighteenth-century texts on the direction of emotion and memory. Many modern studies look at the Picturesque from the perspective of twentieth-century interests, such as tracing the genealogy of Modernism or Abstract art.[2] Here, however, instead of this somewhat proleptic approach, the Picturesque will be reconsidered in terms of the traditions in artistic theory from which it came. What to us may appear to be a very incomplete treatment of a defining issue becomes, when considered against that background, not so much a sketchy discussion as a series of understated allusions whose meaning however was clear to the educated public of that time.

245

'A situation not unlike that of a moth fluttering around a candle': Picturesque views on the effect of art on the spectator

The tradition of looking at nature or architecture as if they were paintings was inaugurated by William Gilpin's *A Dialogue Upon the Gardens of ... Stow* (London, 1748). He there defines 'picturesque' as 'that which is suited to pictorial representation'.

Sir Uvedale Price, in *Essays on the Picturesque as Compared with the Sublime and the Beautiful* (London, 1794), takes Gilpin's definition as a starting point:

> In general, I believe, [the word 'Picturesque'] is applied to every object, and every kind of scenery, which has been, or might be presented with good effect in painting; just as the word beautiful (when we speak of visible nature) is applied to every object, and every kind of scenery, that in any way gives pleasure to the eye; and these seem to be the significations of both words, taken in their most extended and popular sense.[3]

But Price observes that such a definition is at the same time too restrictive and too broad, since it implies that all objects of a painting that give pleasure therefore possess the property of being Picturesque. The Picturesque for Price, however, is not a subspecies of beauty but an independent aesthetic category, on the same level with the categories of the Beautiful and the Sublime. Price's aim is to enquire whether there exist properties that will always, in similar circumstances, produce similar effects on all the senses. Properties that always cause a sensation of the Picturesque are roughness and 'sudden variation, joined to that of irregularity'. He illustrates this by pointing out our reactions to Greek temples: when they are still in perfect condition, we call them beautiful; when they are in decay, they become Picturesque.[4]

The Picturesque, therefore, is not just a matter of something being a suitable object for painters; only if nature and architecture also possess the properties of roughness, sudden variation and intricacy can they rightly be called Picturesque. For Price, it is not an inherent, objective property, reserved to gardens, architecture or music, independent of the beholder; he also considers the effect on the public, lifting the discussion on the nature of the Picturesque to a more abstract level, namely that of the aesthetic discussions of David Hume, Edmund Burke and William Hogarth.

This aesthetic setting is more apparent in the work of Richard Payne Knight, whose *An Analytical Inquiry into the Principles of Taste* (London, 1805) is a reaction to Price's work. In it, he argues that it is not tenable to think that the Picturesque is an inherent property of things. Instead, it consists in the effect, that is, the associations it causes by it in the mind of the observer. The Picturesque – or rather, the sensation or experience of the Picturesque – consists of these effects, not of some objective and independent fitness of parks and buildings to serve as the subject of a painting. The starting-point of his *Analytical Inquiry* is the statement that there exists no fixed and definable combination of colours, lines and forms, which in itself gives pleasure to the senses or the mind.[5] The pleasure that architecture, music or paintings give us is located not in these works of art themselves, but in their association with the sensations they cause in us.[6]

The connoisseur will enjoy a landscape in a higher degree than somebody with an untrained eye, because he or she is familiar with the work of Giorgione, Nicolas Poussin or Claude Lorrain. Once a particular train of associations has been made, it will haunt us, whether we like it or not, 'so that we feel ourselves in a situation not unlike that of a moth fluttering around a candle'. Every work of art or nature will excite associations with those we already know, recall these works to the mind in their former vividness and throw new light on them, so that 'recollection enhances enjoyment, and enjoyment brightens recollection'. The philosopher or the natural historian will find in the insect that is thoughtlessly crushed by a peasant occasion for unlimited speculation and reflection; and the blue vault of the sky will be transformed by means of a train of associations leading from the 'lowest dregs of animated matter' to the 'incomprehensible throne of Omnipotence itself'.[7]

The Picturesque is a perfect example of this process: only those who know the history of painting will enjoy Picturesque landscapes, gardens or buildings. They give pleasure, because by association they cause the same kind of enjoyment as the painting of which they are an imitation. Like Gilpin and Price, Knight connects the Picturesque with the Italian term *pittoresco*, though the implications of this connection are made much clearer by his account. The Italian term was coined only after Giorgione and Titian had developed a typically 'painterly' way of depicting landscape. They had realised that the detailed and faithful copying of nature, which the Flemish School had brought to perfection, did not represent what the eye saw, or the visual appearance of things, but presented only an image of the knowledge, not of the perception, of the mind. Consequently, they developed a technique of representation, which Knight calls 'massing': they concentrated on the play of light and shadow, the fusion of colours and lines, and a sketchy way of drawing, in which only those objects are selected that have mixed colours, an irregular lighting and a harmonious mixture of light and shadow:

> this very relation to painting, expressed by the word *Picturesque*, is that, which affords the whole pleasure derived from association; which can, therefore, only be felt by persons who have correspondent ideas to associate; that is, by persons in a certain degree conversant with that art. Such persons being in the habit of viewing, and receiving pleasure from fine pictures, will naturally feel pleasure in viewing those objects in nature.... By thus comparing nature and art, both the eye and the intellect acquire a higher relish for the productions of each; and the ideas, excited by both, are invigorated, as well as refined, by being thus associated and contrasted.[8]

These views by Price and Knight are part of an aesthetic discussion on the nature of the Picturesque which was characterized by two questions: what is the nature of the Picturesque, in particular in relation to the Beautiful and the Sublime? and is it some property inherent in the object itself, or does it only exist as a sensation of the spectator in beholding particular objects?

However, theories on the Picturesque were developed not only in the context of aesthetics, but also as theories of design of landscape gardening and architecture. Thomas Whately (d. 1772) proposed in *Observations on Modern Gardening* (London and Dublin, 1770) the first English treatise on the aims, methods and achievements of landscape gardening. He stressed the importance of considerations of character in

Caroline van Eck
'The splendid effects of architecture,
and its power to affect the mind'

designing a landscape garden, by which the imagination and sensibility of the visitor are affected. Ruins are particularly effective in this respect:

> they are a class by themselves, beautiful as objects, expressive as characters ... imperfection and obscurity are their properties; and to carry the imagination to something greater than is seen, their effect ... besides the characters expressed by their style and position, they suggest ideas which would not arise from the buildings, if entire. The purposes of many have ceased ... and certain sensations of regret, of veneration, or compassion, attend the recollection.[9]

A somewhat different view of the Picturesque is taken by eighteenth-century architects, among whom Sir John Soane has left the most articulate statements on the ways in which buildings affect the spectator. Like Robert Adam and Sir Joshua Reynolds, he considered the work of Sir John Vanbrugh, and in particular Blenheim Palace in Oxfordshire, as the culmination of Picturesque architecture:

> His great work is Blenheim. The style of this building is grand and majestically imposing, the whole composition analogous to the war-like genius of the mighty hero for whom it was erected [the Duke of Marlborough]. The great extent of this noble structure, the picturesque effect of its various parts, the infinite and pleasing variety, the breaks and contrasts in the different heights and masses, produce the most exquisite sensations in the scientific beholder, whether the view be distant, intermediate, or near.[10]

Again, the power of ruins to awake trains of associations and a wide range of emotions in the mind of the beholder is demonstrated:

> The monuments of the Horatii and Curatii fills us with respect for the patriotic and the heroic deeds to which it refers, whilst the remains of many towering structures, broken arches, and massive walls, bring back to our recollections interesting, important and instructive incidents of history which call forth all the nobler feelings of the sympathetic mind ... when such sensations are raised, if the ruins of buildings bring the recollection of such deeds fresh to the mind, as if then acting, we are only anxious for time to spare such monuments, that the same effect may produced to the latest ages. Here there is no delusion, no imaginary colouring: the effect on the mind is complete....

Soane is more detailed than most of his contemporaries on the actual working of the mechanisms of association. He noted in his preparations for the Academy Lectures, adapting Quintilian, that 'the art of architecture consists of the effect which the perfection of a work has upon the eye'.[11] These effects depend on the union of building, painting, sculpture and landscape gardening in architectural design. However, the way in which these effects were achieved are described by Soane in terms taken from rhetoric

248

and poetics, as he repeatedly stressed the affecting power of the architecture of the ancients, and as he likened the experience of seeing and walking through a building with that of watching a play:

> The front of a building is like the prologue of a play, it prepares us for what we are to expect. If the outside promises more than we find in the inside, we are disappointed. The plot opens itself in the first act and is carried on through the remainder, through all the mazes of character, convenience of arrangement, elegance and propriety of ornaments, and lastly produces a complete whole in distribution, decoration and construction.[12]

The concept connecting the visual arts with rhetoric and drama is that of character, the visual or outward appearance of a building by which its true nature and that of its owner is revealed, just as the character of a dramatic personage is revealed by speech, actions and gesture.

The passages quoted above concentrate on the effect of gardens and buildings on the beholder; to find a discussion of the way these effects are actually achieved, one has to turn to Archibald Alison's *Essay on Taste* (1811), which offers the most extended discussion of the way association works, and in particular to Francis Jeffrey's very clear review of the *Essay on Taste* in *The Edinburgh Review* of 1811. Like so many theorists on the Picturesque, Alison and Jeffrey distinguish between inquiries concerning the mental faculty that experiences the sensation of the Picturesque, and inquiries into the nature of Beautiful, Sublime or Picturesque objects, only to argue that the Picturesque is not a property of an object, but a sensation, 'produced … by the recollection or conception of *other* objects which are associated in our imaginations with those before us'.[13] These objects affect us 'on the common and familiar principle of being the natural objects of love, or of pity, or of fear or veneration, or some other common and lively sensation of the mind. . . . All objects are beautiful or sublime which signify or suggest to us some simple emotion of love, pity, terror, or any other social or selfish affection of our nature'.[14] The connection between these objects and the emotions that they arouse is either that objects may be natural signs or 'perpetual concomitants' of happiness, grief, anger or suffering; that they are accidental or arbitrary concomitants of these feelings; or that they show some analogy or fortuitous resemblance to circumstances or situations in which these emotions occurred.[15] Thus, an English landscape considered as a combination of lines, forms and colours does not affect us; but one finds it beautiful insofar as it presents us with a picture of human happiness that starts a train of associations and emotions in our minds: 'The mere forms and colours that compose its visible appearance, are no more capable of exciting any emotion in the mind, than the forms and colours of a Turkey carpet. It is sympathy with the present or the past, or the imaginary *inhabitants* of such a region, that alone gives it either interest or beauty.'[16]

In these passages on the mechanism of association, Alison and Jeffrey formulated a theory that very closely resembled David Hume's analysis of the laws of association in *Enquiry Concerning the Principles of Human Understanding* (London, 1777), where all possible varieties of association are reduced to three principles: resemblance, contiguity in time or place, and cause and effect.[17]

'[T]he splendid effects of architecture, and its power to affect the mind': how does association work?

In spite of the close resemblance between the position of philosophers such as Hume and Alison on the way association works and the views of theorists of the Picturesque, the associationist position does not offer a very satisfactory explanation. This is mainly because both in the case of Hume and of Alison, the relation between objects and the emotions their perceptions arouse is described in formal terms, varying from spatial and temporal contiguity to accidental resemblance or connection in the beholder's mind. The associationist view does not offer a satisfactory explanation of the reasons why a particular object sets in motion a particular train of emotions and memories, but only a general principle explaining the way associations are combined in very abstract terms. As a consequence, it is merely descriptive, and its view of the working of association can hardly function as a guide for design, because it does not really make clear how particular objects affect individual viewers. However, rather than dismissing the Picturesque as a defective theory, I would propose to look beyond the associationist elements for other clues to understand how the reactions of the spectator may be influenced.

First, Picturesque theories of art do not take as their starting point the innocent, uneducated eye of the beholder. On the contrary, all authors stress the importance of education, both visual, literary and historical, for art to make its effect. The artistic education young gentlemen received by looking at Italian art during their Grand Tour was one of the elements that contributed to the development of the Picturesque; but as Alison, Knight and many others argued, one enjoys looking at nature or art because an education enables one to attach meanings and emotions to what is seen. Alison formulated an application of this principle that went very much against one of the most ingrained and widely received views of that time, by arguing that the beauty of the classical orders did not reside in their proportion, but in the associations of Roman grandeur, Grecian culture and the classical past they evoke:

> for they are the GRECIAN orders; they derive their origin from those times, and were the ornament of those countries which are most hallowed in our imaginations; and it is difficult to see them, even in their modern copies, without feeling them operate upon our minds as relics of those polished nations where they first arose, and of that greater people by whom they were afterwards borrowed.[18]

In Soane's insistence that the union of the visual arts accounts for the most powerful effects architecture can have on the mind of the beholder, one finds a more detailed and precise version of this doctrine formulated from the point of view of the artist. The use of the visual arts, landscape gardening and even drama in architectural design is not meant to be merely a display of academic erudition, a late flowering of the Academic doctrine of the Sister Arts. Instead, elements taken from other arts serve both as clues for the spectator to grasp what is offered to his or her eyes, and as a design strategy for the artist. Thus, he admonished his students that 'In every poem we seek for a distinguishing and chief object; in every picture, a principal figure or group, a principal colour, a principal light, to which every other must be subservient; from these as so many radii, the other parts diverge'. In a more indirect way, this double function of the use of elements taken from other arts both in creating and in perceiving allusions is also illustrated by his comparison of the passage through a building with watching a play quoted above, and by his description of the house he rebuilt for himself, Pitzhanger Manor in Ealing (Fig. 14.1):

> Describe the front. No man will suppose that the architect or owner had attained civic crowns for saving the lives of his fellow citizens. . . . To judge of this species of building we should endeavour to discover the object to be attained: for example, in the building before you, if we suppose the person about to build possessed of a number of detached pieces of ornament, such as eagles and wreaths, demiboys and foliage, columns and statues, pedestals and acroters &c, and that from a desire to preserve them from ruin, or to form a building to give a faint idea of an Italian villa . . . this building may thus be considered as a picture, a sort of portrait.[19]

In a very literal sense, much more precisely defined than in most formulations of the Picturesque, painting for Soane is the language of architecture. Not so much in that the architect must design buildings and their surroundings resembling the landscapes of Claude or Poussin, but in that buildings are a portrait of the character of their inhabitants or architect. At the same time, this view of buildings as portraits of characters enabled him to use devices of plot as they are found both in historical painting and in drama. The best-known instance of this use of the sister arts is of course his own house in Lincoln Inn's Fields in London (Fig. 14.2), where the succeeding rooms, passages and their decoration offer a portrait of the many aspects of Soane's personality, his pursuits, his education and the cultural milieu of which he made himself a part, that gradually unfolds as the visitor walks through the house. Similarly, the façade of Pitzhanger Manor, with its sarcophagi, isolated elements of the orders and fragments of classical statuary, offers a view of the architect almost as a deconstructor of the classical style: here are some of its essential elements, together with the funerary and sacrificial associations that are so essential to its original functions and meaning, but presented almost as building blocks which the architect may assemble as he likes. But the drama in Soane's buildings is not only a drama of character; it is an architectural drama, and therefore one of the handling of light and space, of the direction of movement, and of a progression of points of view. Soane's buildings can never be grasped completely by looking at the façade and ground plan: one has to walk through them. The secret of their beauty lies not, or not only, in their

Caroline van Eck
'The splendid effects of architecture,
and its power to affect the mind'

14.1 Pitzhanger Manor, Middlesex, by Sir John Soane. The building was originally built by George Dance in 1768, with the main block by Soane (1800–3). Photograph by Martin Charles

handling of proportion or of classical ornament, but in that they make the spectator see and feel what it is to create and handle space by the manipulation of light and shade and mass.

Another clue is provided by Jeffrey's observation in his review of Alison's *Essay on Taste* that the effect of art or scenery on the emotions is achieved through a creative act of the mind:

> When we are injured, we feel indignation, — when we are wounded, we feel pain
> … without any effort of the imagination, or the intervention of any picture or

14.2 12–14 Lincoln's Inn Fields, London by Sir John Soane (no.12 was built in 1792–94, no. 14 in 1823–24). No. 13 (1812–13) is now the Sir John Soane's Museum. Photograph by Martin Charles, reproduced by kind permission of the Soane Museum

vision in the mind. But when we feel indignation, or admiration, in consequence of seeing some piece of inanimate matter that merely suggests or recalls to us the ordinary causes or proper objects of these emotions, it is evident that our fancy is set to work, and that the effect is produced by means of a certain poetical creation, or a train of images and conceptions that are conjured up in the mind … we are employed, therefore, partly in composing and delineating this inward and ideal picture of the objects of our emotions, and partly only in receiving the emotions which it excites.[20]

Caroline van Eck
'The splendid effects of architecture,
and its power to affect the mind'

In other words, the experience of beauty consists of an act of creative visualization by the human mind. When we call some building or piece of scenery beautiful, we really mean to say that we are moved by it in some way; this affection sets in motion a train of associations in the mind. But this is not a passive, mechanical reaction through which already formed links between objects and feelings are re-activated, but a creative act of the imagination through which the objects which originally caused us to feel pity, anger, love or hatred are composed and visualized before the mind's eye. All associationists link objects or situations with the arousal of emotion, and mainly describe these links in terms of contiguity, contrast and likeness; but Alison is important because he draws attention to the active role of the mind in forging these connections.

Now both the very essence of the Picturesque, which is to move the spectator through the allusive image set before the eyes; the doctrine of the sister arts through which that richness of meaning is constructed, and the stress on active visualization as part of the aesthetic experience are core issues in classical rhetoric, which was an essential part in the school curriculum and provided many of the key concepts and principles for artistic theories until the end of the eighteenth century.[21]

Of course rhetoric is all about moving and thereby persuading the public; but already in the work of Cicero and particularly Quintilian it developed into a general theory of civilized human communication, including not only speech, but also the visual arts. However, the conviction that all arts are intimately linked was not simply an Academic tag, as the *ut pictura poesis* doctrine was to become in the seventeenth century. Instead, classical rhetoric considered all the arts in the first place as communication, meant to convey a point of view in the most persuasive fashion possible. Art that exists only for the sake of art is a typically nineteenth-century view.[22] Given the general nature of this theory, rhetorical concepts and principles – such as style or composition, or the orator's duty to accommodate his speech to the situation and the public – could easily be used in formulating theories of the visual arts, as is shown in Vitruvius' *De architectura libri X* (first century BC) or Leon Battista Alberti's *De pictura* (1435).[23]

But the visual and the verbal are also associated in another way, in the rhetorical analysis of the creative process and of the ways and means by which emotions in the audience are to be manipulated. In both of these, visualization is essential. In preparing his speech, the orator has to visualize on the one hand his public, the occasion on which he will speak, and the setting; on the other hand, he has to form vivid mental pictures of the subject about which he will speak in order to experience himself the emotions he plans to excite in his audience. As Quintilian put it:

> The prime essential for stirring the emotions of others is ... first of all to feel these emotions oneself. ... But how are we to generate these emotions in ourselves, since emotion is not in our own power? ... There are certain experiences which the Greek call *phantasiai*, and the Romans *visions* [*visiones*], whereby things absent are presented to our imagination with such extreme vividness that they seem actually to be before our very eyes. ... From such

impressions arises that *enargeia* which Cicero calls *illumination* and *actuality* [*illustratio et evidentia*], which makes us seem not so much to narrate as to exhibit the actual scene, while our emotions will be no less actively stirred then if we were present at the actual occurrence.[24]

Language is the medium of oratory, but the orator speaks in order to make his audience see.[25] As in Alison's associationist aesthetic, active visualization is the means through which the public is moved.

Conclusion

Picturesque theories of landscape gardening and architecture may be considered as a late variety of a rhetorical theory of the arts rather than the precursor of nineteenth-century stylistic developments both because of the Picturesque focus on moving the spectator, and because of the central role rhetorical concepts such as movement and variety play in statements on the Picturesque in architecture by Joshua Reynolds, Adam and Soane. But rhetoric also offers a useful framework to understand some other aspects of the Picturesque, and in particular to offer an explanation of the working of associations in terms of rhetorical views on the role of visualization both in design and in perception.

The Picturesque, of course, derives its name from the close association in design between painting and landscape gardens or architecture; but as has been shown, for Soane this connection was both more far reaching and more precise, in that for him the façade offered a portrait of the character of its designer, and a visit to the house could be compared to watching a play. That is, for him the analogy between architecture and painting was not centred on the use of light and shadow, mass and empty space both in landscape painting and in garden design, but on the outward representation of character by visual means, and their architectural equivalent by means of dramatic effects of light and darkness. As in classical rhetoric (which he had studied very thoroughly), Soane was able to transpose the way effects are achieved in one art to another. Just as the orator uses the vividness and directness associated with painting in his descriptions of events and characters, Soane transposed the expressive tasks of painting, namely to give a visual representation of character, to architecture. Similarly, he used architectural means such as the manipulation of light and darkness, or the contrast between enclosed and open space, to achieve effects similar to the sudden changes of mood and situation achieved by careful handling of lightning and plot in drama.

255

Picturesque theories are based on the conviction that in order to have meaning, buildings and landscape gardens must refer to something outside themselves and their own medium. Yet at the same time, they are among the first writings on architecture to show interest in the handling of space, and the role of what one would now call abstract qualities in painting, such as the play of light and darkness, and the grouping of masses. This has led earlier historians of the Picturesque such as Christopher Hussey to consider them as precursors of twentieth-century abstraction and formalist aesthetics.

Caroline van Eck
'The splendid effects of architecture,
and its power to affect the mind'

But given the rhetorical context for the Picturesque argued here, its location of the meaning of architecture outside itself, and the various uses of painting in architecture and landscape design, may both be also understood as expressions of the rhetorical concern to situate all works of art firmly within human life and passions. As Richard Payne Knight observed, to the uneducated observer, the night sky is meaningless, and so are the masterworks of painting and architecture. But one might also turn this around: works of art that do not in some way refer to the life and history of the community for which they are made do not possess any meaning.

Notes

1 Richard Payne Knight, *The Landscape, a Didactic Poem in Three Books. Addressed to Uvedale Price, Esq.* (London, 1795), II, p. 162.

2 For example, J. Mordaunt Crook, *The Dilemma of Style: Architectural Ideas from the Picturesque to the Post-Modern* (London: John Murray, 1987), ch. 1, which locates the origins of the preoccupation with style of the debate on architecture in the nineteenth century in the Picturesque; or Christopher Hussey, *The Picturesque: Studies in a Point of View* (London: Country Life, 1927), where the Picturesque is presented as one of the precursors of abstraction in twentieth-century painting. A notable exception to this trend is Andrew Ballantyne, *Architecture, Landscape and Liberty: Richard Payne Knight and the Picturesque* (Cambridge: Cambridge University Press, 1997), which offers an interpretation of Knight's life and work against the background of contemporary concerns.

3 Sir Uvedale Price, *Essays on the Picturesque, as Compared with the Sublime and the Beautiful; and, on the Use of Studying Pictures, for the Purpose of Improving Real Landscape* [1794] (London, 1810), I, p. 37.

4 *Ibid.*, pp. 51–52.

5 Richard Payne Knight, *An Analytical Inquiry into the Principles of Taste* [1805] (London, 1884), p. 4.

6 *Ibid.*, pp. 143 ff.

7 *Ibid.*, p. 136.

8 *Ibid.*, pp. 152–153.

9 Thomas Wateley, *Observations on Modern Gardening* (London and Dublin, 1770); reprinted in John D. Hunt and Peter Willis (eds), *The Genius of the Place: The English Landscape Garden 1620–1820* (Cambridge, MA: MIT Press, 1988), pp. 305–306. For similar sentiments see William Shenstone, *Unconnected Thoughts on Gardening* (London, 1764); reprinted in Hunt and Willis, *Genius of the Place*, pp. 289–297.

10 David Watkin, *Sir John Soane: Enlightenment Thought and the Royal Academy Lectures* (Cambridge: Cambridge University Press, 1996), p. 563. Also *The Complete Works of Robert and James Adam, Esquires* [1778], ed. with an Introduction by Robert Oresko (London and New York: Academy Editions, 1975), pp. 45–46; and Sir Joshua Reynolds, *Discourses* [1797], ed. with an Introduction and Notes by P. Rogers (Harmondsworth: Penguin, 1992), p. 298.

11 Cf. Watkin, *Sir John Soane*, p. 187.

12 Soane, reprinted in *ibid.*, pp. 187–188.

13 Anon. [Francis Jeffrey], 'Review of *Essays on the Nature and Principles of Taste*, by Archibald Alison', *The Edinburgh Review*, 18/35 (May 1811), p. 3.

14 *Ibid.*

15 *Ibid.*, p. 11.

16 *Ibid.*, p. 13.

17 David Hume, *An Enquiry Concerning Human Understanding*, reprinted from the posthumous 1777 edition and edited by L. A. Selby-Bigge (Oxford: Oxford University Press, 1975), pp. 23–25.

18 Archibald Alison, *Essays on the Nature and Principles of Taste* (London, 1790; repr. Hildesheim: Olms, 1968), II, pp. 156–157, quoted in Jeffrey, 'Review', pp. 32–33.

Caroline van Eck
'The splendid effects of architecture,
and its power to affect the mind'

19 Soane, quoted in Watkin, *Sir John Soane*, pp. 186–187.

20 Jeffrey, 'Review', pp. 26–27.

21 Brian Vickers, *In Defence of Rhetoric* (Oxford: Clarendon, 1988), esp. chs 1, 7.

22 For a discussion of this as a deliberate breach with the rhetorical view of the nature and
    function of art, see *ibid.*, pp. 351–359.

23 Caroline van Eck, 'Rhetorical categories in the Academy', in *The Blackwell Companion to
    Artistic Theory*, eds P. Smith and C. Wilde (Oxford: Blackwell, forthcoming, 2001).

24 Quintilian, *Institutio Oratoria*, with an English trans. by H. E. Butler (Cambridge, MA: Harvard
    University Press, 1921), VI.ii.26–32. Also Aristotle, *Rhetorica* II.ii.23; and Cicero, *De Oratore*
    I.185, I.350ff., where remembrance or *memoria* is almost the active counterpart of the
    passive process of association.

25 On oratory as a way of making the audience, see Jas Elsner, *Art and the Roman Viewer: The
    Transformation of Art from the Pagan World to Christianity* (Cambridge: Cambridge
    University Press, 1995), pp. 21–49; and M. Fumaroli, *L'Ecole du silence: Le sentiment des
    images au xviie siècle* (Paris: Flammarion, 1994), p. 8.

Contributors

Hannah Lewi

is a lecturer in Architectural History and Design at Curtin University of Technology, Western Australia. She recently completed her PhD on '*Post* Terra Nullius: *the re-making of Antipodean place*', which explores particular urban place-studies from post-colonial and heritage theory perspectives. Other recent publications include *Working Papers in Australian Studies*, no. 112 (University College London) and 'Inventing a space to house (post) colonial memories', in *The Architecture of the Museum: Symbolic Structures, Urban Contexts*, ed. M. Giebelhausen (Manchester: Manchester University Press, forthcoming, 2000). She is also a practising architect.

Paul Walker

is a Senior Lecturer in the Faculty of Architecture, Building and Planning at the University of Melbourne. He graduated B Arch (Hons) from the University of Auckland in 1981 and completed a PhD there in 1987. He has worked in architectural practice in Auckland and Wellington, and taught architectural design and theory at the School of Architecture, Victoria University of Wellington from 1989 to 1999. His research is concerned with the reception of architecture and landscape theory in colonial and post-colonial situations and he is currently collaborating on a book on post-war architecture in New Zealand to be published in 2000.

Anne-Catrin Schultz

studied in Stuttgart and Florence and obtained her Diploma in Stuttgart in 1997. She was a Visiting Scholar at MIT, and has been, since 1997, the Editor of the News sheet of the European Association for Architectural Education. She lectures at international conferences and workshops. Since 1997–98 she has been Assistant Professor in Stuttgart. Since 1998 she has been in practice in San Francisco.

Paula Young Lee

received her PhD in Art History from the University of Chicago in 1999. Her interdisciplinary work addresses architectural history/theory, history of science, and philosophy in the context of late eighteenth–nineteenth century France. Her research in the areas of architectural history and museum studies has been published in, for example, *Art Bulletin*, *Assemblage*, *Journal of Architecture*, *Journal of the Society of Architectural Historians*. She has taught at the Harrington Institute of Interior Design, Chicago, as well as at DePaul University. Currently, she is Assistant Professor of Humanities at the University of South Florida, Tampa, where she teaches courses in modern European and American Culture. Ongoing projects include the preparation of her dissertation, 'The logic of the bones: architecture and the anatomical sciences at the Muséum d'Histoire Naturelle, Paris, 1789–1889', as a book.

Jan Birksted

is the Editor of *Relating Architecture to Landscape* (London: Routledge, 1999). He is currently finishing a monograph on the Maeght Foundation. His research interests cover architecture, art and landscape. He is Chair of the DoCoMoMo international Specialist Committee on Urbanism and Landscape and the UK corresponding member of Réseau Architecture Philosophie. He is Senior Research Fellow at the Leicester School of Architecture, De Montfort University.

Edward Eigen

received an M Arch degree from Columbia University and a PhD in the History of Art, Architecture, and Urban Form from the HTC section of the Department of Architecture at MIT. Currently, he is writing a study on building materials and the theory of architectural economy.

Karen Lang

teaches art history at the University of Southern California. She is the recipient of fellowships from the National Endowment of Humanities and the Getty Grant Program, and has published essays on Kantian aesthetic theory and the history of the German monument. Her current research studies the construction of the viewing subject in the history of art.

Stanislaus Fung

is Director of the Asian Architecture Research Unit in the University of New South Wales, Sydney. He is a Consulting Editor of the Penn Studies in Landscape Architecture, a book series of the University of Pennsylvania Press.

Alessandra Ponte

is an architect (Diplôme) and an historian (PhD). She has taught at Harvard, Princeton, and the Cooper Union and in Venice. She has published widely in the USA and in

Europe on museology and landscape. She has been Assistant Professor at Princeton since 1994. She is currently Visiting at the Centre Canadien d'Architecture in Montreal.

Rhona Richman Kenneally

is a Faculty Lecturer at the School of Architecture, McGill University, Montreal, and also teaches Design History and Theory at the Department of Design Art, Concordia University, Montreal. Her multidisciplinary education includes a BA (Hons) in English Literature, an MA in Social History, and a professional degree in architecture. She is currently completing a doctoral dissertation in nineteenth-century English Gothic Revival architectural theory and its appropriation into the field of popular culture. She has published both in this area and in the wider field of material culture, with particular attention to the application of material culture methodology to travel writing and perceptions of landscape.

Katherine Wentworth Rinne

is an Urban Designer and an Associate Fellow at the Institute for Advanced Technology in the Humanities at the University of Virginia. She is a Senior Fellow at the Dibner Institute for the History of Science and Technology at MIT, Massachusetts. She is the author of '*Aquae Urbis Romae*: the Waters of the City of Rome,' (http://jefferson.village. virginia.edu/waters), an interactive history and archive of Roman hydrology and hydraulics published by The Institute for Advanced Technology in the Humanities at the University of Virginia. She holds the Master of Architecture degree from the University of California, Berkeley.

Ursula Seibold-Bultmann

is an independent art historian currently based in Cambridge. She writes on art and architecture for the Neue Zürcher Zeitung of Zurich, and has been a lecturer at the University of Münster.

Philippe Nys

is a philosopher working on gardens and landscapes. His most recent book is *Le Jardin Exploré* (1999). He is also the Co-editor with Monique Mosser of *Le Jardin, art et lieu de mémoire*. He was *Directeur de programme* at the *Collège International de Philosophie* and teaches at the Sorbonne and at the landscape school in Versailles.

Caroline van Eck

is a Senior Research Fellow at the Vrije Universiteit of Amsterdam, where she directs a research programme on the role of rhetoric in the visual arts and architecture, funded by the Dutch Foundation for Scientific Research (NWO). Her publications include *Organicism in 19th-Century Architecture: An Enquiry into its Theoretical and Philosophical Roots* (Amsterdam: Architecture and Natura, 1994) *and* 'Rhetorical categories in the academy', in *The Blackwell Companion to Artistic Theory*, P. Smith and C. Wilde, eds (Oxford: Blackwells, 2000).

Index

263

270